WATERSTONE & CO

Berlin—Two Cities Under Seven Flags
A Kaleidoscopic A–Z

KARIN & ARNO REINFRANK

BERLIN

Two Cities Under Seven Flags
A Kaleidoscopic A–Z

Berlin-Charlottenburg
Belvedere

T. Bettenstaedt
1983

Illustrated by J. Bettenstaedt

OSWALD WOLFF BOOKS
BERG PUBLISHERS
Leamington Spa/Hamburg/New York

Distributed exclusively in the US and Canada by
St. Martin's Press, New York

First published in 1987 by
Berg Publishers Limited
24 Binswood Avenue, Leamington Spa, CV32 5SQ, UK
Schenefelder Landstr. 14K, 2000 Hamburg 55, W.-Germany
175 Fifth Avenue/Room 400, New York, NY 10010, USA

British Library Cataloguing in Publication Data

Reinfrank, Karin
  Berlin: two cities under seven flags: a
  kaleidoscope A–Z.—(Oswald Wolff books)
  1. Berlin (Germany)—Description—
  Guide-books
  I. Title   II. Reinfrank, Arno
  914.3'15504878   DD859

  ISBN 0–85496–530–0

Library of Congress Cataloging-in-Publication Data

Reinfrank-Clark, Karin.
  Berlin—two cities under seven flags.

  'Oswald Wolff books.'
  Bibliography: p.
  Includes index.
  1. Berlin (Germany)—Description—Guide-books.
  I. Reinfrank, Arno, 1934–   . II. Title.
  DD859.R35   1987   914.31'5504878   87–11621
  ISBN 0–85496–530–0

Printed in Great Britain by Billings of Worcester

Contents

Illustrations

A

All Aboard

Ready to go? Don't forget your "most noble part"! It was a famous German writer who so described that unequivocal proof of your existence—your valid passport. He spoke from experience. His most noble part got him around: from Berlin to Denmark (out of the way of the Nazis) in 1933 via Austria, Switzerland, and France, then on to the United States by detour of Sweden, Finland, and the Soviet Union, and back again to Berlin in 1948 after months of delay in Switzerland. The superiority of this most vital part of a human being, so the poet–playwright explains, is self-evident. A human being may come about by negligence, a passport is never issued without good reason. If the document is in order, it is universally accepted. An individual may be as worthy as they come, in the end it is the stamped and sealed certificate of identity which assures recognition and acceptance. Visitors to the twin cities of Berlin, whether they travel by land or air, should mark these words. They are by none other than Bertolt Brecht.

When Brecht, like many others, had to flee, he left Berlin and Germany both still in one piece. By the time he returned both lay in ruins and had been quartered—Berlin into sectors, Germany into zones of occupation—under U.S., British, French, and Soviet command: Hitler's legacy. One year later, in 1949, the consolidation of the American, British, and French zones (and sectors) gave birth to the Federal Republic of Germany (and West Berlin) on the one, and the German

[1]

Democratic Republic (with its capital of East Berlin) on the other side of a deep political divide.

West Berlin emerged as an island inside the territory of the German Democratic Republic (GDR for short), surrounded by a border and connected with the "mainland" of the Federal Republic of Germany (or FRG) by a number of "corridors." Access rights had been negotiated among the victorious Allies. Bertolt Brecht died in 1956, on the "other" side, in East Berlin, which was separated from its Western counterpart by the border which five years later was to solidify into the Berlin Wall. So from wherever to Berlin, not least from one of the twin cities to the other, there is no getting about without your most noble, most accepted part.

Building a border wall is far from original. Chinese and Roman history provide models, even Berlin itself does. In the Middle Ages the town hovered inside its protective fortification, expanding the system of walls as it grew, with armed patrols at each of the many gates. The tradition of border guards, severe penalties for attempting to cross illegally, red tape at customs—all these have been with us for longer than we care to remember. Public executions of young men objecting to military service, however, were last documented in the eighteenth century. Yet during the last days of the Hitler regime Berliners throwing away their weapons and turning their back on a senseless war are known to have been shot.

Between June 1940 and April 1945 310 air attacks destroyed about two-thirds of the city's living quarters and most of its public buildings, producing 70 million cubic meters of rubble. The debris disappeared from view. Artificial mountains, now overgrown and developed into attractive recreation areas within the city limits, little betray their content matter. The people that built them received small memorials in comparison. A statue of a "Trümmerfrau" or "rubble woman" stands close to one such elevation: Rixdorf Heights in the park of Hasenheide (West Berlin). Near the "Rotes Rathaus," the red-brick town hall in the center of East Berlin, two additional sculptures—one of a rubble woman and the other of a construction worker—also bear witness to the will of the townspeople to dig themselves out from under the disaster with pickax and shovel. Gone without any trace are the endless kilometers of narrow-gauge freight-car tracks on which the rubble was carried off. The older generation of Berliners remembers them, and the immediate postwar years, with a shudder.

[2]

Berlin's history and present are full of the most unusual occurrences and the most ordinary everyday events, which have shaped the city and its people. Today Berlin is two cities in fact, under seven flags, and we wouldn't know whether to call that unusual or quite ordinary. It all began on May 2, 1945 at 6:00 a.m. when Hitler's troops capitulated to the victors of the Battle of Berlin: the Soviet forces. Two months later, on the basis of an Allied agreement signed in London as early as 1944, the Americans, British, and French, also entered the town with a contingent of 25,000 each. The division into four sectors of occupation had become a reality, and the first four flags were flying over the defeated capital of Germany. The year 1949 saw the establishment of two distinctively different administrations on German soil, each adding its national flag, bringing the number up to six. Number seven is special. It serves as a reminder of what survived of Berlin and will remain, and it symbolizes for both Berlins of today their common historical roots: the traditional city colors with the silhouette of the Bear of Berlin. The black and white banner with the royal Prussian eagle has long disappeared from the flagpoles: it belongs to a past that will be revived often enough in our A to Z kaleidoscope, and we hope not only in black and white.

Trümmerfrau am Rathaus Ost-Berlin   J. Bittershausen

Americans Just Love It

For most American tourists "doing" Europe, Berlin is a must. The western half of the city maintains a lifestyle close enough to home, yet offers plenty of old-world flavor and eccentricity. Few will forego the chance of a firsthand look into East Berlin from the platform at Checkpoint Charlie in the American sector—and the eery feeling it promises. In a nearby building they may wander through the standing exhibition on the Berlin Wall (now that they have seen it for themselves), watch one of the documentary movies, or relax in the cafeteria. Some will even dare to venture through the checkpoint on a sightseeing bus and take in the heart of Old Berlin, now pulsating in the capital of the GDR. American military personnel cross the border unhindered, in full uniform—thanks to the Four-Power Agreement—stroll around, or go on a profitable shopping spree in socialist shops and department stores. Records, toys and even baby cribs are the main objects of attraction. Foreign civilians would be better advised to abide by the visa and customs regulations laid down for them.

In East Berlin the United States is, of course, far less represented than in the Western counterpart. But the Stars and Stripes fly above the entrance to the U.S. Embassy for everyone to see, just around the corner from the famous Unter den Linden boulevard. Humboldt University offers a program of American Studies and Literature. And let us not forget an industrial product of American origin which even today is of vital economic importance for both parts of the city. Emil Rathenau, engineer (and father of the famous foreign minister of the Weimar Republic who was assassinated in 1922 by right-wing radicals), acquired Edison's patent for the incandescent electric lamp in 1883 and founded a company from which the General Electricity Company (known by its German initials AEG) emerged in 1887. Berlin became the main producer of all types of electrical lighting equipment. To this day the people of Berlin profit from the American invention as well as from the German spirit of enterprise. On both sides of the border successors to the AEG of old are still engaged in the original (and newer) lines of production.

Curiosity about the United States, one may safely say, has been with the Berliners ever since the discovery of the continent by Christopher Columbus. From the beginning, impul-

Berlin chem. Kongresshalle   J. Butteuta

ses skipped across the ocean, eagerly awaited in Berlin.
Letters from the New World, with the latest news about the
Mennonite congregations in Kansas, caught the Berliners'
imagination in the mid-1880s. A few years later a Berlin
lance corporal brought from the United States knowledge of
the latest in machinery for the manufacture of ammunition.
So it seemed natural that Chancellor von Hindenburg appointed him director of the arms factory in Spandau. The
noise on the testing range little resembled the ragtime music
from overseas pressed on the first wax disk in Berlin as early
as 1899. The influx of American tunes from jazz to musicals
and of New World fashions and styles turned many Berliners
into ardent fans of the culture from across the Atlantic.

Even today American music, whether live or canned, has
an equally strong following either side of the dividing line
and is the number one cultural messenger. For years, GDR
officials tried to stem the tide but with little success: the
young generation was won over by jazz and rock. Now East
Berlin officially invites American and other Western bands
and orchestras. To honor Paul Robeson, the black American
singer, they even named a street after him. But it is only in
West Berlin that the music scene gets really hot with the
occasional concert boiling over into all-out battles and chaos.

A concert hall and congress center of a special kind was
donated to the West Berliners through the untiring effort of
Eleanor Lansing Dulles, sister of the former U.S. secretary of
state, John Foster Dulles. In her diary she describes how she

[5]

managed to realize this concrete symbol of American friendship for the "islanders"—not without some clever cunning. Berliners soon found nicknames for this original showpiece of modern architecture that reveal both their appreciation and their caustic wit. The center became known as the "orange peel" or "baby scales" or more widely as the "pregnant oyster." The shell-shaped roof of the Congress Hall, as it is properly called, collapsed at the beginning of the eighties due to structural weaknesses. The cost of reconstruction has been giving the Senate of Berlin a major headache.

For its military personnel the U.S. garrison maintains the usual PX shopping facilities, a baseball stadium, and the like. As a private American foundation a radio station was installed in the American sector: RIAS, staffed by German journalists, became famous not least for its big band. The American Memorial Library, holding more than 700,000 volumes, is a gift from the American people to the people of West Berlin in memory of the airlift operations during 1948–9. Scholars from the "other" part of the city may make use of it as well.

The semicircular structure at Tempelhof Airport dates back to Nazi times, when it formed part of the Air Ministry. In front of it rises a high memorial of concrete, symbolizing the three air routes by which vital supplies reached West Berlin during those winter days when the Soviets had cut off the city's lifelines in one of the worst political crises of the cold war. A "rake of famine," Berliners quipped. The Americans' role in this dramatic support operation remains unforgotten—a "Day of the Air Force" is celebrated every year as a popular festival in West Berlin.

While walking through a nondescript street in the Schöneberg district we chanced upon a memorial plaque. It was here that one of the supply planes ("raisin bombers" in flippant Berlinese) crashed, killing the pilot and civilians on the ground. To avoid a repetition of such a disaster, air security was stepped up immediately, and a watchful eye is now kept on all air movements from the heavily-secured U.S. radar station on the peak of the Teufelsberg (Devil's Mountain). In respectful distance from these installations West Berliners frolic about on skis and sleds in winter. Wrapped up in warm shawls, with steaming breath, we watched them—a remarkably peaceful sight.

Animals Wild and Tame

Among the three species of inhabitants—Berliners, domesticated pets and wild animals—it's the last category that comes into view only to a keen observer. There is no lack of feathered guests from the surrounding forests making Berlin their home, including the great tit, the robin and other songbirds. Swallows nest in the casing of a doorbell, putting it out of action. Two redstarts, unconcerned city brats, move into a mailbox for good, forcing the mailman to throw letters and papers across the garden gate into the wet grass, alerted by the big cardboard sign: "Out of use. Bird breeding!" Along Berlin's streams and lakes, between footpath and sandy bank, swans rear their young. Better not get too close! They charge with furiously beating wings and surprisingly tough beaks. Wild ducks and coots become more visible in winter. In Fasanenstraße (appropriately enough this means Pheasant Street) in West Berlin, a bird fanatic mounted a plastic stork on top of his roof with a nest made from the same material in the hope that perhaps his invitation might be accepted; though it seems very unlikely that so shy a creature would settle right near the tracks of the railroad. The descendants of those peacocks once reared by the royal gamekeepers still populate the island Pfaueninsel, which was named after them.

The city dwellers in large numbers heed a particular piece of biblical wisdom, though they may be unaware of the chapter and verse where it is recorded: "A dog alive is better than a dead lion." Zehlendorf registers one dog for every nineteen people, which really means twenty, since our four-legged friends treat Mom or Dad strictly as one of them. West Berlin takes in a round ten million deutschmarks in dog taxes. Bismarck, who loved to show off his two Russian borzois, was well aware of his metropolitans' weakness from the outset. The "Iron Chancellor" imposed a tax on the owners of those barking darlings for the first time, and soon was able to show off Berlin's paved sidewalks into the bargain. Not that the darlings were much impressed; they left their traces on the pavement with the same relief as before. And no one parted with "Prince" for mere money.

The capital of the GDR has organized its animal lovers in special sections of the League of Culture; an occurrence that the erstwhile founders of the former emigrant organization

Panzernashorn

Bettenstadt
1979

could hardly have envisioned. "Vivaristics" is the heading under which they pursue their hobbies. The aquarians are in the lead; apart from tropical fish they rear frogs and salamanders behind glass. Youngsters rave about their favorite birthday gift—even if the goldfish later makes its exit through the sanitary system! Snakes find plenty of *aficionados* too. A West Berliner who kept his cobra in the bedroom couldn't understand the fuss his wife made. She moved out, and he, rather than paying alimony, solicited his roommate's poisonous bites. He was saved, and what was worse, had to kill his companion. An unforeseen and, for him, unwelcome end to a dramatic situation. Whether the snake found its resting place in the animal cemetery could not be ascertained. There, gracing a meticulous lawn, tombstones for beloved dogs, cats, hamsters, and pet mice carry inscriptions that would melt any heart of stone. The funeral director has a strong cup of coffee ready for his clients. There is no extra charge for the verbal comfort in case of a breakdown.

Deer still roam freely in areas of Greater Berlin. Hunting parties from East Berlin proudly register their gaming success around Müggelsee or in Grünau. They also keep the population of buzzards, owls and foxes in check. Once upon a time, the upper crust hunted on horseback with packs of hounds for wild boars and rabbits—a practice no longer held in favor. A relief on a house wall in Charlottenburg (West), where Bismarck- and Leibnizstraße cross, shows the oversized image of the Baron of Münchhausen. Remember the famous tall tales about the baron? It was he who fired a load of cherry pits so cleverly between a buck's antlers, that the following year he was able to recognize the beast immediately for the fruit-bearing cherry tree it carried on its head. The baron really

[8]

existed and hunted in the fields of Charlottenburg. The ballads of a literarily gifted descendant of his had a sizeable following during the Nazi period. However it was Rudolf Erich Raspe, a university professor, convicted embezzler and refugee from justice sheltering in England who first put the baron's stories in writing and published them in London in 1785.

An awful stench from a basement alerted neighbors to call the West Berlin police. The men came quickly, broke through a wooden partition and discovered the badly decomposed carcass of a cat. Suddenly every one of them began scratching and tearing at his clothes. They got in their van, but the itching became worse instead of better; the host of fleas from the dead cat's body was just getting started on them. A strict order from the station came over the car radio not to dare approach it until men and material had been thoroughly fumigated. For hours the fleas kept a whole team of homicide detectives out of commission providing their colleagues with a good hunting tale that was not tall in the slightest.

Architecture

With that sarcastic streak of a true Berliner an architect observed: "We are the only town in the world managing to destroy our buildings twice." He was referring to the fact that after 1945 the wartime debris was ground by special machinery to brick dust and recycled into new construction material. The archeologists of the future will look in vain for fragments from the Berlin of old. Everything was pulverized. The political division of the city radically cut into urban planning as well. Diverging concepts based on different economic realities created two distinct physical styles. For a long time, state financing of all building efforts accounted in East Berlin for a uniformity of style by no means absent from the West Berlin scene, although here much of the reconstruction was privately funded. Development in the GDR capital by necessity went at a much slower pace than in its more af-

Berlin   J. Bettenstadt

fluent Western neighbor able to rely on investment and subsidies from the Federal Republic. But money alone does not assure inhabitable and beautiful surroundings. In the words of a native author: "Since the postwar generation of architects had no time to spend much thought on either past history or the future, their vision led to a mere agglomeration of high-rises. With the variety of nineteenth-century architectural forms, long-established conditions of human habitation and life were discarded as well. Driving through the city today one gets the clear impression that forces hostile to it have been at work."

Apart from the towering television needle with its shining

sphere, which dominates the whole of the metropolis from East Berlin territory, it is the remains of the Kaiser-Wilhelm-Gedächtniskirche that catches the eye of the visitor to West Berlin. The war-damaged steeple of a nineteenth-century church structure with its modern appendages stands at the northern end of Kurfürstendamm and was soon nicknamed "lipstick with powder puff". Why was this carefully maintained ruin preserved at all? Perhaps, once the frenzy of postwar construction had begun, Berliners did not want to part with every one of their old landmarks. The church was originally consecrated on September 1, 1885. Its patron, Emperor William II, in typical humility, accompanied the laying of the foundation with the following words: "In honor of the Almighty, in memory of my unforgettable grandfather who said: 'I wish that religion be preserved for my people.'"

Not in Berlin's infamous old tenement barracks but in traditional middle-class apartment houses one occasionally still encounters an architectural peculiarity which developed from floor-plan economy: the Berlin Room. A connecting link between different sections of the apartment rather than a proper room, its window always looked out into a somber back courtyard. The natives didn't seem to mind much that the room was hard to air. An outsider might have wondered why the family welcomed their guests here, amidst the smell of smoke and coffee. The room had one advantage however. During cold winter days you could remain oblivious to dirty snow and slippery ice on the streets outside and cuddle up in cozy comfort. It was for different reasons that architectural oddities were created during the Nazi regime. Under Hitler's order his minister in charge, the architect Albert Speer, set out to design a cityscape in line with the prevailing megalomania. Luckily not many of his plans materialized, for obvious reasons. Prophesied victories (which luckily did not materialize either) were to be celebrated in the splendor of the Nazi "Millennium", immortalized by a Victory Boulevard through the center of Berlin. Adjacent houses were to be torn down, the wide avenue was to be lined on either side with enemy tanks and cannons and other spoils of war. Next to the building of the Reichstag a gigantic domed chancellery was to be erected, more powerful than St. Peter's in Rome. Berlin would be known as "Capital Germania." Speer's father, upon taking a look at these designs, is reported to have exclaimed: "You have gone completely crazy!"

For the mere fun of it, Berliners did build the occasional

[11]

frivolous whimsicality which came to fame before disappearing again. The best known of these was Café Vaterland (or Fatherland), a sensation in its time. It fell victim to World War II. Each room was shaped and decorated according to a different theme and served by staff in the appropriate costume. Waiters bringing tiny cups of hot mocha to their customers wore a Turkish fez. Next door waitresses in dirndls were heaving steins of beer. Surrounded by the landscape of the Rhine, complete with the Loreley, guests could marvel at the thunderstorm staged every hour. In all, they had the choice of a dozen different specialty restaurants, all under one roof. As early as 1894 a rich family from Pankow by the name of Wollank had their Oriental Palace fashioned in the shape of an Indian mosque on a raft floating freely in a park lake. Dances were held there until 1928, when it finally burnt down.

East Berlin's Karl-Marx-Allee is not without its peculiarities either. Among them are the ceramic tiles which fall off of the facing of outside walls. Wire cages are attached to catch the falling pieces. On leaving the underground station at Marchlewski-Straße you may soon find yourself in front of a noticeably unimaginative residential block. Hans Scharoun's name is listed among the designers. He later went westward, where he became famous for similarly noticeable buildings in the other Berlin. This apartment house was a quixotic creation, built for a remote heating system before such a system was available. As a remedy, the public landlord parked a steam locomotive in the backyard to provide the much-needed heat for the apartments. Tenants who still remember those days have been paying the same low rent for the past thirty years. This particular part of a traffic artery rebuilt from the ground after the war no longer bears Stalin's name but its prior one, Frankfurter Allee.

Soon after the change, or more correctly after the reversion, the young son of a writer otherwise never at a loss for words wanted an explanation for the change. The father hesitated. How could he possibly explain to the five-year-old about world history and the recent falling from grace of Stalin? Before he had found his composure the rascal looked up at him, worldly-wise: "I know, dad, Stalin got married. . . ."

Art and the Art of Belonging
to the Scene

The municipal art gallery of West Berlin, one of numerous show facilities for the fine arts, is located on the second floor of an inconspicuous building on Budapester Straße. A window halfway up the staircase opens up onto an unexpected view, the monkey cage of the zoo bordering on the back of the house. The species kept there is known for the redness of their hind ends. No satirist has so far availed him- or herself of the inherent metaphorical material for comments on the state of modern art and art criticism.

Satire has long characterized the Berliners' association with their artistic community, which in turn fired back in a similar vein. Adolph von Menzel, an artist living during the reign of Emperor William II, was of rather small physical stature, and for that reason an easy target for derisive remarks. Once, in a café, he could not help overhearing two gentlemen and a lady showing off their wit and high spirits in an exchange of supposedly droll comments about him. Soon, much to the annoyance of the two male escorts, Menzel began to draw energetically, his gaze fixed on the lady. The gallant self-appointed protectors objected pompously: "Infamous to draw her portrait without asking permission!" "Destroy the sketch or hand it over immediately." "Well, of course!" the painter drily replied, "If your lady feels I captured her likeness, you are more than welcome." He handed over the sheet of paper showing the naturalistic drawing of a goose.

Berlin's fine-arts scene appears as farcical at times as do those who actively or passively populate it. A highly respected professor decided some ten years ago to patronize a well-known sculptor by acquiring one of his works. He got a tour of the studio, accepted a few drinks, came to a decision, and left by taxi with the statue of a kneeling boy in bronze. Two years later the artist's wife learned by mere chance that the sculpture had reappeared at a junk dealer's. Retracing the route of the "Kneeling Boy" it came to light that the merry professor had proceeded to a pleasure boat on the Spree River, had continued to drink happily and forgotten all about his purchase. On board the piece of art was in the way, and a cleaning lady rescued it and lugged it home. Her grandson in turn sold it to a junk dealer for the price of the metal. In the end, the artist's spouse repurchased the work for little more and presented it to its creator. In this fashion, art in Berlin provides pleasure all around.

In West Berlin, the Emperor Frederick Museum Club, founded in 1898, comes to public attention occasionally with astonishing signs of an active, though private existence. The club owns the famous painting *Man with a Golden Helmet*, once believed to be a work by Rembrandt. Its members are wealthy Berlin families whose pictorial assets may appear on loan in the best of exhibitions, as did ninety paintings from the Dutch baroque period for example. Neither showings of this caliber nor the treasures collected in the museums of West Berlin can cover up the fact that the arts trade is more successful selling depictions of bellowing stags and alpine landscapes all aglow.

Beginning in 1933 Berlin, the city of academies, temples, galleries, and students and disciples of the arts, was "liberated" from the majority of its master artists and modern masterpieces thanks to Hitler's cultural policy. Max Liebermann, the outstanding impressionist, commented about the development: "I couldn't possibly stuff myself with as much as I want to puke up." His early natural death spared him the fate of his wife, who, late in years, committed suicide in 1943 shortly before she was to be transported to a concentration camp. Other artists, Jewish or not, fled the country to foreign shores, wherever they were granted asylum. Today, West Berlin maintains an open-door policy to fill old and new artist colonies with life again.

The fostering of pictorial arts in East Berlin rests almost completely within the public domain. Samples of indigenous modern painting and sculpture decorate the walls and the grand hall of the Palace of the Republic, easily accessible in the center of the capital. A West German chocolate and sweets manufacturer, in exchange for permission to open up a branch factory at his own expense in the GDR, presented the East Berlin art world with a collection of Picassos and younger modernists on permanent loan.

Important art exhibits are held in galleries throughout the center of the GDR capital, although their number is not quite a match for those all over West Berlin. In the most authentic historical part of Old Berlin, the Otto Nagel House keeps alive the memory of its patron, just as it presents artistic and documentary material from Berlin's social history and the labor movement. In all, East Berlin can pride itself on three

[14]

and a half million visitors annually to its twenty-five museums.

In East Berlin we found ourselves walking around pleasantly humorous sculptures and well-executed portraits of such greats as Käthe Kollwitz with children from the deprived area of Prenzlau cuddled up in her lap. Heinrich Zille can be seen sketching, while a nosy shoemaker's apprentice is looking over his shoulder to catch a glimpse of the master's drawing. You find yourself waiting for the stone figures to come to life.

In West Berlin the modern statues and sculptures in public places hardly produce the same sense of identification with their whimsicality and grotesqueness. What do you expect from a metallic hand (with a watch), cut off at the wrist, gripping a cube? Or from a pair of aluminium legs on two left feet? Only they know why they are on a pedestal.

B

Balconies—Sanctuaries With a Bird's-Eye View

Berlin without balconies would be like Venice without gondolas. There is no traditional building in the middle-class strata without balconies to the front, from where life in the street can be comfortably supervised. In some residential areas, however, dilapidated "observation decks" had to be dismantled or their access barred for safety reasons, as in many streets of the old district of Kreuzberg. Since the building boom of the turn of the last century, the possession of such a balcony conferred upon the lucky ones a nimbus of special wealth. Here, on a few square meters, they could enjoy their Sunday afternoon coffee in the open air and leisurely devour mountains of pastry, cake, and tarts. The balcony doubled as a health resort, an oasis of recreation they could reach in slippers.

A whole industry provides all you may desire for your balcony comfort: small tables and plastic chairs to match; sunshades and awnings; flower stands and boxes; gaudy clay reliefs; brightly colored posters; pictures and other "original" wall adornments; even floor covering as soft and green as a lawn. One could almost speak of a new science of "balconology," considering that the Women's League of East Berlin offers special consultation to those seeking advice about balcony plants and their care. Weekly office hours are advertised in the paper.

Not all newly-constructed blocks of flats are equipped with

these spas in miniature any longer. Where they fell victim to economic considerations, positive thinkers soon rationalized and expounded on the benefit of avoiding such nuisance: now there was no longer any need to take all that noise and pollution from the street.

The urban centers of today have rendered the balcony obsolete. Cars, buses and elevated trains were sending their roar and dirt up to the highest stories: there was no escaping it. In Neukölln people have been known to turn up their radio to defend themselves against the thunder of busy streets. The German Institute for Urban Studies came to the conclusion that every third Berliner considered his balcony wasted space, hardly ever used it and resented the extra rent it cost. Granny's paradise has become an outdated pocket of freedom. The outlook becomes gloomier still when we realize that an increasing number of senior citizens and others use their balcony as a springboard to ultimate freedom. But that in no way increases the usefulness of these once-treasured vantage points.

In the past, balconies in Berlin have been closely linked to important phases in German history. Hitler used to make his appearance on the balcony of his chancellery in Wilhelm-Straße, making a gesture with which other people chase off wasps. The entire building was razed to the ground: no sign of it remains. The frontispiece of the old city palace, damaged in 1945 and torn down later, was preserved and incorporated into the façade of the State Council Building in East Berlin in 1965. From this balcony the socialist Karl Liebknecht had proclaimed the "Free Socialist Republic of Germany" on November 9, 1918, after Emperor William II had abdicated. Almost simultaneously the Social Democrat Philipp Scheidemann announced the founding of a "German Republic" from a window of the Reichstag. This republic prevailed, outright socialism was out. Neither the burning of the Reichstag early in Hitler's days as chancellor nor war damages in his final hours managed to destroy the Reichstag. Only visitors to the standing exhibition in the Reichstag entitled "Questions to German History" cast an eye on it, as it lies off the beaten track near West Berlin's no-man's-land on the border wall. In contrast, no East Berlin tourist guide will fail to point with pride to the showpiece on the State Council Building.

Balconies in Berlin are not only a drain on the purse, they may be regular mints as well. At least for the lawyers called to represent litigant parties. And what do they fight about?

[17]

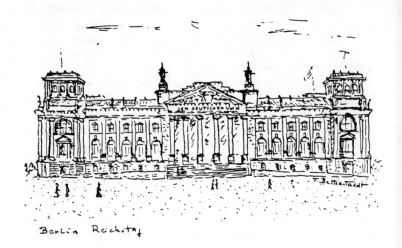

Berlin Reichstag

About the right to water one's plants, of course. The flowers on the upper level have barely received their daily nourishment when traces thereof appear on the lower level, defacing a beautifully painted ceiling or ruining a new awning. If the first exchange of letters cannot bring about reconciliation, the courts are asked to intervene. The legal profession isn't a bit sorry.

On national holidays recalling events of triumph or defeat, Berliners will go all out to decorate their airy palaces. Formerly flags and banners were the craze. Today it is streamers and candles under glass in the Eastern half of town, or electric lights in the national colors on fir branches even in the West, turning an otherwise secular balcony into a proper altar. Whoever thinks this is for the birds is right, too. The local feathered population just loves the hospitality, but not only in winter, when crumbs and grains fill the custom-built feeders. One summer, a pigeon set up house in a vent pipe leading from our balcony to the bathroom. No broomstick was able to reach the perfect hideout, and unperturbed, the bird reared its chirping brood, while our bathtub was forever decorated with what looked like specks of dried-up shaving foam. Our neigbors had more luck. Their son became the hero of his class in "show and tell," when he presented a stag beetle that had landed on their balcony. Is it any wonder that the evaluation of balconies varies from one person to the next?

Banking on the Past and Future

The old stock exchange of Berlin! Once it was an inexhaustible fountain of witticism and Berlin jokes that traveled through the whole of the banking district faster than the latest financial quotations. And they did not have far to go, as the major banks were centered around Unter den Linden, Behrenstraße and Gendarmenmarkt, now located east of the border. In a peculiar way the political transformations which have taken place since 1945 changed the face of this area as well. Under the new social and political order the stock market became obsolete—the war-torn building was pulled down, as was the old Imperial Bank nearby. The dark blocks of granite were put to a different use, one even the toughest market bulls could not have dreamed about: they reappeared in the panorama wall of East Berlin's zoo right behind the polar bear enclosure. The zoo management points out that they form a splendid contrast to the pale bearskins.

Money and share markets, sticky business that they are, tend to stick to their traditional terrain. By the thirties, when inflation ran rampant, traders in foreign currency gathered at a corner of Kurfürstendamm. They dealt in hard dollars then. A few steps away stands the Zoo Station (now on West Berlin territory). Once a money market, always a money market: here illegal trading took place in German marks from both the Eastern and the Western sectors during the immediate postwar years, when free traffic between them was hardly checked. Five marks of "their" currency had to change hands in the end for a single one of "ours," the stronger mark. Police usually kept one eye closed to the black-market transfer; only on special occasions would they swarm in for an all-out raid. Today only one peaceful private money changer's office remains. Should you want a 100-mark bill changed into smaller denominations though, beware; ninety-nine marks is all you get in return. One deutschmark finds its way into the changer's purse for commission. Imagine our surprise in the official exchange office of Friedrichstraße Station (East Berlin) when we got the very same bargain. The division of Berlin has apparently failed where ripping off unsuspecting travelers is concerned.

Most banks in West Berlin nowadays are but branches of institutions operating with their main offices in Frankfurt,

Düsseldorf, or in foreign countries. Since Bonn was selected as capital of the Federal Republic of Germany, the significance of West Berlin as a financial center has shrunk considerably. East Berlin often filled old bank buildings with a different type of life, housing the Academy of Science in the former State Bank of Prussia building, and the main offices of the trade unions in some large bank. The Central Committee of the Socialist Unity Party (SED) even ousted the GDR Ministry of Finance from the drab functional edifice of the erstwhile Imperial Central Bank, thereby breaking that last bond between past and present economic systems. The strong vaults safeguard secret cadre files now.

The State Bank of the GDR—all private banking has been abolished—resides today in the block of the former Dresdner Bank, which continues to function under its old name only in the FRG. In West Berlin, according to the Four-Power Agreement, this financial institution was forced to provide its branches with new nameplates to foil any revisionist tendencies that might attach symbolic meaning to the old Dresden connection. (Dresden lies in the GDR.) The scenario of Berlin's banking world has always been marked by change of companies, nameplates and functions. In one respect, however, the dual city did remain an important junction for the financial transactions of so-called "German–German" business and for international East–West trade.

Share quotations of industrial concerns, banks, insurance companies, and investment trusts are noted at West Berlin's stock exchange, situated in a plain modern building on Fasanenstraße. Though far from the hustle and bustle of Wall Street and the City of London, West Berlin experiences its share of crashes and financial scandals. A few of them were of such magnitude that Senate majorities tumbled and administrations were toppled. Some speak of earthquakes, others of a storm in a teacup; but world-shattering they were not.

Carl Fürstenberg, a Berlin banker who was feared for his biting wit, would have been delighted. He preferred losing a good friend to losing a *bon mot*, and when asked to tell about a reception given by the Prussian minister of finance, he shrugged: "Madam Minister appeared in a low but unsuccessful *décolleté*. She always reminds me of her husband. He keeps on sporting an uncovered deficit, too."

Barrel Organs Cranking Out the Nostalgia

An old man in extravagant attire pushes a box on four wheels across the pavement. There are pipes visible in front and from the side a crank protrudes. If asked, the old gentleman would certainly claim a prominent place in the hierarchy of Berlin's maestros, second only to the director of the Philharmonic Orchestra, Herbert von Karajan. And rightly so, for as soon as he begins to turn the crank, the air around fills with immortal Berlin melodies.

Barrel-organ music has been a Berlin trademark for ages. Occasionally an organ-grinder would drag along a dancer, a singer, or even a trained monkey for added attraction: a mini-band, entertaining Berlin's poor. Whenever one appeared in a sunless, stifling courtyard inside the maze of walls of those notorious Berlin tenement barracks, excitement spread into the farthest of the back courts. Disabled war veterans in particular took this opportunity to stretch their meager state pension with the help of voluntary contributions. A few coins wrapped in newspaper were always thrown out of a window or placed into the hat by eager children.

Times changed, and it seemed our dear old barrel organ had been pushed into the corner along with other antique collectors' items by radio, tape recorder and Walkman. Then it reappeared in public places, churning out the old favorites. It reappeared in East Berlin, where it had been banished in the immediate aftermath of the war as a symbol of poverty and human degradation to be abolished and not mystified. On West Berlin's Kurfürstendamm every July now an international array of organ-grinders gathers to compete for the attention of the public. The festival-style atmosphere almost glorifies our old-fashioned music center into a proper concert instrument.

Considering that our organ-grinder makes up for a whole orchestra of violinists, trumpeters and percussionists, the weight of his musical apparatus reaching around seventy-five kilograms is hardly surprising. Most precious are the barrels. New ones are rarely produced and finding someone to repair an old one is a difficult enterprise. Each cylinder keeps eight tunes trapped for reproduction when the time is ripe, to recall the "Lumber Auction in Grunewald," or the sassy angel who invites St. Peter to a fling on the merry-go-round, not to forget that amiable tippler groping his way home "sticking to the wall, all along the way."

The famous artisan families who crafted the barrel organs have disappeared, as have their workshops. It is now up to the expertise of museum personnel to mend and maintain the antique pieces. Consequently the most outstanding samples of the instrument are carefully preserved in the instrumental collections of Berlin museums. Much to the delight of young and old the music machines exhibited in East Berlin's Märkisches Museum are played one day a week at a set time.

The heart of a Berliner is full of sentiment and nostalgia, a wealth of emotion unexpected in a metropolitan who tends to hide it all under a veil of brassiness. There are even tears glistening when that corny postwar pop song intones: "Dear old barrel-organ man / let me hear your tune again. . . ." These nostalgic touches stand in marked contrast to the quickly vanishing waves of the contemporary pop–rock–punk–what's-next music scene, and represent the Berliner's stubborn line of defense.

Rules and regulations have a way of surviving with the same stubborn conservativism. In the *Ministerial Bulletin* issued by the royal Prussian ministers of finance and the interior in 1898 we find the following: "Shows in public pathways, roads and squares which consist of the exhibition of tableaus depicting murders, catastrophes, and other sensational events and include the singing of short explanatory verses to the accompaniment of barrel-organ music are to be considered entertainment within the meaning of tax section No. 39 of the Stamp Duty Act of 31 July 1895."

Eighty years later an American student, Harvard-educated, in West Berlin on a so-called "airlift" scholarship, set out to develop the barrel-organ idea further and augment his pocket-money. He was banking on a neat plan really. He positioned a man-sized cardboard box, a sort of Punch and Judy theater, on Kurfürstendamm. Forty-two labeled buttons adorned the lower front part of his contraption; the upper part could be opened from the inside. For one deutschmark and at the push of a button the window would open, he would break out into the requested song: a live music box. He had not counted on Berlin's Engineering Department, though other authorities had granted their permission. The underground engineers, fans of the barrel organ that they were, found fault with the fact that the box had no wheels! That trained singer and doctoral candidate in comparative literature, should he have worn his roller skates?

Bear of Berlin

Since the bear appeared on the municipal arms Berlin has protected the animal most caringly from the sharp bite of local humor and wit. One neither provokes nor pokes fun at one's patron genius. Other animals get it instead: the monkey for instance. The owner of a pet store chased a crowd of unruly spectators from his window protesting: "The monkeys feel sick enough just looking at you, there is no need to incite them any further." It was left to a Rhinelander to immortalize in a satirical ballad the shaggy beast so jealously kept out of harm's way in Berlin. Heinrich Heine's "Atta Troll" nevertheless can count on friends in the city. Besides, the verses were dedicated to a famous Berlin personality, August Varnhagen von Ense, husband of the equally famous Rahel, noted for her intelligence and charm and for her literary salon, which made history. "Listen, listen," proudly proclaims Atta Troll, "I'm a bear, / Not ashamed of my descent, / Just as proud as if I stemmed / From one Moses Mendelssohn!"

The origin of Berlin's heraldic figure goes back to at least the thirteenth century. Berlin was but a small market town then. In 1709, Frederick I combined Berlin with four other settlements, namely Cölln, Friedrichswerder, Dorotheenstadt, and Friedrichstadt, to render it worthy of its status of capital of the realm. The red and black eagle, long associated with the other constituent townships, had to accept the bear's presence on the coat of arms from here on. Since then, the animal has marched in triumph onto coffee cups, ashtrays, streamers and city banners, milestones and jumpers, into publications, even into the popular song "Little Bear of Berlin."

There are plenty of real Berlin bears around: in East Berlin's Tierpark (or animal gardens) and its Western equivalent, the Zoo, their magnetic appeal works wonders. They are displayed in both parks, clearly visible even to casual passers-by without a ticket in hand. Madison Avenue could not have

come up with a more attractive advertising campaign. Just a few steps from the Märkisches Museum in East Berlin, safely fenced off and attended by a loving keeper, a single bear family enjoys its very own pit and the curiosity of those strange animals on the other side of the moat.

Long before anyone got the idea of cutting Berlin into two halves, the sculptor Hugo Lederer, in an act of endearing historical foresight, saw to it that his two bear fountains were fairly distributed, one each, in the Eastern and Western sides of town. In 1958, thirty years after his work in red tuff had originally been set up near Werderscher Markt, East Berlin authorities had the sculpture reconstructed and installed in its rightful place. His other monument is of granite as tough as the reputation of the Internal Revenue Service, whose Zehlendorf office is located nearby. It depicts a bear mother nursing her four cubs, or in the vernacular: "Mother Berlin and her four sectors."

In either of the twin cities photographers may get on tourists' nerves, offering their services with a special bait, a partner in bear costume. With a small crown on the beastly head (the Eastern version) or a bright sash across a bearish beer belly (the Western edition), these "bears" dance around the sidewalks and motion their half-willing, half-repelled prospective clients to cuddle up for a picture to remember their visit by. Probably the oldest of these prancing monsters is a smallish, 84-year-old man working the Tiergarten district west of the Brandenburg Gate. In temperatures of over forty degrees Celsius everyone else would keel over, but not Paul. "When you get to be my age," he chuckles, "your body forgets to perspire." For that unforgettable snapshot taken by his colleague, Paul in his time has embraced politicians, film

[24]

stars, and pop singers. Prepaid to be on the safe side—these photographs have been sent as far away as Mexico, Australia, and the United States. Stingy West Germans attempting to get away scot-free have frequently hastened to take a shot with their own camera. But Paul is quick to notice, quicker yet with his Berlin tongue from the bear's jaws: "Nothing doing, you cheapskate." And true to the local motto, "Anyone can be nice, but growling is a form of art," he continues: "Jump into the pit in the zoo and get yourself a bite in the ass. Then you'll have the Berlin souvenir you deserve."

Berliners For Better or Worse

There are a million and one ways in which to characterize a typical Berliner. He is irked by something, anything really, at any given moment. And as a consequence he is known to complain continuously. What he himself dishes out, he has to take back from his fellow citizens manifold, and he reciprocates with a quick tongue, sharp and point-blank. The following reply was sent by an infuriated mother in response to a letter received from the principal: "What is this about my girl's bad odor? You are there to teach Elsie, not to smell her out!"

A Berliner who identifies with his hometown is recognized by the way he breathes in the air about him, the perfumes of his city, *Berliner Luft*. Around Schönhauser Allee it's the aroma of smoked fish from brown coal briquettes still used in abundance. In Charlottenburg the sweet-and-sour odor of cabbage from a window above the street mingles with the mouth-watering mixture of herbal scents from a pizzeria below. On rare and luckly occasions these and more float like a bouquet of flowers on a cloud of pine from the surrounding forests. A faraway look will appear on every Berliner's face, half melancholic, half longing. Oh, to be out in the country now! But the fail-safe antidote brings him quickly back to his senses, the irresistible fragrance of beer and cigar smoke and sour pickles trailing from every bar window. Sanity is restored.

For over a generation now, women have outnumbered

men in both East and West Berlin, and that very fact has given prominence to their special timbre in the concert of a population of 1.8 million to the west and 1.2 million to the east of the border. Their power of repartee has much of the flippancy for which Madame Dutitre was famous a hundred years ago. Descended from a Huguenot family, but a true-born Berliner, her tongue was so irreverently quick that her son-in-law actually refrained from inviting her to a dinner party for his sophisticated circle of friends. Resolute as she was, the lady positioned herself in front of the villa in Wilmersdorf greeting every guest arriving with a reproachful: "See, you got invited, but not me." On her deathbed, she was still overcome by such rage against her pretentious brood that she was heard to say: "When I think of who is going to get their hands on my beautiful money, I'd rather not die at all."

In his love for Berlin the true native spares nothing in boasting to chauvinists from other parts. "If the Mississippi were flowing over here," he might brag, "it would be much wider." Or, shown a beautiful building or an elegant street far away from home, he would assert: "But our toilets are much more comfortable." No one can get under a Berliner's skin, though, the way a pseudo-Berliner will, and none more than a Saxon. There are a great number of Saxons living in GDR Berlin for instance. These "immigrants" try hard to assume the customs and characteristics of the natives, which gets them into the strangest of competitions. Is it any wonder that the newcomers bear the brunt of most jokes? "Do you know," we were asked by a casual acquaintance from across the table, "why the television tower is as high as it is?" Not a clue could be gathered from his dead-pan face. "Just to give Saxons a better vantage point to scout for an empty apartment." How could anyone dare push his way around the metropolis without "Berlin" stamped on his birth certificate!

Metropolitans find it difficult, wherever they may be, to abstain from indulging in the idea that they personally tip the scale in all matters, legislative, executive, and judicial. The pride of living so close to the center of command, where decisions of greatest importance are reached, their illusion of grandeur seems all the more ludicrous, when, as in the case of West Berlin, circumstances have changed drastically and the seat of government has been moved elsewhere, i.e. to Bonn. The presumptuous air has stayed behind. A Berliner without at least a trace of arrogant insolence simply does not exist. Only the steady stream of new settlers generates a softening of the effect. Hasn't Berlin's population always benefited from the influx of different regenerating cultures—those of the Dutch, the Slavs, the French, the Jews, and of course the Austrians? Viennese film actors and directors, barkeepers, restaurateurs still maintain a stronghold on Berlin. And what about the West Germans flocking into town? The Federal government in Bonn keeps on subsidizing its most expensive problem child with millions to assure the functioning of social services, economy, and the lure of its most eastern outpost.

In this respect, to those arriving from southern Europe, the Balkans, and Turkey, Berlin appears like the world of wonders of a thousand and one nights. Their offspring adapt to the new lifestyle, idiom and nonchalance with the speed of Berlin's proverbial wit. Thunderstruck, a grandmother from Ankara remained silent when her grandson fended off her reproach with a cool: "I'm not dumb at all. I just look that way." Another Berliner in the making.

Botanical Treasures and Pleasures

Most typical for Berlin is a plant known as much for its infinite variety of shapes and sizes as for its resilience and toughness, blooming in spite of a shadowy existence in the concrete urban surroundings. Blossoming in rather pale colors, this species, always of the feminine gender, actually thrives on Berlin air and that mixture of asphalt and sandy soil for vitality. Please consider the thorny shrub marketed under the name "Berliner Pflanze" (Plant of Berlin) by a clever gardener in Frankfurt on Main: a sorry fake and an insult to the original, which exhibits qualities no would-be replica can match. *The* "Berliner Pflanze" is in the spring of her life, bouncing, and though as vulnerable as any other girl, toughened by a strong will to survive. Her street sense, acquired the hard way, is the one characteristic she always manages to preserve through her inevitable mutation into a professional or housewife in the city or anywhere else.

Botanically speaking much of what is firmly rooted in

Berlin's soil today traces its origin back to foreign imports. The 250-year-old mulberry tree in the former Huguenot quarters between Friedrich- and Reinhardtstraße still bears witness to this fact. This exotic veteran no longer supplies its leaves to feed hungry silkworms raised by French immigrants, but its berries still leave pink, sticky traces on people's fingers.

It was in the eighteenth century that a merchant with worldwide trading connections presented the Prussian monarch with a veritable cornucopia, a treasure which took well to the local ground. The Arabian acacia, planted in the park of Sanssouci in Potsdam, flourished and multiplied, and soon grove after grove of offsprings appeared around town. Traders from seaports as far away as Hamburg began a regular run on the timber, which was so tenacious and thus excellently suited for the production of wooden nails for ships' planks. The coffers of the Berlin treasury filled, the merchants retained their share of happiness, shipowners and sailors greeted the security of their boats in rough waters, and successive Prussian kings and their subjects were assured of Berlin's "presence" across the Seven Seas of the World.

Botany is a matter close to the Berliner's heart, and not only from this practical point of view. Linden trees, which gave the stately promenade Unter den Linden its name, used to line the historically younger avenue of Kurfürstendamm to the west as well. Poplar and lime trees, horse chestnuts and others offer shade in summertime throughout every district in town. If the season is extremely short of rain, newspapers in both East and West Berlin, as in one voice, call upon their citizens to water the trees, even if with the contents of their bathtubs, since soapsuds do not affect the roots of the trees. Saved from withering in summer, the trees are lucky to make it through the winter, not so much for lack of water, as for the effect of all that salt strewn against ice and snow. Immediately the papers, once again in one voice, demand prompt replacement from the cities' administrations for the victims of traffic safety. In former times that seemed easy. A gardener came, dug a hole, and planted a tree. The costs were minimal. Today, the road has to be closed, traffic rerouted, a crane appears on the scene, and a team of experts including a horticulturist, a tree root specialist, and of course a civil servant from the municipal accounting office must be present. As a result the whole procedure comes to a total of 15,000 deutschmarks for all of one newly-planted tree.

For a quiet hour of rest we retreated to a bench in one of the old cemeteries, in a part no longer in use. Whatever trees were damaged by war artillery in 1945 have long been replenished. Forsythia were glowing in golden yellow, almost blinding our eyes. Birds were chirping and rabbits hopping amongst overgrown graves. Where the rabbits had scraped the ground, light sand lay bare—the same material used by Prussians for centuries to blot the ink on letters and documents. If the gravestones had not been in view, it would have been hard to believe that these times when sand was used to blot the ink on public and private correspondences ever existed in Berlin at all.

Berlin's parks and gardens and tree-lined avenues have been admired all over Europe since the master landscape architect Peter Joseph Lenné, a descendant of the Huguenots, became Royal Director of Gardens in 1821. His successor, Gustav Meyer, followed in his footsteps. The very first botanical garden, however, planted in the pleasure park of the city palace, dates as far back as the seventeenth century. A model garden and herbarium in the Schöneberg area was not long to follow. Here the romantic poet Adalbert von Chamisso was employed from 1819 until his death in 1838.

The examples Lenné and Meyer set kept bearing fruit, if not to say blossoms. All over town, from Schöneberg to Friedrichshain, from Treptow to Gesundbrunnen, delightful public gardens were cultivated. Berlin went on an aesthetic rampage. The arboretum on Baumschulenweg (appropriately called Nursery Way) is maintained by East Berlin's Humboldt University as a botanical research center in the Department of Natural Sciences. Dahlem's Botanical Gardens (now West), founded in 1910, lure visitors into the greenhouses and along informative and beautiful nature strolls. The Botanical Museum next to the garden's entrance was not reopened until 1963.

Each year in early spring, when cherries and magnolia are in bloom, the public park in Mariendorf is haunted at night. The ghosts of insomniac Berliners roam through the dark with phantom saws. When the apparitions have vanished, the prettiest branches with the most gorgeous adornment of buds and blossoms have disappeared along with them.

In the immediate aftermath of the Second World War, public gardens not only supplied Berliners with otherwise unattainable heating material; they also offered ground for private and clandestine cultivation of vegetables. Don't look

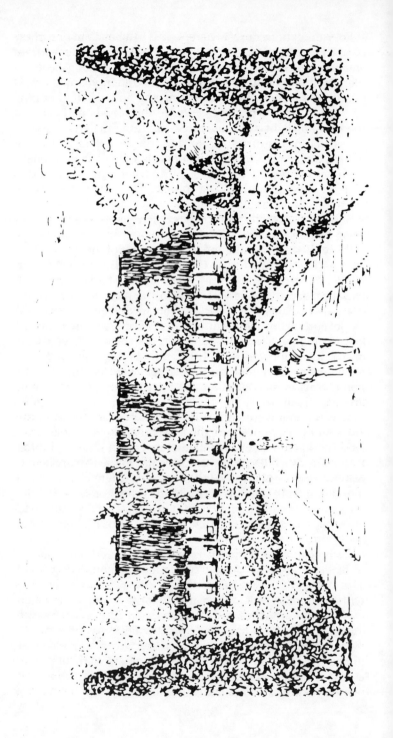

at it from too narrow a perspective, the natives keep on telling everyone. Which has brought us full circle back to the practical side of botany.

British Through and Through

Anything and everything British was the rage of the sixties in West Berlin, from the lingerie shop "My Fair Lady" to the men's hair stylist "Mylord." Kurfürstendamm, too, came out of its traditional reserve of high-class and high-priced elegance, adopting the Carnaby Street look, with street vendors and flashy wares spilling from the display windows out onto the pavement. East Berlin could not help catching a milder form of the virus. On Alexanderplatz kids licked "soft ices," and grown-ups in jeans carried a "broiler" home for dinner instead of what had previously been called roasted chicken— or "rubber eagle" in good old Berlinese. Not least surprised by the new fad were the many British businessmen and trade union officials in town on a promotional or negotiating mission.

As early as a century ago the Prussian Ministry of Trade and Commerce welcomed the import of English coal, iron goods and cloth. The last, labeled "cheap and nasty" by the promoters of home-produced materials, was manufactured into "Fashions from Berlin" in thousands of textile firms. The "English Waterworks" at the Stralau Gate as well as the first gasworks in Berlin owe their design and construction to the know-how of engineers from the British Isles. Sewage disappeared from the street gutters of Berlin only after the introduction of that noble English invention, the WC, but as late as 1870 no more than half of the city's households were equipped with so genteel a device. An outbreak of cholera then shook the city fathers out of their complacency and forced them to provide the funds necessary for a canalization system long advocated by the eminent doctor and health official Rudolf Virchow. He had returned from a journey to England an ardent supporter of this newfangled British idea. Greenwich Pier in Tegel continues to remind the initiated that the first steamer on the Havel River, too, was built according

[31]

to British models. The uninitiated board a pleasure boat there thinking nothing of it, and set sail just the same.

The famous Prussian architect Karl Friedrich Schinkel was in for a crushing disappointment when he came home to the city after an extensive educational tour of Britain. However brilliant the ideas for light and airy factories and humane living quarters he had brought back, nobody was interested. What his clients wanted from him were construction plans for mock-Scottish castles in miniature, ornamented with the greatest possible number of brick turrets or for mansions with balconies in English Gothic style. The *nouveaux riches* had made it in the world, finally, and what the royals had, they could afford easily now. World War II reduced much of this architecture to rubble.

The British garrison in West Berlin houses a contingent of 3,500 soldiers to defend their sector, which comprises the Tiergarten, Charlottenburg, Wilmersdorf, and Spandau districts. Their headquarters are located near the Olympic Stadium Hitler had built from scratch for the games of 1936. The annual parade in honor of the queen's official birthday is held on the "Field of May," while the stadium itself is used for drill and sports purposes by Her Majesty's subjects all year round. The gala birthday celebration displays the appropriate trimmings, complete with regimental mascot—be it pony, ram, or donkey—and the occasional member of the Royal Guard fainting in the hot summer sun. Should the four-legged talisman in all innocence misbehave in any way, punishment is not far off: favorite ration cut by one glass of beer. On that particular day, military musicians in red jackets with shiny instruments make their appearance at the British Embassy on East Berlin's Unter den Linden. The ambassador and his guests are treated to a birthday serenade, which more often than not fills the air with cheerful tunes from light operas. Prussian souls expecting snappy marches have been known to betray their culture shock by raised eyebrows.

Among the West Berlin papers those with a special affinity to the British all belong to the press empire built by the late Axel Caesar Springer. In the years immediately following Hitler's fall, it was the British military administration which granted Springer his first publishing licenses. Rumor has it that in the early morning at Windsor Castle Prince Philip peruses the Springer products, among other German tabloids, for the latest revelations about his family, just to be able to start the day with hilarious laughter.

East Berlin papers keep their imaginative faculties well under control, which makes them less funny too.

With the assistance of the Shropshire Horticultural Society and a generous donation from the British Royal Household, an English garden was laid out in Tiergarten. The grounds were officially presented to the public in 1952, with the British foreign secretary, Sir Anthony Eden, giving the opening speech. No wonder Berliners quickly referred to it as their "Garden of Eden."

C

Cabaret—Willkommen, Bienvenue, Welcome and Good-bye

The Golden Age of Berlin's cabarets is a thing of the past, brought to a sudden end in 1933 by the forced closure of these small stages and intimate theaters loved and feared for their great political satire and wide influence. And whatever was revived in the postwar years seems but a pale second brew, only faintly resembling the strong original stuff. Cabaret Berlin style was not like an American floor show or a program of sassy ballads in the English music-hall tradition. It was sassy alright, and musical, too, but there was more: biting wit, poignant satire, outright sarcasm attacking the failings and deficiencies of the socio-political system and its propagators. The salty puns of a Claire Waldoff or the irreverent lines of a Joachim Ringelnatz, both of whom came to fame in Berlin, still prop up their hard-working, honestly striving but misaiming emulators.

A Berlin cabaret personality was writer, actor, entertainer, political commentator, economic analyst, social critic; a sage smiling at human foibles and a fighter endowed with the courage of a gladiator, all wrapped into one. He or she knew something about music, couldn't always match Maria Callas or Caruso, but played an instrument well, and ideally possessed the business sense of an entrepreneur. There was only one thing he or she was not fit to be: a conformist. Consequently the most admired cabaret artists emigrated at the beginning of the Hitler era, if they were lucky. Some, like

Werner Finck, were taken into state custody as a warning to others.

Berlin offered the liberal attitudes the cabarets needed to exist, as well as the intolerance and intolerable situations to assail. Such a precarious balance never holds for long, especially not in Berlin; too much on either side of the scale and the sharp weapon of satire and irony finds no target or breaks down altogether. Only in the twenties and early thirties could the caustic wit of the cabaret hit as much against the enemies of liberalism as against liberalism itself. The texts sparkled and cut like diamonds, and not just those written by the likes of Kästner, Tucholsky, and Brecht. The names of Mischa Spoliansky and Hanns Eisler remain a trademark for musical quality. Trude Hesterberg and Curt Bois could count on their fans old and young, unlike any pop star of today. American swing had barely conquered Berlin between the two devastating wars when, in cabaret fashion, Bertolt Brecht and Hanns Eisler termed it "misuc" to reveal parodistically the *mis*leading smoothness of its pleasing beat that only superficially covered the sharp edges of the times. They had a model, of course, in Adolf Glaßbrenner, the father of Berlin cabaret artists and satirists. He invented a club for all reactionaries who were striving for the return of Prussian absolutism, the "Zaruck" Club (a bowdlerization of "zurück," which means backward, and "Zar" for emperor). But neither the cabarets nor their followers were able to establish a bulwark against the forces stirred by Hitler.

The divided city certainly offered absurdities enough, and new cabarets could have prospered after the war. They appeared on the scene soon after 1945—Insulaner (Islanders) and Stachelschweine (Porcupines) in the West, Distel (Thistle) in East Berlin. But some basic ingredient had been replaced. The "common enemy," once the target of chansons and sketches, monologues and verses in the name of common sense and decency, now no longer lay on one's own doorstep but "over there" in the other political camp. From whichever side the jokes were fired, at least half of them had become conformist. By now, both sides have begun to clean their own dirty laundry, and the Distel has opened a second location in Hohenschönhausen, since the old Admiral Palais in Friedrichstraße cannot hold all those eager to see the shows.

To capture a share of the cabaret business before it started waning, radio and television stepped in, particularly in the

[35]

West. For young aspiring artists, the chance of instant large-scale success proved an invitation to unprofessional careless-ness. Each mistake could be erased on tape and rerecorded. The well-versed cameraman knew how to bridge weak pass-ages in live performances by a quick turn of the lens. Profes-sional qualities decreased, while the fees rose, creating new financial demands. The art of bundling energy and keeping the audience spellbound was all too easily lost in the process.

A number of small theaters opened in West Berlin, bring-ing the old magic show and miniature vaudeville back to life. Sit-com jokes take the place of witty commentary. Kids love it. Young East Berliners have developed their own mixture of show concert and cabaret. Not all critical arrows hit the mark, but that doesn't really matter. Applause is assured, and since whistling counts among the signs of approval, no negative reaction remains. Pop music gets things going again should a punch line fall flat.

Cafés

Berliners are known for their sweet tooth as much as for their sociability, and what better way to cater for both at the same time than with a leisurely rendezvous in their favorite café. These earthly colonies of heavenly delights come in all styles, from plain to elegant: with a trace of Viennese *Kaffeehaus* here and a touch of French bistro there; some as functional as an American coffee shop or as cozy as grandmother's living room; and some in the splendor of a royal palace. Breakfast is served until closing time at night, as well as the ever-tempting variety of pastry, cakes and tarts, chocolates, and candies, not to forget the array of beverages from coffee to the most potent liquor.

Swiss confectioners were the first to introduce their Prus-sian cousins to these calorific traps that crush the strongest New Year's resolution. Heinrich Heine raved about the cream puffs from Unter den Linden. A century and a half later, Chancellor Kohl raved about the rhubarb tart from Kur-fürstendamm. One hundred and fifty years of intellectual controversy melting on the tongue like sweet nothings: all

Berlin Kurfürstendamm

from a Berlin pastry shop. Through the window of a café in a West Berlin side street we could see fat flies on their backs. Lifelessly they lay sprawled between cakes on white paper doilies, gorged to death.

Theobald von Bethmann-Hollweg, a prominent politician under the last of the German emperors, had his breakfast regularly at Möhring's. The room he lounged in still carries his name, but the wallpaper is of a more recent design. The house burnt down and had to be rebuilt. George Grosz, the eminent graphic artist and satirist, was still able to recognize the old decor, when he returned to Berlin (where he died in 1959) from his exile in the United States. This "phenomenon of sadness" (his self-description) saw himself surrounded by nothing but old acquaintances. No matter how much time had changed, the physiognomies about him, male or female, had lost none of the traits he had caricatured before the war. No budding artist takes these faces seriously enough anymore to capture them with quick, sharp, and revealing strokes of the pen. And alas, the wealthy young American who lifts a coffee cup with trembling hand would be too sad a model even for George Grosz. Wide eyes in an emaciated face betray an addiction to stuff stronger than the sweet delicacies offered here.

A new Romanisches Café opened its doors on Budapester Straße, not far from the original location of what was once the number one gathering place for the literary talents of the day.

When thumbing through the Nazi-period edition of a leading literary reference work, you'll find that the names are missing of all those who frequented the Romanische and brought it to fame. No one was or has been able to take their place, not in the café, nor in any lexicon of authors. The new generation of writers, artists, and intellectuals in West Berlin meets to chat and argue in cafés and pubs on Savigny Platz that conform with more modern lifestyles, while at the same time displaying customs that have survived with the proverbial local stubbornness. According to a golden rule faithfully observed in Berlin for ages, nobody has money, and if by chance they have some, it belongs to someone else. The principle of borrowing off Peter to pay Paul is so generally and consistently applied that it welds even these most staunchly individualistic creatures into a community of common interest— excepting perhaps those pledged to lifelong hatred—renewable weekly. Our friend M.L., journalist and cynic, maintains that Berliners are cannibals devouring one another. He is doubtlessly right, considering their appetite for that jelly-filled donut they themselves call pancake, but known by the rest of Germany as "Berliner."

East Berlin follows a slightly modified café tradition. The clientele consists more often than not of people who should actually be working but have allowed themselves an "out to lunch" party. With lunch it may start; the waiters and waitresses have a pretty realistic idea of the massive orders for coffee, cake, and alcoholic beverages to follow. The waitresses of East Berlin usually don the same type of footwear: sensible, comfortable sandals that an understanding union had specially designed and produced for their friendly neigborhood long-distance runners. Guests from anywhere outside the republic are just as welcome as the locals. Older ladies from West Berlin love to come and munch their way through mountains of strawberry cake and plum tart with whipped cream. They are easily identified by the pill containers they set down next to their plates with a deep sigh, and by their grumbling about the few coins charged by the toilet attendant for the use of a towel. In *their* part of town that is included in the overall price which, all things considered, is markedly higher. And wasn't that the very reason they came across the border anyway, forsaking Kurfürstendamm with its famous Café Kranzler and Möhring's?

The intellectual set of East Berlin only occasionally resorts to public cafés for their get-togethers. They prefer their clubs, as much for their privacy as for the coffee shop *and* bar service they provide. In wanting such choices under one roof the intellectuals may have been trendsetters, but they are not alone. New establishments tried to match the trend. "We are not strictly a café in the coffee-and-cake sense," explained the manager of the Arkade, located in an historical setting near the reconstructed Großes Schauspielhaus or Grand Theater. He referred to the café-snack bar with mirrored walls and exotic palms for added atmosphere up front, and the rooms further to the back: modernized, spruced-up versions of the old-fashioned Berlin *Kneipe* or drinking bar. In the city center such newfangled combinations have their justification. The average Berliner, however, shies away from too much elegance. Unpretentious in taste, he will feel more comfortable in less stylish an ambience. The widely-known and loved Zenner, a garden café established in 1822 as part of Gasthaus Treptow (Treptow Inn), has drawn in the crowds now for over 160 years. Weather permitting, there is space enough for a thousand hungry strollers.

In the olden days, garden cafés of this kind would sell their cakes and pastry and supply the hot water for families to brew their own coffee. If veteran Berliners are to be believed, those were the "good old days."

Castles, Once for Royal Pleasure Only

The most ardent celebrity-watchers may consider themselves lucky today if they catch a glimpse of a state representative in a well-tailored suit. His Imperial Highness, Emperor of Germany and King of Prussia, always appeared on the scene in flashy gala uniform, and his residences shone in regal splendor. Since the German Republic was proclaimed in 1918, glamor has just not been what it used to be. With the fall of empire and monarchy, even the palaces in and around Berlin were one by one turned over to public ownership.

For the old City Palace (dating from the fifteenth century) there was no redress once bombs and grenades of the last World War had taken their toll. The authorities of the republic east of the German–German divide decided to tear the

Berlin Schloss Glienicke   John Bernstädt

ruins down. Seat for over 560 years for the Hohenzollern *margraves*, electors, kings of Prussia, and emperors of Germany, the castle had been one of the major attractions in the capital. By 1950 after a few detonations, and innumerable truckloads of debris had been hoisted off, it had vanished from view. No one had ever been allowed to enter without a pass, sentries stood guard throughout. In that respect at least, not much has changed for the visitor to any of the state ministries in the vicinity. In contrast, the Palace of the Republic erected on the site of the former royal residence thrives on public attendance as perhaps *the* cultural and social center of the GDR metropolis. It goes without saying that the one wing where the People's Chamber holds its sessions remains off limits for the casual passer-by.

Another famous Berlin castle for which you will search in vain is Monbijou, the jewel that once was. Lawns, flower beds, and a children's playground occupy the space of the former pleasure palace, which contained the family museum of the Hohenzollern dynasty from 1877 onward. The beauty of such lost treasures is recalled in preciously bound and exquisitely crafted picture volumes. Photographs show the imperial boudoirs with their ornate four-poster beds and canopies, the state rooms in marble and gold, and the stoves of magnificent Dutch tiles.

It was the youngest brother of Frederick the Great who commissioned the construction of Bellevue Castle in Tiergarten. For the first time, neoclassical style triumphed here over

the "effeminate" playfulness of the rococo period. With every architect who took charge of alterations and expansions the design became increasingly stern. Relinquished into state ownership in 1928, the Nazis remodeled it in 1938 into the "Guest House of the Reich." Then came the war and destruction, followed by peace and reconstruction. Today, Bellevue is regarded as the official seat in West Berlin of the president of the Federal Republic, who normally resides in Bonn.

In the beautiful English garden surrounding Bellevue we saw little devils running about, quite obviously up to nothing good. Waiting until they thought the coast was clear, they would grab their bows and, using bicycle spokes for arrows, begin their hunt for the ducks on the pond. The innocence of the "Garden of Eden" was broken, but perhaps the Berlin rascals simply remembered that this terrain had a long tradition as a riding and hunting ground?

On both sides of the border, Berliners can take pride in nearly twenty castles altogether, many of them erstwhile hunting lodges or summer retreats, the majority of them long smothered by apartment complexes and traffic arteries, all of them put to something other than their original use. Köpenick (in East Berlin) converted its old castle into a museum of modern crafts after it had served for a time as a student's dormitory. It was not until 1939 that the heirs to the princely Klein Glienicke Castle (a relative newcomer among the castles now on West Berlin territory), were persuaded to part with that estate for a very handsome sum, and it then cost the city a bundle to repair.

The park surrounding the castle hotel has become a favorite spot for outings. But it is a bridge in these gardens which has the more curious tale to tell. Built by a romantically-inclined architect as a ruin, it was to symbolize the passing of time and the decay of all cultural phenomena. In 1938, one hundred years later, a no-nonsense realist restructured the bridge into a solid, functional piece: practical but everything but romantic! Then, recently, a building contractor was asked to restore it once again to its original "ruinous" shape, at considerable expense to the public purse.

Of some Berlin castles, as for instance in Buch (East Berlin), only a wing or a few service buildings were spared destruction. Wannsee and Rudow (West Berlin) fell victim to disfigurement by plaster brigades, who smoothed out every façade. Schoeler's manor in Wilmersdorf (also in the West) became a children's home. The former mansion in Niederschönhausen opens its doors to prominent guests of the GDR government only. And since the small renovated palace of Friedrichsfelde lies on the grounds of the East Berlin Zoological Garden, lectures and concerts are held there to the accompaniment of melodious contributions by seals and buffaloes. During the restoration of the Grunewald hunting lodge, now a picture gallery, wall paintings from the Renaissance period were discovered that had been hidden for centuries.

The castle in Tegel, part of the estate of the scholarly von Humboldt family, so delighted the cultural officer of the Red Army that he had it cleared and its contents moved to his homeland. Everything was returned later, but to East Berlin. West Berlin protested. The East Berliners countercharged that many of the treasures belonging to them were held back by the other side, too. Different memories are connected with the little castle in Steglitz, where Field Marshal Friedrich von Wrangel used to live. A typical representative of Prussian militarism, he was instrumental in crushing the German democratic revolution of 1848. He used to walk around the park in full gala uniform, decorated with all his medals. A shoemaker's apprentice once saw the old soldier approach and stopped his whistling immediately. Wrangel was taken in by this respectful behavior, told the fellow so and rewarded him with a small coin. The boy bowed and said: "Thank you, Sir. But when I see you with all that silver tinsel, I have to laugh. And when I laugh, I can't whistle."

Cemeteries for the Famous and the Fast Forgotten

General decree of March 4, 1899 concerning the
bearing of a standard during funerals of members of
war veterans' associations. With view to certain
offenses which have occurred, I hereby once again,
and for the benefit of the subordinate departments
involved in this matter, call attention to the fact that
during funerals of members of war veterans'
associations, those associations in possession of a
banner authorized by the State may bear this standard
and none other.

Berlin, March 4, 1899
For the Minister of the Interior
signed: *Lindig*.

While order has prevailed in Berlin cemeteries since time immemorial, the very peace generally conceded to the dead never has. Visiting the Garrison Cemetery on Columbiadamm you may find yourself thunderstruck by the awesomeness of the World War I memorials in honor of the First Dragoon Regiment of Guards or the First West Prussian Foot-Artillery Regiment or, even worse, by that black granite monster erected for the Augusta Grenadier Regiment of Guards. Resting on a catafalque a soldier lies covered by a military blanket, his fist clenched, embodiment of the vindicative spirit stirring in German military circles after the defeat of 1918. Nazi architecture, too, manifested itself from 1936 to 1939 in a demonstratively horrid structure in the graveyard on Lilienthalstraße, Neukölln. Only in 1966 did the Federation of German War-Graves Commissions undertake some corrections, even if only minor ones.

Eternity and respect for eternity are measured in Berlin by other than the usual gauges. In 1943 the Secret State Police of the Nazis destroyed the Jewish Cemetery consecrated in Große Hamburgerstraße in 1672. Many gravesites could not be reconstructed any more. Only a memorial stone erected by East Berlin authorities serves a a visible reminder that the great Jewish philosopher Moses Mendelssohn lies buried here. Jewish graves along Schönhauser Allee were also ransacked by Hitler's followers. Neither was the monument spared which Mies van der Rohe, the architect of interna-

[43]

tional acclaim, had designed for the tomb of Rosa Luxemburg and Karl Liebknecht. The two leading representatives of the Left had been brutally murdered in 1919 after having been kidnapped by uniformed men. Liebknecht's body was found a few hours after the murder; Rosa Luxemburg's corpse was discovered floating in the Landwehrkanal months later. Political friends raised the memorial in 1926, and nine years later the Nazis tore it down.

An evening college teacher from Charlottenburg organizes tours to the burial places of famous Berliners, poets and writers in particular. The bus takes off from the Charlottenburg town hall. Many a name inscribed in the annals of European culture can be discovered on a tombstone in the cemeteries of Berlin, as, for instance, those in front of the Halle Gate. In the course of modern street planning some cemetery walls have been demolished, a transgression comparable to the one against the Invalidenfriedhof (originally for war invalids only) the western end of which was cut through by the Berlin Wall. Since 1748 mainly high army officials had been buried here. The Nazis abused the place by incorporating it into their hero cult, and in order to prevent any flare-up of old militaristic and nationalistic demonstrations, the burial grounds remain closed to the public at most times.

On the benches of the Dorotheenstädter Friedhof (East Berlin), Western intellectuals may frequently be seen to rest and contemplate. Bertolt Brecht lies buried here, his modest gravesite but the size of a divan, just wide enough to grant his wife, petite actress Helene Weigel, a final resting place as well. G.F.W. Hegel's gravestone stands not far away.

In the idyllic Waldfriedhof in West Berlin, visitors can find solitude in a landscape relatively untouched, a part of the Grunewald, where in days past wild boars were rutting about in the underbrush. That's why the cemetery pond bears the name "Saukuhle," or sow pit.

Not even the history of the cemeteries in Berlin is without traces of the burlesque. Arno Holz, the poet, was first buried in a child's grave for lack of space, before he received a more dignified tomb. In 1982 there was the interment of Friedrich Schröder, who had also adopted the patronymic Sonnenstern to annoy a wealthy family in his native Pomerania. He had been a painter and a dreamer, fond of the bottle, a frequent guest in psychiatric clinics, and an eccentric long before his old age. Some of his artist friends had brought nettles along instead of flowers, and vodka bottles with which to console themselves before converting them into vases. In the end the bouquets were lowered into the grave near the bottom of the casket—according to a last wish of the deceased—as a remedy for his eternally cold feet.

King Frederick William I had set an early example for this sort of funeral celebration. In 1731 he had his court jester and cellar master buried in what resembled a wine barrel. When no clergyman could be persuaded to conduct the ceremony, the jester's archenemy stepped in and held the *laudatio* to the barely disguised amusement of the small congregation. The tombstone raised not long afterwards depicted Minerva (for cleverness), three peacock feathers (for vanity) and a hare (for cowardice).

Charlottenburg
alias Lietzenburg Castle

When the foundation was laid for Charlottenburg Castle, then just west of Berlin city limits, the Prussian monarchy was not yet born. Elector Frederick III had not crowned himself Frederick I, King *in* Prussia, yet. Nothing more was planned than a pleasant, unassuming summer palace for the elector's second wife, Sophie Charlotte, to be called Lietzenburg after the adjoining village of Lietzen (Lietzow). That was in 1695. Half a dozen years later, in 1701, Frederick was king and Lietzenburg rang with the sounds of royal celebrations for six months. The palace had been enlarged several times already; a small opera house premiered with the performance of an Italian favorite. So far, so good. But there was a new role to be played now. The country, consisting of not much more than smallish towns and villages, needed stature, needed a building boom. The layout of Lietzenburg was provincial, lacking luster. And so the Swedish architect Eosander was appointed to draw up plans for the development of Lietzow into a more modern settlement—and to enlarge as well as embellish the palace, making it both a landmark and an abode fit for royals.

What he was able to accomplish in decades of construction and conversion, what his successors added and reconverted

Berlin Schloss Charlottenburg

over centuries—all was blown to pieces in only one night, during the air raid on Berlin of November 23, 1943. Postwar reconstruction was essentially completed by 1956, by sheer good luck—literally. The purchase of period furniture, the acquisition of precious china to replace the once famous collection that was lost, and the piece by piece accumulation of works of art worthy of the tradition were all accomplished with the proceeds from the Berlin lottery.

Sophie Charlotte, in a few brief years, turned her castle into the intellectual and cultural center of the realm. Loved and admired, she attracted leading scholars and artists to Lietzenburg, including the philosopher Leibniz. Charlottenburg

[46]

Castle, as it was renamed after her untimely death in 1705, never again lived up to this initial high reputation. The new settlement, into which Old Lietzow (so called for the "Lietzen" or coots nesting in the surrounding waters) was incorporated in 1720, received a town charter as Charlottenburg and kept on growing.

During his younger days Sophie Charlotte's son, later Frederick William I, better known as the "Soldier King," could be found indulging in his favorite pastime: floating toy boats on the Spree River, which bordered the palace gardens. To him they constituted the "Turkish Fleet," which he sank, men, mast and all, jubilant about his victory over the "heathens." The "heathens" residing in Berlin in large numbers today provide living proof that such victories do not last. By droves they stroll through Charlottenburg Park during their leisure time or make themselves comfortable on the grass for a picnic, not far from the place where the martial king long ago ordered a carp pond to be laid out. Back then, a bell regularly called the fish to the surface for feeding, at least until the harsh winter of 1864, when the pond froze solid and the fat and mossy carps died, all thirty-six of them.

The graceful Belvedere tower can be seen glistening through the trees in rococo serenity, giving no hint of the strange passion indulged in there by a Prussian king. Frederick William II was initiated into the Order of the Rosicrucians in 1781, and henceforth firmly believed in ghosts. With a few like-minded friends he would retreat into an upper chamber of the pavilion to conjure up whomever or whatever. Then, one day, having gone up with high expectations, he stumbled down again white as a sheet. The spirits of his forefathers and other historical personalities of the past as far back as Caesar hauled him over the coals so forcefully that he had the entrance to Belvedere nailed shut, never to return again.

Devoted fans of pomp and ceremony are personally insulted that West Berlin no longer has occasion to shine with festivities of the diplomatic corps and receptions of state, since it was stripped of its status as a capital. Prestige and glory seem to have vanished as well. And what makes matters worse, East Berlin did not suffer the same fate. The only hope left is Charlottenburg Castle. Following the annual military parades of the three Allied forces, festive crowds gather here, or the descendant of the last emperor makes an occasional appearance for a visit of his family's former resi-

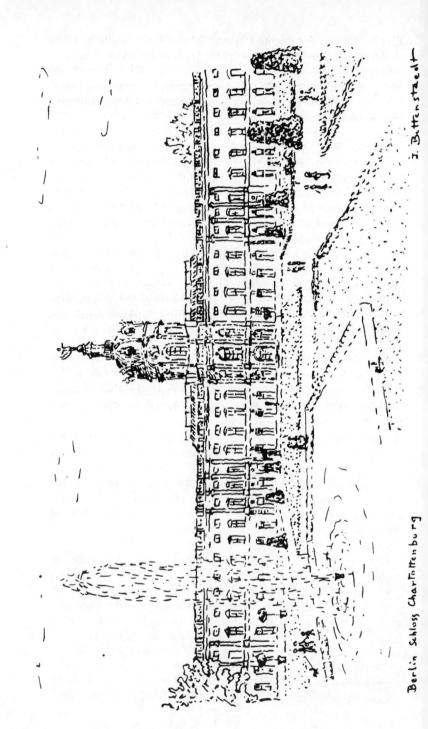

Berlin Schloss Charlottenburg

J. Battenstaedt

dency. Then some of the old splendor shines through, even if, for security reasons, the Berliners are banished to a spectators' position at a safe distance from their castle. The press, however, are right there, reporting on even the smallest item on the menu. Something like the gossip of court gazettes rustles through the daily drab; a change for a change, a touch of *noblesse*, nostalgia, delusion.

Berlin's most beloved Queen Luise lies buried in the park of Charlottenburg. Above her tomb a mausoleum rises in somber grey in the style of a nineteenth-century memorial temple. It also enshrines the urns that hold the once fast-beating hearts of some of her noble relations, cut from the bodies of the deceased as in Pharaonic times. Karl Friedrich Schinkel, the architect of a number of relatively recent alterations to the castle, perfected the design of the mausoleum begun by Luise's widower Frederick William III. In honor of Queen Luise nationalistically-inclined women of Berlin had knitted patriotic socks for their men in the field during the wars of liberation from Napoleonic rule: a magic formula, adapted from classical antiquity, to assure victory.

Above the front entrance to the shrine the Greek letters *xi* and *rho* bear witness to the Christian belief of the Hohenzollerns as much as to their preference for days gone by. The alpha and omega displayed on either side irrefutably attest to the fact that everything has a beginning and an end.

Churches in Use and in Shambles

Berliners live under the constant fear of being mistaken for provincials. To ward off this unwelcome reputation they keep on reiterating—in the manner of a magic formula—"Berlin ain't no village." But the double negation can't hide the historical fact that the city developed out of just that, and even today it is but an agglomeration of different villages grown together, some fifty in all, each centering around a church spire. In 1539 the Prussian rulers converted from Catholicism and joined the Lutheran Reformation, from which they withdrew again in 1613 to enter the Reformed Church influenced by Calvin. While theological tensions and

Berlin: Dom

competition ensued between the older Lutheran congregations and the Calvinist newcomers who enjoyed the patronage of the ruling dynasty, Catholics had to take a back seat. Most Berlin churches are Protestant now, even if they began in the Roman papal tradition which had increased its influence in the territory between the Oder and Elbe rivers from the tenth century onward.

The name of an East Berlin street and subway station, Kloster-Straße—or Monastery Street—reminds us of the Franciscan monastery founded in 1271 near this spot. Its church, considered the first all-brick building in Berlin, has been retained as a ruin. The building material was originally carted here from the brick kiln in Kreuzberg, which had been a donation. The Franciscans still wore a grey habit then, and the people attached this color to their monastery as well, calling it "Graues Kloster." Yet in 1571, as a direct result of post-Reformation decrees—the order had been forbidden to accept novices and the last of the monks had passed away—the monastic buildings were put to different use, as a laboratory and school. A student of Paracelsus (Europe's foremost medical authority of the day), one Leonhard Thurneysser, scientist, alchemist, businessman, and medical practitioner all in one, moved in.

The elector had appointed Thurneysser as his personal physician and given much of the monastery over to him for medical research and pharmacological experiments. Held in high esteem by his superiors and admired as much as feared

by the general public, the scientist experimented and con-
cocted medications from the produce of his herb garden,
while superstitious rumor had it that he regularly dined with
Satan himself. In 1572 Thurneysser depicted in a woodcut the
gruesome quartering of the court Jew Lippold, who had
fallen from official grace. Two years later part of the monastery was taken over by the first "common," non-parochial
high school of Berlin, which was to survive in East Berlin
until 1958 and whose tradition was revived in West Berlin
from 1954 on.

The churches of Berlin can look back on a turbulent history.
In 1615 the people of Berlin stormed and looted the cathedral.
The domed episcopal church of St. Hedwig was severely
damaged, like many others, in the Second World War and
was not restored until 1963. Toward the end of the nineteenth
century the former royal Prussian capital turned metropolis
of the German Empire could pride itself on having more
churches than Rome. Due to the rapid growth in population
up to a hundred christenings had to be performed after each
Sunday service in the Bethanienkirche. Baptism was of course
obligatory back then. For coachmen and cabbies special early
services were held in the old Spitalkirche, the hospital church,
today part of the Economics Department of East Berlin's
Humboldt University. These services had to be canceled once
participation rapidly dwindled as a result of a law that gave
every third coachman free time until twelve noon on Sundays.
To illustrate the Old Testament miracle of bountiful manna,
the pastor of the newly-constructed church in today's modern Hansa Quarter of West Berlin distributed American pop-
corn among his congregation. In other respects, too, the
church is special, with its roof within easy reach for drunks,
who can climb up at night and entertain the sleepy neighborhood with songs not found in any hymn book.

Among the treasures of art history found in East Berlin, the
Marienkirche with its white marble altar and the wide wall
relief of the "Dance of Death" of 1484 is outstanding. Not far
away rises the Imperial Cathedral—modeled after, but not
matching, St. Peter's of Rome. Its repairs were funded by the
public purse of the GDR, with contributions from the
churches of both German states. The edifice is maintained as
a national museum rather than as a place of worship. Its crypt
holds the tombs of many of the Hohenzollern line. Prince
Louis Ferdinand, grandson of the last emperor, William II,
recalls that his grandfather still considered himself bishop

[51]

Berlin: St. Hedwigs-Kathedrale   J. Bittenstardt

and head of the Protestant Church of Prussia even after his abdication in 1918 and while in exile in the Netherlands. The prince is also known as the composer of the music played by the peal of bells which sounds from the tower of the Kaiser-Wilhelm-Gedächtniskirche (the Emperor William Memorial Church) on Kurfürstendamm. To the great sorrow of the vicar in charge, he cannot prevent the entrance and even the interior of his church being mistaken time and again for a public toilet.

The times of the demolition of Berlin churches for fear of collapsing structures have gone. In West Berlin an occasional prayer hall is offered for sale. Religious East Berliners acknowledge with relief that the GDR Building Academy has presented their cardinal bishop with a brand-new house of God in the modern development of Marzahn; a church which carries the name "Maria, Queen of Peace." The Nikolaikirche in the center of the GDR capital is being restored, possibly to become a concert hall. This, too, has tradition in Berlin, where once the so-called "Polka Church" rang with bouncy organ music at every wedding celebration.

Circus World

Tightrope dancing, lion taming, and fire-eating rank high among favorite entertainments of Berliners who, after all, have had plenty of occasion to become experts in these arts. Thus the stage is set for any type of circus games, not excluding those of world politics.

In 1821 a certain G.F. Richter, master carpenter and entrepreneur, built a first circus hall just outside Brandenburg Gate. More about him, his venture, and the history of the circuses of Berlin can be learned in the "Documenta Artistica" section of the Märkisches Museum in East Berlin. In the western twin city a private collector has gathered what he could find about the love of his life. When he advertises in the papers his offer reads: "Admission Free! Forty years of circus performances in Berlin, a cultural–historical documentation. My circus museum is exclusively financed through my old-age pension. Edgar Falkenberg, Jüterborgstraße 9, Berlin Kreuzberg."

Between Schiffbauerdamm and Karlstraße (now Reinhardtstraße) a market hall went up in 1868, which from 1870 to 1919 saw the dare-devil acts of Salamonsky's, Renz's, and Schumann's circuses in succession. After major conversions the building became one of the sanctuaries of German theatrical history, under such high priests as Max Reinhardt and Erwin Piscator. Nevertheless, Das Große Schauspielhaus (the gigantic people's amphitheater Reinhardt had envisioned and realized) was forced to close in 1923. The stars had wandered off into the more lucrative film studios. The house, at the address Am Zirkus 1, was to serve other purposes. In the Hitler years light and trite amusement programs were produced here to raise the morale of the uniformed audience on temporary leave from the front and to get them ready for active duty again in a murderous war. In 1946 the site, then known as Friedrichstadtpalast, provided the backdrop for the first of a number of first-night performances in real splendor. But the ground was slipping, literally. The foundations slid ever more dangerously down the Spree River's bank into the mud. By 1984 the company was moved just around the corner into an ambitious new home at the very spot where the State Circus of the GDR had maintained its winter quarters. Water basin, skating rinks, and larger and smaller stages provide a splendid setting for all sorts of variety shows.

Animal acts and acrobatic numbers are incorporated into the program to preserve some of the circus atmosphere. For as long as the inner city border was still open, West Berliners enjoyed a trip to the "Palast," too. Now, as a result of well-known checkpoint problems, they flock into their own Deutschlandhalle, when "Holiday on Ice" is in town. A house built specifically for circus and variety shows is still lacking in West Berlin.

In both parts of the city the desire for sensation is satisfied with different attractions. When a team of acrobats runs their high wire between the Europa-Center and the Kaiser-Wilhelm-Gedächtniskirche, West Berliners fill the streets to get their thrill, shuddering, wondering whether someone might not accidentally . . . . East Berlin trains their artistes in a state-run circus school, where highest skill and utmost security are law. Above a specific height all performers are secured by either a rope or a safety net. Once they have graduated they are on tour with the state circus most of the time, throughout the world and sometimes even in their own country. The state circus maintains its winter home in Dahlwitz-Hoppegarten outside Berlin. No spectacles here, just hard work and training, training, training.

Berlin's most famous Zirkus Busch was once housed near the city railroad station, Börse (or Stock Exchange). Its successor, Busch-Roland, pulled up its tents again west of the border after the last war, and when not on tour in the Federal Republic or in other West European countries it is stationed on West Berlin's Reichpietsch-Ufer. No matter how spoilt the audiences have gotten by T.V. programs, it is something else to see "live" seven Siberian tigers hiss and gnarl at a young woman tamer who fearlessly scratches their necks as a reward. The grand old lady of the circus, daughter of the erstwhile founder and herself later director of the family enterprise, also took up writing. Paula Busch, with indestructible Berlin humor and in typical Berlin dialect, recalls in her book *Wasserminna* the adventures and misadventures of that city brat Minna, nicknamed Waterminna, whose world was the circus. That girl, probably the first stuntwoman in Germany, with the drive of a locomotive and a heart of gold, would jump, on horseback, from a height of 6 meters into a huge water basin in the arena. Or she would spend hours underwater in a diving bell trying new and dangerous stunts. She also worked on the trapeze or with giant snakes.

Her courage only left her when it came to men. About love

she skeptically philosophized: "Five minutes of apprehension, and then that whole rubbish all over again."

Climate and Other Atmospheric Conditions

When Berliners talk about the weather they think of winter. When they think about summer the possibilities double. East Berliners plan their holidays in one of the labor unions' recreational facilities on the Baltic Sea, in Thuringia, in the Harz Mountains, or in a foreign locale within the socialist sphere of influence. West Berliners look forward to leaving their walled-in part of town in any direction. Those who stay behind vacation on their garden plot or their boat. Boats of all descriptions and sizes, with or without a private landing place, are so much a part of the natives' life-style that you will find the "islanders" near rivers and lakes (if not on them) even far away from their city. Wherever irises bloom in the reeds, where the reed warbler sings its crackling tune, where one can splash about with or without a bathing suit, Berliners find their natural habitat.

During the summer months Berlin (either side of the divide) is a tourist attraction in its own right. Across Alexanderplatz march groups of farmers, male and female, who know their way better through dusty Kazakhstan or the Siberian taiga than in this world wonder of a western metropolis. They appear in delegations and sit at hotel and restaurant tables especially reserved for them, an interpreter always close at hand. From Poland and Czechoslovakia there are visitors traveling in their own cars to the capital of the GDR, where their passports only take them as far as the Wall. Many West Germans in air-conditioned buses arrive near Funkturm, be they members of a Christian women's association, schoolkids from Bavaria, or bowling fans from the Rhineland. Then there are the other Europeans, from Spain or Belgium or some other place. During these weeks and months the western half of Berlin lives off entertainment tax. Every district of the city fills up, every free space has been reserved for a summer festival. In that respect the situation in East

Berlin differs little. One hundred and sixty individual events are on the agenda of the Köpenick festivities alone. Treptow promises to go up in flames, which is a fraud, since it is still standing. Only its huge fairground will be all alight.

July temperatures reach 24 degrees (Celsius) regularly. From the vantage point of Grunewald Tower (West) and its counterpart Müggel Tower (East), you cannot see the sandy beaches for all the bare legs during those glorious days of summer sunshine. No matter how refreshingly cool the lakes and rivers become, temperatures generated along their shores and banks greatly exceed the metereological values measured. In winter the thermometer falls well below the freezing point. The janitor or house owner who fails to shovel "his" part of the sidewalk free of snow or pick away the ice is breaking the law and will be held responsible.

Already in 1822 the following warning was issued by the royal Prussian authorities: "Due to the present snow and frost it is particularly vital to obey faithfully the legal provisions for the prevention of accidents according to which it is neither permitted to drive a sleigh without a shaft or the ringing of bells nor to drive or ride through the streets at excessive speed. Any violation thereof will be punishable at the rate of 5 talers or the equivalent."

The traditional Dutch-tiled stoves for producing comfy warmth have the disadvantage that the dust from their ashes spreads throughout the entire house. Central- and remote-heating systems considerably raise the amount of sulphur dioxide that pollutes the air. More visible in cold weather than in summer, smoke clouds rising from power stations are registered by the Berliners with extreme distrust; and the results of pollution monitoring are not published too willingly by the authorities. You may blame the weather as much as you like, but it won't abide by your wishes, and the civil servants go by their rules anyway. The meteorologists at Potsdam station are tuned into a Soviet computer which converts satellite information into diagrams West Berliners do not trust. The meteorologists within the U.S. security area at Tempelhof Airport have their weather report transmitted from Offenbach on the Main. Berliners are therefore lucky enough to be enlightened about the same rain or sunshine in duplicate.

Whenever it rains, pours, dribbles, hails, storms, freezes, or snows, the best place to be is in a pub or *Kneipe*. In 1902 Minister of the Interior von Hammerstein decreed that any innkeeper's license would be taken away, who "during the daily gathering of numerous customers neglects to provide for appropriate circulation of air," that is, anyone who did not have a ventilating system. To which staunch Berliners retorted with the proverbial: "Frost is a known killer. Have you heard of anyone dying of the stench?"

Crime and the Hard Facts of Life

During the celebrated Golden Twenties "chic" sightseeing tours were organized for the well-to-do to visit hangouts of the Berlin underworld: the troughs of pimps and prostitutes, thieves trained in long-finger academies, professional safe-crackers, and worse. Young West Berlin policemen today could easily acquire a bad case of nostalgia when being told of the good relations between their colleagues and the heavies then. Nowadays the police are sent out to crack call-girl rings and drug syndicates and to chase after murderers, maimers, and muggers (whose victims frequently tend to be senior citizens). Even if their work may sometimes be almost routine, the crimes they fight have increased in sheer number, brutality, and organization. Or they are called out on the streets again and again during demonstrations which are often accompanied by chaos and vandalism and by violence on both sides. Not that the street battles of the thirties have resurged, but for many Berliners what is, is bad enough. For comic relief they may have grinned about the news item of the old granddad, detained several times for entering a bank and shouting: "Everyone to the floor. This is a bank robbery!" He was harmless, and a bit simple too, just relishing the sight of everybody down at his feet.

West Berlin's legal system is affiliated with that of the Federal Republic, but when a case takes on typical Berlin characteristics even criminal judges may have something to hide, if only a chuckle. The door of the courtroom opens lightly and a befuddled granny pops her head in. Seeing that the gentlemen are in session already she chimes: "Couldn't you speed me up a little? The long wait outside is so boring." Her file is pulled out and her case heard out of turn. Petty theft in a department store, a pair of gym shoes. "You see," explains the defendant, "my son ran out on his family and my grandson is such a nice kid. And since all my pension money goes for booze, I needed a gift for the boy and took these shoes. The store is full of them." With a few words of warning added, Grandma receives a probational sentence. Coming up out of a cheerfully low curtsy she beams: "Thank you very much, Your Honor, for being so merciful and for having set me right so well."

In East Berlin similar violations of the law, such as insult and slander, disturbance of domestic peace, evasion of compulsory school attendance, or absenteeism, are matters within the realm of a lieutenant of the People's Police, who is officially called something like "precinct commissioner." He and some volunteers, at times accompanied by a lawyer, will appear with the offender in front of an arbitration committee convened in the district for a public hearing. Here fines are decided upon, admonitions proclaimed, or work for one of the social services ordered. Once the dues are paid the culprit is readmitted into the ranks of the righteous. In this manner municipal and district courts are not overloaded with cases of petty crime and civil disputes. There are few independent lawyers left in the capital of the GDR, most work in the public sector or in state-run notary offices. The GDR Supreme Court resides in the building of the former Academy for Military Medicine on Invalidenstraße erected in 1905. The head office of the People's Police has moved from its original place of operation but has remained well within the vicinity of Alexanderplatz where Berlin police have always had their traditional headquarters.

The West Berlin jails and penitentiaries are overcrowded, and many have been around for a long while. Tegel, for instance, was mentioned in Alfred Döblin's 1929 novel *Berlin Alexanderplatz*. Most terrifying memories are connected with Plötzensee Prison, one of the places of execution for the victims of Nazi henchman Roland Freisler, president of the infamous People's Court of Justice. Plötzensee has been enlarged over and over again and since 1945 has been converted into a detention center for primarily young offenders. From the highway we were able to look over a light-colored wall secured by a mass of barbed wire and searchlight and catch a glimpse of the modern pavilions. The sight must be surely prettier from the outside than from the inside.

On either side of the Wall economic crimes are on the rise.

In the GDR, where the press does not indulge in sensational reporting at all, these offenses are publicized as a warning. Given the fact that West Berlin makes full use of the advances of high technology, fraud and theft by computer—as enticing as it is lucrative for the crafty crook—have relieved banks and ministries of enormous sums. In general the scale and scope of criminal activity in West Berlin differ little from that in other Western European metropolitan centers.

Berlin police will not give up the belief that making people shudder is one of the best and most effective educational methods to prevent those who easily stray from the right path from joining the ranks of the criminals. Prior to 1961, when customs officers had not yet every meter of the border under their control, the smuggle of foodstuffs to West Berlin was in full bloom. They were (and are) inexpensive in East Berlin and would be paid for in hard Western currency so highly in demand. As a deterrent measure, East Berlin criminal police arranged for public displays of confiscated items, like underwear of all types with sewn-in pockets which had been stuffed with chops and frankfurters when their wearers were arrested. These garments in their dirty, grimy state turned many a stomach and accomplished what had been intended: to spoil the appetite of West Berliners in particular for illegal goods carried across the border in this unhygienic manner.

West Berlin police, too, prove their taste for creepy displays in their criminal museum. They exhibit the plaster cast of a hand which strangled over fifty couples in Berlin and the surrounding areas. The murderer named Bruno Lüdke was caught in 1943, and, as the official information goes, died 1944 in a Viennese hospital "as a result of medical experimentation." Experiments of this sort were undertaken under Nazi influence in great numbers, and the thought of one crime compounding another makes one's flesh crawl even more.

D

Department Stores for All and Sundry

Before World War II you would have heard: "For clothes and household goods you simply must try Jandorf. You won't find any lower prices anywhere. No! Better still, go to Manheimer on Oberwallstraße. For family needs Hermann Tietz is tops, except perhaps for A.C. Steinhardt, which offers marvelous children's suits, underwear, and ties!" The older generation will remember some of the more famous prewar stores of Berlin. West Berliners, however, can still shop at Wertheim's, part of the Hertie concern now, and that came into being in direct consequence of economic sanctions by the Nazis against the Jewish owners of the Hermann Tietz chain. Only the initial letters of the name have been retained. The linen and lingerie company of Carl Joel, a mail-order house, was transferred through a Berlin bank into the "Aryan" hands of Josef Neckermann at circumstantially "favorable" conditions, the circumstances being shaped by the forced expropriation of Jewish firms and property.

Tietz, Wertheim, and Jandorf owned department stores on Leipziger Straße, now in East Berlin. Adolf Jandorf had his organized according to American models, a pioneering feat. All fell to ruin, and with the debris excavators removed the remains of Doric columns and tiled walls after 1945, before Leipziger Straße received a completely new and different face. East Berlin stores, unless in private hands, now belong to the state trade organization, the cooperative society or H.O. for short. Department stores on Frankfurter Allee,

around Alexanderplatz, and along Rathausstraße find their equivalent in those privately run shopping paradises along West Belin's Kurfürstendamm only in terms of size, not in terms of supplies they offer. West Berlin's KaDeWe (Kaufhaus des Westens) with its incredible food-hall selection could turn any major city green with envy. What has been preserved of the Alexanderplatz branch of Tietz is the grey concrete block built at an angle, which houses the Alexander Department Store, a number of smaller stores, and administrative offices in the upper stories. Opposite eager shoppers crowd the new Centrum store, next to the 39-floor Interhotel. Just as in West Berlin's Europa Center long walks and tired feet have to be taken into account when shopping, in spite of the concentration of shops into one area.

Numerous small shops provide a pleasant alternative to the centrally located superstores. Those who loathe department-store ventilation visit the stores along Schönhauser Allee. They are not as colorful as they once were, but the manager will find time to advise her customers, and the saleslady time to chat for a while. Steglitz, in the western part of town, provides the same personal and homy atmosphere, which is enhanced by the architectural beauty of the old house and store fronts still on view. A gigantic department store complex had been planned for this area, into which a financial scandal tore like a bomb. The project of the so-called Steglitz Gyroscope resulted in a changing of the guards in the city government. Today the Senate, to get at least a little out of the money spent to prevent all-out bankruptcy, has taken over part of the block for administrative offices.

A peculiarity of East Berlin's merchandizing system are the Intershops. You pay in Western currency for goods which are imported by the state's own trade organization for Western money or which are produced mainly for export into the West. Duty-free stands can be found on the platforms of East Berlin's Friedrichstraße Station which are extraterritorial for West Berlin customs and a kind of grey market in a no-man's-land outside the jurisdiction of the internal revenue service. Bargains for Westerners are alcohol, tobacco, and tobacco products—even Western brands—at a price far cheaper than on the other side of the border. "Exquisit" shops in East Berlin sell high-quality luxury products to the natives for their own bills and coins. Normal consumer goods for daily use are, however, far less expensive in relation to wages earned than they are in West Berlin or the Federal Republic.

A kind of free trade area has developed in those markets, where during the week new, wonderous things are on sale. The assortment is amazingly similar in East and West: pieces of material, rest offers from textile firms, soaps and brushes, "non-slip, foot-warm" bathtub mats, and more. These markets flourish under the communist trees of Pankow as under the capitalist ones in Friedenau. Vegetables, and flowers, fruit, and poultry ready for the oven can be found there, too. At one booth we discovered a special sale on bra padding. A shy young girl—from all we could tell not from Berlin—began to whisper to the saleslady. The latter responded in a loud and brassy voice: "Miss, there is no need to whisper. We have nothing to hide!"

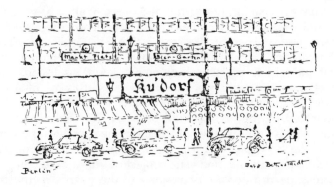

Dialect and Dialectics

Fate jumbled them together, God knows how.
Whatever they were, they are true-born Berliners now.
(Variation on a theme by Daniel Defoe)

God knows: true-born Berliners, should you be lucky enough to meet a few in town, are the proud descendants of a great variety of ethnic groups or any combination thereof. Their language in particular reveals their multi-cultural roots. There are traces of the Slavonic spoken by the earliest dwellers along these river banks, fishermen by trade, and remnants of the Low German dialect of Brandenburg peasant folk. The immigrants from the lower left bank of the Rhine left their mark not only on the dialect of Berlin. These Dutch settlers drained the swamps, cultivated the soil, built their canals. Their princesses even married into the local dynasty, bringing their servants along. Then, around the year 1700, some 6,000–7,000 Huguenots from France arrived in Berlin looking for refuge from the persecution they suffered because of their Protestant creed. They influenced what we know as Berlinese, as did the steady stream of new arrivals from Poland, Silesia, Pomerania, East Prussia and Russia. With the latter waves of immigration that mixture of Hebrew and Middle High German called Yiddish returned into Prussia and Germany, enlivened by linguistic influences from these Eastern European regions.

A brief list of Germanized Hebrew expressions which entered Berlinese via Yiddish and still survive as colloquialisms will immediately convince the uninitiated of the extent of such cross-fertilization:

Dalles = Hebr.: *dalut*, poverty. *Pleite* = Hebr.: *peleta*, to be broke. *Stuss* = Hebr.: *shetut*, foolishness. *Schofel* = Hebr.: *shafel*, inferior. *Zores* = Hebr.: *zares*, bad luck. *Stieke* = Hebr.: *shetika*, silence. In true-born Berlin style even the nickname *Ganovenbrücke* for *Jannowitzbrücke* comes from the Hebrew word *ganaw* for thief. Berliners cheer about their "Bridge of Thieves," elsewhere the name would have provoked irritation, to say the least.

At the court of Berlin, from the time of the Great Elector until the reign of Frederick William II, French *alone* was the language *comme il faut*; German language, grammar and spelling were almost *inconnu* among the sovereigns and their

[63]

courtiers. (Almost *inconnu* among Berliners since those days is the sound of the German "z" as in the English "le*ts*"; they automatically slide into the softer "s" and will call a piece of paper (*Zettel* in German) "settle" rather than "tsettle.") But not every nonsense wrapped into French takes on the quality of *esprit*. Adolf Glaßbrenner had his fictional character Nante, the unemployed loafer, respond to the arrogance of a police-man with an equal amount of folly. The conversation is terse and snappy, much like the exchanges on the drill grounds. Police officer (asking for Nante's personal data): "Born?" Nante: "Yes, je suis." Wit, satire, and irony: a bit of each is wrapped up in this revealing anecdote. For such and other poignant observations Glaßbrenner, a satirist of re-known, had to pay fines, spend time in prison—even leave the city under order never to return.

The language of Prussian drill may also account for other kinds of linguistic sharpness and brevity. Nollendorfplatz is simply "Nolle", and the Gropius-Viertel, that modern resi-dential development, is of course "Gropy." The seconds saved in thinking and talking come in handy as a reserve in the speed of modern city life.

The latest foreign influences on the Berliners' dialect didn't escape our ears. American sounds and expressions top the rest, from "job" to "juice," from "hit" to "beat" to "city," in East and West alike. East Berliners call their summer cottage a "datsha," a comrade is "tovarish," with the same ironic undertone that accompanies the description "playboy" for a Westerner. From the Arabic Berlin took "hash" for hashish, "to kiff" for "kiff-kiff" (to share)—and what is shared is an American "joint," a word every schoolchild knows. Culinary delights kept their original Italian names, such as "pollo" or "pizza"—which a creative linguist and East German patriot corrupted into "krusta," but it did not catch on for long. Balkan "shashlik" and Turkish "kebab" have become stan-dard fare. But other Turkish words have failed to enter the vernacular so far, in spite of the large Turkish population in West Berlin. Austria's "servus" and the Italian "ciao" have been all but completely adopted into the Berlin dialect.

The distance between tongue and brain is shorter in the indigenous population (anatomical proof yet outstanding) than in members of most other German-speaking cultures. No matter which is set in motion first, what comes out of that famous Berlin "trap" leaves nothing to be desired in precision and brazen imperturbability. Whatever worked as a self-

[64]

defense mechanism against Prussian authoritarian rule holds its own today against the oppressions of urban concrete, wholesale living, Bureaucratese and Party Chinese. A party badge on the lapel of an East Berlin functionary is called: "His eye of make-believe." And a visitor to the annual Protestant church convention at the stadium had to digest his taxi driver quip: "Where to? To God's own Olympiad?"

E

Entertainment Galore

In this city in duplicate, entertainment—officially staged or simply available—comes in quadruplicate. On both sides tourist programs, however multifaceted, cannot and should not outshine the festivities and amusements of the indigenous population. Visitors are advised to hang on to natives or Berliners-by-assimilation for dear life and the highest expectations for the greatest of fun will come true. They take you where no 100-mark bill can open the door and elicit a cheesy grin but where an introduction of "these are our friends" brings out a warm welcome and a ready smile. Soon everyone has moved a little closer together, and suddenly there is room enough.

West Berlin offers a selection of nearly fifty performances nightly in its theaters and smaller playhouses; East Berlin lags not far behind. Lovers of classical and popular music find the repertory full and rich. City tours begin at Zoo Station or Alexanderplatz, depending on whether you are west or east of the Brandenburg Gate. Guests from far and near are admitted to meetings and events by cultural clubs. "What's all that running about?" we were asked by a well-versed Berliner. "Afterwards you are as sober as before."

Walking tours around town, which need not leave out an occasional stop for a refreshing drink, alcoholic or otherwise, you can best organize yourself. Guidebooks on how to discover the cityscape on foot, even if the bookseller has to pull them out from under a dusty stack in the corner, are a treat in themselves. Where else would you learn so many hair-raising, exciting details about the history of Berlin (with exact location given) as, for instance, why the city railroad squeals around so many curves? It follows the line of the moat around the city's old fortification, that's why. Or that Woltersdorf Lock, on the outskirts of East Berlin, has been in operation since 1557; that the playwright Gerhart Hauptmann had a museum dedicated to him in Erkner (East Berlin), where he lived from 1886–9; or that you can join a club in West Berlin's Zehlendorf which owns a palisade village erected according to original designs. On Sundays old-style German bread (recipe from the twelfth century) is baked here and you can enjoy a glass of mead along with it, either as a club member or a paying guest.

In addition to these guidebooks, local museums are an ideal source of information about local lore and history. Almost every district of town has established its own "treasure chest," usually located not far from the public library. Dedicated laymen and professional historians overflow with love for their area and their folk, and their enthusiasm— beware—is catchy, soon afflicting even the most casual of the curious visitors. They can also tell you about the strangest festivities. In Pankow the cloth makers still celebrate their "Festival of the Flies," which, like that of the wool weavers in Lichtenberg in honor of the moths, is ages old. The gluttony of the celebrated guaranteed a continuing demand for the merchandise of those celebrating. These times are held in loving and grateful memory even in our days of synthetic fibers, socialist bureaucracy, and ever-present fear of war. Wouldn't one like to wish the moths a prosperous future?

The A-1 attraction for the townspeople themselves is undeniably the arrival of spring with its blossom and flower festivals. When the cherry trees display their first white shimmer, migration begins to Buckow and the rural charm of Werder in the East, to Britz in the West. It goes to show that Britz is not only famous for the vicar who, after the Thirty Years War, slammed the cemetery gates right in front of a funeral procession in defiance for not having been paid by his congregation. As early as 1760 garden centers, nurseries, and rose cultivation were documented in Britz. Nowadays the splendor of Japanese cherry blossoms just seems to be an excuse for washing down last year's fruit wine as if it were beer: speed in drinking assures maximum effect. It is advisable therefore to travel by subway or bus to Britz, as the experienced Berliners will tell you. And what is more, public transport gives you a chance to deal the first round of cards for a game of "Skat."

From the nineteenth century onward "Skat" has been the Berliners' passion. An East Berlin paper summons fans to participate in a "Skat" tournament every year, and on the average some 4,000 players respond. "Were the trees in bloom already?" a pale-faced factory doorman was asked by his buddy, who had had his ears talked off about Britz and the blossoms and the fun of it. "Howda I know?" was the apathetic answer. "We didn't stop playing Skat."

There is dancing at these festivals, too. Actually there is a lot of dancing going on in Berlin. They spin around to the left and to the right and roll their eyes, no matter what the size of the waistline. Even during the aftermath of World War II, a plywood plank surrounded by rubble and sporting a rather unveiled female figure lured: "Come into the St. Pauli Dancing Cabaret." The establishment flourished in the basement of a bombed-out, "topless" house.

In the ballrooms of Berlin, at "Clärchen's" for instance, in the former red-light district in the eastern part of town, ties are obligatory. The cloakroom attendant has a cardboard box full of cravats or bow ties from which to choose according to one's taste—for a deposit and fee, of course. The days are gone when women would appear at "Clärchen's" wearing long red gloves and holding long cigarette holders. Prices have become affordable, even for the apprentice with his date. Every Wednesday the advertisement promises "Ball in Reverse"—a chance for the ladies to select their dancing partners. Whoever assumes that West Berlin's Café Keese (Café Cheese) is different is mistaken. In order to make the choice of partners easier there, buttons or tags with signs of the zodiac are distributed. Just when the night has reached its highest point the lights go on, the band spreads blankets over their instruments, the chairs are stacked on the dance floor. Those whose fun has ended sway happily home. Those who still have stamina and money take a taxi and move on to the next bar.

F

Farming Within an Island City

East Berlin children have no problem getting out into the countryside—it envelops their part of the city, except of course to the west, where it draws a wider circle around the island of West Berlin. Without passport or entry permit school classes may venture into green pastures and through forests and farmland. Large garden centers, too, penetrate the metropolitan areas from the northeast. For pupils in the "other" Berlin the experience of fresh country air is a rare adventure—the border around them cuts them off from the countryside completely.

But still, on 1,750 acres, West Berlin cultivates cereals, potatoes and animal feed. Almost three hundred dairy cattle roam the green patches in summer and are kept in stables during wintertime. The terrain only supplies a minimum of green fodder, so fresh milk and dairy products have to be imported. Some 50,000 tons of milk roll across the motorways through GDR territory annually in special trucks, from areas such as Lower Saxony. Another 10,000 tons are brought in from the GDR. A West Berlin supermarket chain, the Bolle Co., is one of the reminders of the good old days. Once upon a time Bolle supplied the budding metropolis with milk delivered by horse-drawn carts. Even then the firm was so famous and successful that the owner, who had gone bankrupt as a herring merchant, had a church built for his coachmen and other staff. There they gathered for morning service before going on with their daily routine. Bolle's light-hearted disposition has remained proverbial in Berlin, East and West. The milk wagons have disappeared and yet, in Schöneberg, between apartment buildings and commercial enterprises, there still exists a last stable full of cows which supply hundreds of liters of fresh milk daily. Customers must be willing to make the trip and buy it from the producer.

Schöneberg once laid claim to having the richest farmers in Prussia, which was partly true, and partly not. The farmers became rich only after they had parted with their land and sold it to real-estate speculators. The expansion fever of the Founder Years around the turn of the last century saw the value of every square inch of ground shoot up sky-high and the speculative maneuvers resembled acrobatics, some of which ended in fatal crashes. However, many an area farmer became wealthy. Their palatial mansions bore witness to their new status. A visit to Schöneberg cemetery, to their fancy mausoleums and gravesites will teach you a history lesson *par excellence*. These times of American-style "from-rags-to-riches" stories achieved literary fame, too. A novel about a millionaire farmer in Schöneberg sold in several large editions, but in North America, not Berlin.

Pigs' belly and pigs' knuckles, Berlin specialties, are reared on the outskirts of town. Where some 400 sheep graze on Tempelhof Airport terrain, Prussian efficiency also counts 500 bee colonies collecting honey to satisfy the Berliners' sweet tooth. The sandy soil produces generous harvests of white asparagus in late spring, when you can spot the bended backs of seasonal farmhands moving through row after row of asparagus beds, much like they do along the Dutch/German border in the lower Rhine area. Under Frederick I settlers from that area introduced the delicious vegetable. His Majesty's interest in his new subjects extended to their expertise in dairy farming too. In fact, so a chronicler emphasizes, dairy products including butter were at the center of ambitious royal plans, and a prize of 100 talers was promised for major quality improvements, a bonus for which the Dutch competed with industry and undisputed know-how.

Alt-Lübars still retains its fame as a cereal-growing area and a haven of peace, where storks can occasionally be seen nesting on barn roofs. We rubbed our eyes: a hog was trotting leisurely on the road right in front of a bus. It had escaped the confinement of its enclosure on a nearby farm. Then the farmer came running to take his property by the tail and dragged it, over squealing protest, to where it belonged. The bus driver heaved an appreciative sigh: ". . . one more pig-headed than the other."

Dahlem, once a domain of the state, contributed an anecdote of its own to Old Berlin's lore and legends. A sharecropper sowing peas mumbled and grumbled in his beard: "If they come, they won't. If they don't come, they will." The overlord, who was passing by, snarled at him, asking what he was up to. The peasant answered reverently but firmly: "Sir, I was saying that if your pigeons come, my peas won't, but if your pigeons don't, my peas will." The legend does not let us know whether the noble gentleman refrained from letting his pigeons fly or not. For us today, the question no longer arises. We buy our peas in cans, in cellophane, or by the packet.

Fashion Fantastics and Fantasies

From the twenties into the thirties Berlin finally enjoyed the reputation of a leading fashion center in Europe. It had long been a city of the clothing industry, which supplied the military and the masses with moderately-priced uniforms and outfits, was able to collect taxes from a great number of textile manufacturing and trading companies, and had a host of diligent pieceworkers at its disposal. But never before had Lady Berlin been mentioned in one breath with those other great cradles of elegance, individual style, and expensive wardrobe, Paris and Rome. Now it had arrived. Berlin fashions were inspired and inspired the world. Forgotten was that Prussian puritanism and frugality. Lavish gala robes were paraded on the stages of those grand musical shows. As many as 250 herons had to be plucked for one such feather costume that revealed as much as it covered up. The stars, Asta Nielsen, Fritzi Massary, Josephine Baker, set the trend, and the others did not stay far behind. Among the fashionable was everybody who was anybody at all. You were what you wore, and the flair in design and excellence in material of your clothes decided your social status. Accessories from hats to shoes, from purses to jewelry, rounded off the picture. All came to see, to buy, to be seen—and some even to be bought.

[71]

Berlin's fashion magazines made sure that the top show, the most recent costume of a star, the newest style, and the very latest gossip became the talk of the town.

The Nazis were able to burst the bubble and change the backdrop and scenery of Berlin's fashion fair within a few years. Many textile firms had been traditionally owned by Jewish families and had to close down: Reimann's art and fashion school shut in 1938; the house of Gerson disappeared from the business register of Berlin in 1939 once and for all. There was no more competition for and with Paris and Rome. The style of the German "Mother" had arrived (Hitler needed new blood for the military). On special occasions "Mother" was perhaps allowed to bear herself as a Spartan lady in long, flowing, neoclassical robes. The rest was drab and dreary on command—which did not keep officers of the German occupational forces in Paris from attending more flashy fashion shows there in their drab and dreary uniforms. What followed was the latest in "poverty," or (literally) "turn-coat" style, the one that turned old things and made them into something new.

The division of the city did not help the fashion industry any either. For fear of being cut off in West Berlin and out of the mainstream, many designers, fashion studios, and companies left the "frontier town" for West Germany. While the other centers began to re-establish their fame and fortune, West Berlin stayed behind. True, by now it has become Europe's most prolific manufacturer of ladies' clothing with a turnover of just under a billion deutschmarks; but it's mass production, copied from Roman, Parisian, New York, or London trends. True also, three times a year a fashion fair is held in town, heavily subsidized by the Senate, but without more than a fleeting impact. There is no fashion magazine to speak of left in West Berlin. Recently some young fashion artists formed a group to get some new initiative going, either creative avantgarde or anti-chic; this project again is sure to receive Senate support, which may help it to steer clear of mass production and dependence on the bulk industry.

A glance across the border reveals that, at least among top male functionaries of state, a dress code has been upheld—leaving no room for the imagination—which is uniform and functional, but no more. The fairer sex, however, does benefit from outside influences. In recent times some courageous designers have appeared on the scene in Moscow and have found favor and protection. Their output, and everything in the way of fashionable novelties from the West, are eagerly taken up, modified, and multiplied.

The Fashion Institute of East Berlin is not run along individualistic lines. The everyday need of the average citizen worries teachers and students alike. Some of the latter are from the Third World and trained to help build textile industries in their own countries. A young lady from the Mongolian Republic was confident she would one day hold a leading position in a company back home. She was sure of one thing above all, that she would be promoting brighter, more colorful patterns. Even in this respect East Berlin is rapidly improving. Cheerfully colored apparel on view in the streets of the capital is not necessarily a gift from relatives or friends in the West. An East Berlin fashion journal and regular features in other magazines tend to lead the way as far as taste and design are concerned. The problems that remain are those of price, the need for high quality exports, and the question of where to get suitable material. Shortages, though they may test the creative flexibility, can also cause unwelcome interruptions in the steady flow of production. Everyone has experienced it—the shortcomings are not concealed.

Then there is television playing a formative role in the fascination of fashion, not through films from the West but via the clothes worn by lady announcers who double as star models. East Berlin's television station employs a special wardrobe advisor and anyone can recognize whether she is ill or on vacation. Something, or rather everything goes or looks wrong when she is away.

As in West Berlin, East Berlin has flea markets and second-hand shops, has exquisite boutiques and special stores as well. About two hundred tailors working privately and individually in East Berlin cater to the wishes of the fashion-conscious male clientele. They are training a large number of apprentices, too, and some continue sitting on the table cross-legged while sowing by hand—not to crease the material they are working on—just like their colleagues "over there." While Eastern models present tomorrow's look today at the Babylon Film Theater when it hosts its "Music and Fashion International," West Berliners gather in hotels such as the Conti, Steigenberger, or Kempinski to see what they are supposed to dress like. The latest creations from young Berlin designers take off from the rock and punk and funk scenes and take you wherever their imagination carries them; far-out is in, didn't you know?

[73]

Film—Features and Fates

When the Red Army stormed the UFA film studios in Berlin, they entered where some few years before *Münchhausen*, the first color picture, had been shot: a sensational novelty rooted in yet another Berlin first, the AGFA color system. The Soviet soldiers interrupted the making of a Nazi comedy. The star had recently been killed by shrapnel from a bomb. Director Heinz Rühmann, loved by audiences during and after the Hitler years for his acting, had to accompany the officer in charge and relinquish his liberty for a spell.

Under Soviet cultural administration film production was moved into the less devastated UFA studios in Babelsberg near Potsdam. Here the acclaimed German postwar movie *The Murderers Are Among Us* was produced under the directorship of Wolfgang Staudte, who died in Munich in 1984. During those days in 1946, when the classic was first shown on screen, a Berliner commented: "No one leaves the theater the same person he was going in." The newly formed film company DEFA produced a number of further anti-Nazi features, few as impressive as the initial one.

Berlin entered the movie scene in 1884. A Herr Paul Nipkow had applied for a patent for his "electrical telescope" the very same year Eastman and Goodwin developed the first photographic film overseas. But as early as 1859 "living pictures" had been presented by Max Skladanowsky in a "bioscopic show," for which he had rented the Wintergarten variety theater. A Pankow inn, too, left its mark in the history of film as one of the first movie showrooms. Even today the Tivoli Cinema, standing on the spot of the old inn, is keeping up the tradition. Many of the feature films shown in East Berlin originate in the Soviet Union, while the Westerners flock to pictures from the United States. Doesn't that say a lot about the former film metropolis Berlin?

None other than the Postal Service of Berlin transmitted the very first television signals over a 50 kilometer radius from their broadcasting tower. The year was 1932 and the era of television was about to grow like an offshoot next to an old rosebush. Bit by bit it sucked the life out of a once blooming feature-film industry. Paul Nipkow was still alive to see the first experimental television program shown in a "public television room" in Pankow in 1935.

During those days Berlin's film world was not yet past its

prime. The greatest names in the art of acting and directing were associated with the city. By 1929 Marlene Dietrich, born just after the turn of the last century, was well on her way to world stardom after sixteen roles in silent movies. Charlie Chaplin had reached the heights too. His fans so harassed him in 1931 on Unter den Linden that he had to make his escape in a maneuver which cost him the buttons of his suspenders. Thus embarrassed he waddled in his character-istic manner through cheering crowds and disappeared be-hind the revolving door of his hotel. The very night of her triumphant success, the 1930 premiere of *The Blue Angel*, Marlene Dietrich emigrated to the United States. No Nazi lure, not even the offer of a starring role in a 1937 film, could bring her back into the city until after the war. Her first gala concert in West Berlin in the fifties was marred by gangs of incorrigibles shouting "traitor, traitor." The police could shield her from the stones, if not from the shocking verbal abuse.

The Allies, in a rare case of unanimity, took great care that Berlin did not lose its reputation as a movie capital. During the Berlin Film Festival international as well as German film artists gather in the western part of town. The "Berlinale," an annual event since 1951, is held in a cinema complex with a seating capacity of over 3,000.

One hundred and seventy tons of material from seventy years of film history are now stored in the GDR National Film Archives in Rahnsdorf-Wilhelmshagen. In 1963 West Berlin answered with the founding of a similar film library in Steg-litz. It is an occasion for a film collector to chance on a lost treasure—a West Berliner did find himself so lucky. When rummaging through cans of films in New York he discovered a copy of a feature produced in 1935. *A Star Falls From the Skies* had never before been seen in Germany. The world-famous tenor Joseph Schmidt played the lead. Schmidt, a man of small stature, had waited long for a stage career, until the picture *A Song Goes Around the World* brought him instant acclaim.

Among the younger generation of film-makers more and more women directors have come into focus. However there are hardly more than twenty cinemas left in East Berlin, and there are some seventy in West Berlin. In 1938, still undi-vided, Berlin could pride itself of having 402 film theaters to entertain the crowds of fans. Where have all the pictures gone, long time passing? The answer is not blowing in the wind—Berlin waterworks can easily tell. Once the credits have flickered across the T.V. screen or the final score of a soccer match has faded out with scoreboard, stadium and all, the meters of the waterworks measure astronomical consumption figures within minutes: 15 million liters for West Berlin alone. During these minutes Berliners, in otherwise unheard-of solidarity, rise from their armchairs and couches and individually, but simultaneously, go to pay their bathrooms a visit.

Flea Markets Flourishing

What can you do with the useless treasures found when cleaning out basement or attic in a city where rummage or garage sales have not caught on yet? Berliners have one of two choices: either to offer the objects for their curiosity value to a secondhand dealer or, once a month, unload them on the sidewalk the night before bulky garbage is collected. In the latter case a casual passer-by or a "private collector" will probably take matters into his own hands, carrying off the veritable *objets trouvés*, before the garbage men can, for personal use or to sell them in turn to the next-best antique shop. In this way, nothing ever gets lost in West Berlin. Everything is recycled.

The flea market on Nollendorfplatz even charges 1 deutschmark admission, more than most public museums. But as a bonus you climb up in the world, up into a defunct subway station above street level. The traders have set themselves and their wares up in a compartment of one of the worn-out subway cars. Only one yellow veteran still ferries customers to yet another market near Potsdamer Platz. Here the atmosphere resembles a Turkish bazaar and you are invited to browse among pornographic videos, savor a kebab, or pull your filling with Turkish Delight—firsthand.

On Sundays the area around Ernst Reuter House in Charlottenburg also buzzes with activity. From Grandma's coffee-mill, complete with crank and tiny drawer, to one-eyed dolls, everything and anything is for sale that otherwise would fit perfectly into a garbage bin. The mood is happy and relaxed.

[76]

The tradesman is glad to get rid of six chipped saucers, the purchaser beams about the bargain. If she or he gets bored with the acquisition, there is next Sunday's opportunity to recycle it again at this very spot, marketing rights being free for all. And a free-for-all it is—win or lose. Even tiles illegally chiseled from the hallway of a period building change hands.

What is it all about? Is it the fun of playing store? Finally getting rid of that old stuff? Economic necessity? The background to this flourishing secondhand business in West Berlin remains mysteriously in the dark. East Berlin's Association of Journalists holds its "Solidarity Bazaar" once a year. The day's intake will be sent to Chile or Nicaragua or elsewhere. The work and preparation which go into events of this kind are easily compensated by the success and pleasure they provide. What's important, however, is that to this avail a theater's storage room was opened for plundering, and costumes and props had sold like hotcakes. With greater regularity, out-of-the-ordinary and outright eccentric items make their way into the suburban street markets: stones and rocks, cacti and old playhouse programs among them. Musicians stand by to entertain the crowds with catchy tunes, and the workweek could not end on a happier note.

One single pawnbroker's shop remains open in East Berlin, just north of the Museumsinsel in the Ackerstraße area. The central "lost and found" office is located in the vicinity, too, as is an antique shop with fixed prices that has the reputation of being an inexhaustible source of rarities. Customs officers will get in the way of fans who attempt to take valuable antiques from here (or anywhere else for that matter) across the border to West Berlin without an export permit. An exception is only made when the collector's car sports the sacrosanct number plate reserved for the diplomatic corps.

The degree to which the police have always kept an eager eye on pawnbrokers' shops is easily documented by a quick look at the *Prussian Ministerial Bulletin* of 1902. The owners were obligated to keep not one, but *two* inventory lists for more stringent control: one for dates with even, and the other for days with uneven calendar numbers. This division, at first thought completely ludicrous, was initiated to help, not hinder, daily business. In this manner the shop's owner was able to list the day's turnover in one book, while the police investigated the previous day's list for stolen goods. We purchased the bound volume of the 1902 *Ministerial Bulletin* in a secondhand bookstore, the seal in it expressly stating that it had once been the inviolable property of the Berlin State Library.

Flea market days would be all too boring in the long run without at least a little swindle. A Berlin trader specializing in Nazi uniforms, Hitler insignia, and weapons in good repair, was visited by two young gentlemen who introduced themselves as officers of the Iraqi forces on a private journey and slightly short of cash. Trust against trust: the shop owner let it be known that he had once been a member of the SS and was really delighted to be of assistance. He bought a few gold coins from them, thanked them and accompanied them to the door. He was in for a surprising discovery. The coins were not gold and the two gentlemen were not from Iraq. They had only hoped to teach the former brownshirt a lesson—and how well they succeeded!

A serious fair for collectors of all sorts takes place annually at the West Berlin Funkturm or radio tower. A painted beer mug with a "Prosit" to the reservists of 1900 fetches the trifle of 1,500 deutschmarks. Interested parties from all over the Federal Republic and from foreign parts arrive for the sales show. Certificates of long-defunct public companies are in particularly high demand for their beautiful printing technique. And a colorfully illustrated catalogue documenting bankruptcies of the past is also on display and will go for the right price.

Flying High

Aviation in Berlin got off the ground on the tail of birds and plant seeds, so to speak. A stuffed albatross, its wings spread, is still hanging from the ceiling in a villa which was once the home of Otto Lilienthal and was untouched by the last wars. The pioneer of flight technology had closely studied the aerodynamic patterns of the albatross and stork before he modeled his first flying machine accordingly. The glider succeeded in taking to the air from a mount Lilienthal had had custom-built at his own expense. The lift-off ramp still exists, topped by a memorial which resembles, if anything, a primus stove. The inventor, so honored, died in a crash in 1896. Not much later designers of motor planes were testing

"Der Rosinenbomber
Berlin-Tempelhof"

F. Buttenstedt

alcohol and other propellant mixtures.

Some twenty years after Lilienthal's death a bitter legal fight ensued in Berlin between a German and an Austrian aviator. The grotesque and bitter dispute centered on the question of which of them had first come across the idea to improve flight performance by fashioning a prototype of the "Rumpler Dove" after the wind-propelled seed of a Japanese palm tree. By 1930 Wernher von Braun and others were experimenting with liquid-fuelled rockets, a development which led to Hitler's revenge weapons, the VI and V2. Also called "doodlebugs," these were shot at Dutch and British targets, causing heavy loss of life and major destruction. Their employment could not change the outcome of World War II—predictable as it was.

Flight technology had hardly outgrown its infancy when it became the pet of the military. Berlin began to convert the once imperial drill ground in Tempelhof into an airport as early as 1923. Here town councillor Leonhard Adler realized a childhood dream and had hangars and airport facilities constructed in such a way that they outlined the shape of an eagle (for "Adler" means eagle). No matter that in the end the ground plan was more reminiscent of a plucked chicken, Tempelhof became *the* landing strip in 1948–9 during the blockade of West Berlin by the Russians, when Western Allied planes supplied the "islanders" with food and other essentials. Upon approaching Tempelhof the pilots could plainly see the featherbeds spread over the windowsills for airing, so closely did they have to maneuver in the process. The planes came in at such extremely short intervals that the

[79]

noise pollution cost the people, who were short of food and heating, their last nerve. Since the commercial lines frequent more modern Tegel Airport, Tempelhof has gotten back to normal. U.S. military machines still use the airfield, but the intensity of traffic and noise have notably decreased.

Much that had to do with aviation grated on the Berliners' nerves. Those Tempelhof buildings now occupied by the U.S. Aviation Authority saw Nazi leader Hermann Göring and his subordinates come and go until 1945. Göring had been a favorite target for "whisper" jokes which could easily earn the joker a stretch in a Secret Police prison. The block of the Air Ministry is still standing in East Berlin on Leipziger Straße, having lost none of its threatening and somber grey. During the peak of the cold war period another test of nerves had to be borne. A French general risked a major confrontation with the Russians. He ordered two radio towers blown up which, though under Soviet control, stood on Western territory on the French military base in Gatow, obstructing Western air traffic. The expected revenge measures did not materialize.

In the days when the metropolitans still had a healthier nervous system, Berlin's first airfield was laid out in Johannisthal in 1908. Soon tens of thousands of spectators and flying enthusiasts came on foot or by streetcar to catch a glimpse of, or be part of, the sensational goings-on. As the first aviatrix, Ms. Melli Beese started flying here in a plane built by the Wright Brothers in 1910. One year later she became the first female pilot to be granted an official license. Low barracks constructed during Nazi times along the airstrip of Johannisthal recall other neck-breaking aerobatics. Little did the responsible authorities envision then that after their flying adventures were over the synchronizing studios of East Berlin's DEFA film company would move in to stay. Ever since 1960 national and international flights to and from the capital of the GDR are handled by Schönefeld Airport just outside the city limits. According to the Four-Power Agreement of the Allies, West Germany's Lufthansa is not allowed to service West Berlin, even though the airline does provide charter flights into Leipzig, a major GDR city. Air France, British Airways, Pan American, and Dan Air share the West Berlin route. A transit bus links Tegel with Schönefeld Airport, from where the GDR Interflug line, Soviet Aeroflot, and other carriers, not exclusively Eastern European ones, take over. Above GDR territory all airlines have to keep to clearly prescribed corridors. Judging from the supersonic booms audible all over Berlin, East and West, the airspace above commercial traffic spheres serves as a training ground for hide-and-seek artists from both political blocs. Whoever is caught at the game may expect a reprimand from the opposite team along diplomatic lines.

in Tempelhof Dorfkirche   J. B. Heutadt

Food for Thought, Some Thoughts on Food

When those antagonistic to Berlin accuse the city of cannibal manners, they usually mean the aggressiveness of a metropolitan mentality rather than the culinary preference of the population, even though Berliners do indulge in favorites such as "Stolzer Heinrich" (proud Henry), "Hackepeter" (minced Peter), and "Schusterjungen" (shoemaker's apprentices). One used to be able to buy six "Schusterjungen," made with inexpensive rye flour, for the price of four white rolls. Fresh "Hackepeter," minced meat garnished with onions and served on a bun (the traditional cannibal sandwich), is found on the "cold" side of the buffet table. Henry's pride became proverbial, when rumor spread that Berlin's beloved Queen Luise preferred Henry the Butcher's bratwurst, one seasoned with dark beer, to all others.

Many specialties of Old Berlin are historical evidence of the multi-cultural influences that found their way into the pots and on to the tables of Prussia's capital. In the seventeenth century a ruling elector had imported his kitchen chef from Prague and swore by Bohemian cuisine. Later imported were the French pâtés, and pies and pastries from England. Crayfish, pike, perch and other sweet-water delicacies were closer at hand. The lakes, rivers, and streams around Berlin were full of them. When herring was a lot less expensive than it is today, it was known as the workmen's trout.

With praiseworthy humility Berliners refrain from boasting about their knack for food. The taste of their dishes proves them right. Cabbage, whether white or red, acquired and deserves the reputation of going up in steam leaving behind but a strange-looking pulp for serving. Excellent in contrast is everything offered as fast food. "Brathering" and "Buletten," Berliners' hamburgers, fried with spices, onion, bread, and egg already mixed in, quickly find their way to the customer. "Buletten" even entered *The Guinness Book of Records*. They arrived in Berlin with the Huguenots and were soon exported again. In Australia one such giant meatball, weighing over 2,500 pounds, hit the grill one year. In 1982 a town in one of the Dakotas broke that record, and fed a festive crowd of 6,000 with one single "Bulette."

"Bockwursts," once sold by street vendors (always called "Wurst-Maxe") fresh from a hot-water container in front of their bellies, come in cans now, thanks to the blessings of modern civilization. Much like their smaller cousin, the frankfurter, they are enhanced by mustard, sold on a bun or with a good helping of potato salad at kiosks and carry-out restaurants. In West Berlin, shyly blushing, they are involved in a skin to skin race with their closest competitor, the curry sausage. The addition of food coloring alone cannot possibly be held responsible for the ever rising cost of such palatable

[82]

offerings. In East Berlin, on the other hand, sausages sport their nobly pale complexion with natural modesty and down-to-earth prices. An innkeeper from near Görlitz Station is said to have invented the "bockwurst" in 1890 to go along with bock beer. The sausage tastes cold only to those who enjoy drinking their beer piping hot.

As much as to their traditional foods, Berliners hang on to traditions that are connected with their cuisine. Located at a crossroads in Oberschönweide (East) is a square called Königsplatz. Contrary to the more immediate assumption that this "King's Place" celebrates the royal Prussian past, it in fact still honors a butcher by the name of König, who has long passed on. No plaque, no sign alludes to the historical root. The butchershop exists to this day under a different name and continues to provide for an appreciative clientele. Symbols of tradition are to be found in old signs from the bakery trade. Since 1520 the bakers' guild carries a picture of a pretzel on its mark of excellence, on view at times in front of bakeries as an advertisement. The lore connected with the pretzel has vanished into oblivion as have many varieties unique to Berlin of old. Pretzels strewn or filled with nuts, poppy seed, or almonds are for sale only on rare occasions. But some thousand West Berlin bakeries supply their customers yearly with 35 kg of wheat bread and rolls, 27 kg of rye bread and 4 kg of cakes and pastry per capita. East Berlin has centralized its production of bakery goods. The large factories are joined together in a bakery "combine" called "BaKo." Supermarkets, retail stores, factory canteens, hotels, and restaurants can be sure of their daily delivery of 800,000 hard rolls ("Schrippen" in Berlinese) and much much more.

"Berliner Pfannekuchen" (Berlin pancakes), "Berliners" for short, are, like much else in town, a side-product of Prussian military history. A baker called to active duty in the artillery proved to be so unsuitable that he was discharged. His pride was hurt and he wanted to contribute something very patriotic in the service of his country. He formed donuts in the shape of cannonballs, deep-fried them, and created scrumptious, jelly-filled "Berliners." Prussia's enemies, those with bad gall problems in particular, have to throw up their arms in defeat after just one direct hit.

Berliners of the human species went hungry during both World Wars, very hungry indeed. We were reminded of those times when we saw an old man bending down in the road to pick up a carelessly thrown-away sandwich. A few minutes later we observed him as he fed the pigeons near the edge of a park. After the war young girls flirted with G.I.s for a slice of bread. The Red Army soldiers, too, took pity on kids begging for food and gave generously. Today a West Berlin restaurant advertises Siberian bear-claw soup and antelope steak in peppermint sauce. Far Eastern specialties are offered in many West Berlin places and in a luxury-class restaurant in East Berlin's Palast-Hotel complex as well.

Propaganda for the cultivation of potatoes—introduced in Prussia in 1750—took the form of decrees proclaimed to the accompaniment of rolling drums. Not even a dog took a bite out of those round things voluntarily. The ruling monarch sent his overseers and guards around to make sure that the seed potatoes were properly placed into the soil and cared for and harvested. Twenty-five years later potato fields spread around the outskirts of Berlin and the time was ripe for the "Kartoffelpuffer," a pancake of grated potatoes, usually served with apple sauce, to leave its grease mark on Berlin's dinner tables. Other fruits and vegetables hardly tempt the Berliner's palate. To keep up appearances, there is some sort of gastronomical museum maintained in a restaurant in the Old Supreme Court building in West Berlin. But who cares about oranges or cauliflower when there is beer and schnapps enough to go around? Pickled herring and gherkins are a better hangover remedy.

Foreigners and Other Friendly Aliens

A major city without a sizeable foreign colony is unthinkable, at least in Europe, and the two Berlins developing along different lines since 1945 are no exception. Since by nature and accumulated civilization neither has much of an oriental air about it, arrivals from the Middle East—whether there to stay, to work temporarily, or on a short state visit—are apt to throw the municipal equilibrium off balance. East Berlin was preparing for an incognito visit by the Iranian head of state, Shah Reza Pahlevi, just when he was ousted in Tehran. Thus he lost the peacock throne as well as the chance of ever seeing ancient Persian numismatic and other treasures in East Berlin museums. Earlier, in 1967, a four-day official visit by the shah and his consort in the federal German capital of Bonn had drawn huge crowds of protesters out into the streets of many West German cities. In West Berlin, where anti-shah feelings reached violent proportions, one of the students demonstrating was shot and killed by the police.

Already one of his predecessors, Shah Nasir-ad-Din, had proven a veritable headache for his hosts at the royal Prussian court in 1869. The reasons were not so much political but concerned matters of etiquette. During the banquet in his honor, the oriental potentate kept throwing his gnawed-off bird bones over his shoulder so carelessly that they landed on Queen Augusta's train. While a page picked up the foul remnants one by one, the honored guest enjoyed his food. So much so that it first took an attempt by the master steward, then a try by the queen herself, before finally, at the instigation of the king, everyone including the shah rose from the table.

Some 200 foreigners arrive in West Berlin every week; a similar number leave after a prolonged stay. Of the 240,000 invited or uninvited guests from other shores about 60,000 are proud possessors of unlimited residency permits. They have to register their whereabouts with the police department responsible for aliens. If a foreigner has been granted the right of asylum in the Federal Republic of Germany, he or she can freely move into West Berlin. The prerequisite is proof that one's life is in danger or that one is being persecuted at home for political or religious reasons. Even the occasional emigrant from the Vatican State finds the climate in West Berlin more liberal than in Rome.

Many families of foreign extraction, among them quite a number of Turkish emigrants, have been living in Berlin for generations now.

As early as 1763 the Ottoman Empire dispatched an extraordinary ambassador to the court of Frederick the Great, a certain Ahmed Effendi. His Berlin landlord, owner of the palais where the Turkish dignitary had taken up residence with his entourage of eighty, was terribly worried. Soon after the arrival of his guests he took out a special insurance, "as the foreign visitors are extremely careless with fire, and anything is to be feared." His panic rose when the projected date of moving out passed and nothing happened. Such and other problems are well-known to the house owners of today, even the Senate of West Berlin itself.

[86]

With the choice of Bonn as capital of the Federal Republic the buildings of the foreign representations and official embassies were left empty. The People's Republic of China sold its ambassadorial and consular estate on Kurfürstendamm to an insurance company. Japan agreed to convert its former embassy in the Tiergarten district near Mussolini's ruined mission into a cultural center. In contrast East Berlin can show off the number of international embassies, consulates, and missions expected of a capital. Near East Berlin's Friedrichstraße Station Japanese architects erected a modern high-rise building which today houses the International Trade Center of the GDR. From there under the arches of the railroad bridge one reaches the International Press Club, where a representative of a U.S. news agency can enjoy a drink at the bar with a correspondent of *Pravda*. The only difference between the two is that each has a different set of formalities to go through for accreditation. The numbers of East Berlin's foreign colony remain in the dark. For hotel guests the unavoidable registration with the police is handled by the reception staff, a formality which in West Berlin has been reduced to filling out a registry form casually pushed under your nose upon arrival.

With apparent glee old traditions are held on to on both sides of the Wall. Paragraphs laid down in the early part of this century have retained their force. However some provisions of the "Police Ordinance on Registration" of 1902 are no longer valid, for instance, one forcing foreigners to prove that their civil wedding ceremony was followed immediately by a religious one, be it Russian or Greek Orthodox. Whoever dies a foreigner in Berlin need not worry about anything. Every step of the way has been prescribed by law. For generations now Berlin authorities have been issuing, strictly for the occasion, a passport for a corpse, at a fee to be sure.

The already mentioned Ahmed Effendi was extremely suspicious of Prussia's care for foreigners. Immediately upon arrival in Berlin he had the Islamic Cemetery laid out which is still visited by crowds of Turks on religious holidays. The British garrison, too, maintains its own military cemetery on Heerstraße. And the distinguished old French Cemetery in East Berlin is of historical interest not only for students from Paris. The Edict of Nantes of 1685 and the persecution of the Huguenots, their flight from France, and the arrival of thousands of them in Berlin, are recalled in the Huguenot Museum on Platz der Akademie (formerly Gendarmenmarkt)

[87]

close to Mohrenstraße, where in earlier times military musicians from Africa had been stationed. Bohemian musicians, who once played in Rixdorf, left their trace on the coat of arms of Neukölln: a Hussite communion cup. In 1785–6 Bohemian weavers were the first to show the Prussians the power of a social rebellion. Nowawes, Czech for "new village," was the name of their settlement, renamed under Hitler into Babelsberg at a time when Slavonic was not in demand.

Berlin would be empty without its foreigners, and those who wish it were otherwise should be reminded of the true and yet symbolic, sadly comical example of the Palatinates of 200 years ago. They had been given frugal land to settle in peace, cut off from the main roads and trade routes. Strange as it may sound, soon only baby girls were born and the end of this outpost seemed in sight. But in 1896 an access road was built, and wouldn't you know, with outside traffic baby boys began to reappear in the cribs and wedding bells began to ring again—at times even in reverse order.

Fountains, Fountains, Fountains!

The public fountains of Berlin have a soothing effect on eye and ear, occasionally interrupted during summer days by splashing and squeaking youngsters who frolic about. Some of the old water fountains even do their own squeaking once their handles are set in motion. These few remnants of the traditional cast-iron pump variety had their heyday when in 1945 the water supply system had been put out of action almost completely by war. Where washerwomen once fetched their buckets full of water and coachmen watered their horses a human chain now formed, with people patiently waiting their turn to fill cannisters and bottles and pails. These pumps were held in such high regard that even metal thieves left them alone. With their adornment of shells and dolphins and flower ornaments they present themselves, freshly painted, as monuments of the iron Prussian heritage at many a street corner in Berlin. Survivors of war and ruins, and more recently reconstruction which has its mania of destroying rather than

Berlin
brunnen am Europa-Center

restoring cultural treasures.

Also surviving are a number of public fountains originating from the years after the turn of the last century, each one a vivid illustration of Noah's Ark: ducks, dolphins, foxes, swans, sea-lions, bears and stags appear as allegorical adornment where an ample supply of water jetting into a basin might well have served the basic requirement. The sculptor of a fountain on Pappelplatz, East Berlin, created an athlete endowed with such enormous muscular masculinity that the effect is colossally comic. The sportsman, enormous and naked, is bending down without apparent reason. Where there is no reason, Berliners invent one. Superman is picking up the coins thrown into a wishing well.

Famous far and near is the Neptune Fountain, which has been relocated several times. First the emperor felt himself under surveillance because the water deity was casting his attentive glance straight into the palace's imperial bedchambers. The magistrate found an appropriate solution, turning the figure with its rear—a side which had been particularly well-padded by the artist Reinhold Begas—to the palace. His Imperial Highness was taken aback once more, and was not even consoled by the view of four equally well-padded mermaids, symbolizing the Rhine, Elbe, Weichsel and Oder rivers, gracing the rim of the basin. On the Piazza Navona of Rome a similar idea had been executed with much greater originality, but that was of no concern to the magistrate, who had presented Emperor William II with the sculpture upon his accession to the throne. The authorities of Berlin had to relocate the work again and again, at their own cost. Even though the city palace of Germany's second and last emperor in modern times could not be saved from ruin after the Second World War, the fountain of red granite and green bronze was carefully restored and placed not far from its erstwhile location. Neptune and his mermaids, in water-cooled serenity, bear witness to the fact that nuisances have a long life in Berlin.

On Alexanderplatz East Berlin had the Fountain of Friendship Among Peoples erected when reshaping the well-known square. West Berlin would not stay behind. In the rear of "Little Manhattan," the Europa Center that is, the Weltkugelbrunnen (Globe Fountain) is making its mark. Four hundred thousand liters of water per hour run through its tubular veins. Aesthetically pleasing? You'll have to make up your own mind. High into the sky shoots a water jet at a crossroads in Charlottenburg (West), formerly known as "The Knee," today as Ernst-Reuter-Platz in honor of West Berlin's former lord mayor. In his honor, too, the fountain bears the jocular name "Reuter's Bubble."

Once more, just before time had run out on Germany's imperial days, the kaiser was able to let his imagination run wild—something the public had to swallow, if only grudgingly. To recover lost ground and boost his fading popularity, William II had a fairy-tale fountain set up in Friedrichshain, that part of Berlin which claimed the questionable fame of a densely populated area with overcrowded living conditions. To avoid anger and a feeling of envy of western districts of Berlin, much richer even then, the city park called "Hain" was cultivated and maintained as a tranquilizer. Among the fairy-tale figurines decorating the fountain a man-eating monster could also be detected. In 1970, when the fountain had been reconstructed and rededicated, this time to the people of East Berlin, the nightmarish monster and his daughter had disappeared. The anti-aircraft bunkers, constructed by the Nazis in the complex, are now buried under wartime rubble and debris. Their roofs, accessible by sloping pathways, double as observation platforms.

The greatest and largest basin in all of Berlin stands empty, wetted only by rain water. Designed by the architect Schinkel it is a colossal piece of art. Cut from one single boulder of granite, the vessel, roughly cut, was transported to Berlin by boat in 1834 and there polished to perfection. Twenty-two feet, exactly, in diameter, weighing 75 tons, it was Berlin's wonder of the world. Soon forgotten was a young man crippled during the setting up of the basin in the royal pleasure garden near the palace. Actually it had been intended for the rotunda of the Old Museum, a plan foiled by the basin's sheer size. During 1934 the Nazis, who marched in droves on the square whenever the occasion arose (and they knew how to make it arise), banished it into a corner. East Berlin authorities moved it back to its original place. Among other grand and bombastic sights, good and bad, East and West, the "Schale" as it is called only reveals its dimension and workmanship close-up. The megalomania of a century ago has been dwarfed in the meantime. Forty years after its destruction a fountain in Friedenau (West) figured on the expenditure side of the municipal balance sheet. In 1943 the bronze cherubs resting on its rim had been dismantled and sold off by the Nazis because the sculptor was a Jew. The Erika Fountain, so called for the little girl, daughter of a Berlin politician, who had served as model for the cherubs, splashes its waters about again during the friendlier seasons. In wintertime all fountains in Berlin are shut down as a precautionary measure against cracks from "frost bite."

French Traces Many Places

Unexpectedly and frequently visitors to Berlin will stumble upon traces of French influences on the city's military, art and linguistic history, while alas, too little of their culinary expertise took hold. The garrison of the French contingent in

Berlin, called Quartier Napoléon, in 1982 housed an infantry regiment which Louis XIV had established in 1644 at the beginning of his reign as the Sun King. Napoleon himself entered Berlin in 1806 with 24,000 men, marching directly through Brandenburg Gate. Hardly had his horse carried him through the gateway when it stepped on what was to be known as Pariser Platz (Paris Square), a quadrangle east of the famous city gate fashioned according to royal Prussian command after a square on the city map of old Paris. Consequentially it was known as the "Quarrée." Napoleon took such a fancy to what he first saw of Berlin, including the depiction of a quadriga drawn by four stallions on top of the gate, that he had the sculpture, carriage, horses, Lady Victoria, and her banner dismantled and carried off to Paris. In 1813 military luck had turned around. The last French soldiers had retreated behind the walls of the Spandau citadel inside a Prussian fortress to defend themselves against Prussian cannoniers. The powder magazine blew up. The old warrior General Blücher pursued the French right to the Seine, and the first spoils transported back to Berlin were the quadriga, horses, Victory statue, and all. Not the tricolor flies above Brandenburg Gate today but the colors of the German Democratic Republic.

The original premises of the Royal Prussian Porcelain Manufacture, now as everything else existing in duplicate, were located in the eastern part of Berlin. Given the preference of Frederick II for all things French, period design and motifs on old vases and plates are distinctly French, too, the patterns copies of originals from Watteau's and Boucher's studios. On both sides of the border museums proudly exhibit samples of such beautifully painted chinaware. Any fan of Honoré Daumier and his satirical lithographs might be well advised to take in the world-famous "Kupferstichkabinett," the rooms reserved for copper engravings in the Old Museum. The style of the French social critic stands in marked contrast to the pleasantry of shepherd scenes the court painters concentrated on. Daumier inspired Berlin artists like Käthe Kollwitz and Heinrich Zille.

One need not only point to the times of Voltaire's connection with the Prussian court in order to show the deep-rooted influence of French critical intellectualism here. During the days of Bismarck the empress had called a young Frenchman, Jules Laforgue, into her service as a reader, who knew how to hide his mephistophelian wit and bite extremely well. As if to

BERLIN Der französische Dom

take revenge for the lost war of 1871, he penned sharp and poignant reports for his countrymen about the goings-on at the Prussian court. Jules Laforgue had read his Heinrich Heine and quoted his remark: "Whenever someone steps on my toes in Paris, I tell myself that he is a Prussian." And Laforgue continued: "In the streets of Berlin you are pushed and kicked more often than would be inevitable even on the smallest of sidewalks, and the people don't even apologize. If, in turn, I step on someone's heel on purpose, he doesn't even turn his head. Neither will a lady, when she is jostled." These appraisals appeared in the *Figaro* under a pseudonym lifted only many years later.

Nowadays Berliners step on one another's toes when on their way to the German–French festival, which is held every year on Kurt-Schumacher-Damm, where can-can dancers most convincingly kick their heels for the sake of friendship among peoples. The Maison de France, with library and reading room on Kurfürstendamm helps to make friends via the literary vehicle. When a group of French officers embark on a cultural visit to East Berlin, they easily recognize on the curtain of the Berliner Ensemble, founded by Brecht, a large dove of peace designed by their elective compatriot Pablo

[93]

Picasso. Picasso's message of peace notwithstanding, French military exercises are held regularly between 8 a.m. and 5 p.m. in wooded areas either side of Lake Tegel. Immediately after shooting and drills have ended, though, time is ripe for a non-belligerent roasting of legs of lamb, and an inviting scent of garlic fills the air.

The Frenchmen's contempt for miserable cuisine coined the expression "false mocha" or "mocca faux" for that miserable coffee substitute flavored with chicory. The words were taken right out of the Berliners' mouths for they were forced to drink it during Napoleon's continental blockade, when hardly a coffee bean penetrated the lines. Mock coffee from roasted barley is still "Muckefuck" (pronounced something like mook-a-fook in English) to Berliners and Germans elsewhere.

G

Gardens—Lots and Lots of Gardens

If statistics can be trusted, every twenty-first household in West Berlin is the proud lessee of a small garden plot. Only in very rare cases, not statistically accounted for, is such a patch of green privately owned. These allotment gardens are arranged fence to fence in colonies, and are at times unexpectedly found in the midst of urban areas. Kreuzberg (West) and Prenzlauer Berg (East), most in need of a whiff of fresh air because of their population density and social structure, have the least access to garden colonies nearby. In that respect East and West are in accord.

The closer one ventures toward the outskirts of the twin cities, the more frequently one encounters these kingdoms in miniature, rows and rows of small gardens with shed, hut, bower or cottage. Here Berlin families can live out their creative if anarchical urge of self-expression to the fullest. Once these green colonies began to flourish in the nineteenth century so did Prussia's legislation with respect to them. By law no one was to be allowed to live here throughout the year, but quite a number of the small bungalows erected on the lots became permanent residences more or less secretly, particularly in times of housing shortage or during the war years. The colonies are run as small garden clubs and their tradition has taken strong and deep roots. Who in a metropolis would not love to possess a key to the gate of a colony which lets you know in large letters that you are now entering the "Sunshine Club" or the "Evening Breeze Club"?

[95]

"Trust in the Lord, steal timber board, and prosper in your bower." This Berlin proverb, created by an anonymous poet who must have known what he was talking about, contains a piece of advice still heeded occasionally. Garden lots and the huts or summerhouses in them have played an important role during times of need. In the thirties garden produce fed the hungry who were under pressure from inflation and unemployment. During World War II a number of Jewish citizens were able to hide from persecution in "garden bowers," at least as long as their neighbors closed their eyes. The destruction of the city drove thousands to look for shelter there. Pilfering and looting were everyday occurrences.

In order to build a solid little house in his garden, so a Berliner told us, he and his family salvaged bricks from among the postwar rubble. Several times the building material they managed to collect had vanished by morning. They decided on a nightly watch. They were able to frighten off the thief or thieves who left a small van behind. "But wadda ya do with a van and no gas anywhere?" asked the old man with a twinkle.

Small is beautiful and multiplied it is something with which to be reckoned. The central organization for small gardeners and breeders of small animals in East Berlin has an impressive membership of 60,600. The individual clubs, however, are of a more manageable size. Here a chairperson and a board are elected, a cashier handles the financial side of things, and meetings are held where projects are decided upon and complaints settled. There is even time left for growing fruit and vegetables, and supplying mother's fridge with eggs and meat from small furry or feathered animals. Apples and pears, carrots and strawberries are lugged to the juice press to quench an outdoor thirst. In West Berlin the yield of a plot is no longer the owners' main concern, though the 400 colonies still render a lot of produce, and the biggest head of cabbage still wins first prize. But the mowing of the lawn, by statutory regulation, is limited to certain hours of the day and particularly limited on weekends.

Every colony in West and East could not survive without its own restaurant or drinking place, of stone or wood. In rainy weather everyone retreats under its roof, but otherwise the summer festivals are held in the open. Chinese lanterns or brightly colored light bulbs wind their way from branch to branch, the charcoal grill spreads inviting perfumes, fresh waffles powdered with sugar tempt even the fiercest calory counter. A huge "Welcome" sign is draped above the band-stand, where talented amateurs will soon begin to play the old favorites or the latest from the charts. Highlight of the party will be the never failing ballet parody, when dads and uncles in hula-hula skirts perform oriental belly dances, a guaranteed success and tear jerker given the average size of a Berliner's beer-belly. Quarrels and fights count among the uncontested enrichments of the festive program, and during the follow-up meeting even unusual complaints have to be dealt with, not excluding one posted in black on white on a fence: "The person who threw a lady's slip over on my plot should beware—I have called the police!"

The resiliency of Berlin's "Gartenlauben" (a term as archaic as "garden bower") is well documented. In 1938 the Nazis burnt down the Wilmersdorf synagogue. Two bowers in the immediate vicinity were spared. Twenty years later the ruins of the synagogue were torn down completely, the huts re-mained. Another two decades went by, and a seven-story high-rise was built in the location. The "bowers" to this day stand in oblivious serenity behind their fences. World history passed them by, only the trees that shade them appear older and more tired.

Gates and Towers and Plenty of Steps

When Berlin was nothing but a few wooden houses and clay huts, two churches (St. Nicolai and St. Petri), and a ford across the Spree, it already possessed two gates: one in the direction of Spandau, the other leading toward Bernau. At these gates traffic in and out of town was controlled and the city guarded against possible raids by marauders. In the event of an attack the gates would be slammed shut and barricaded. Thus it could be said that the gates of Berlin were a result of fear of the outside and the will to exert authoritat-ive control over what was inside the city wall.

After a few centuries Berliners had become so accustomed to being guarded and watched over that they took each addition to the city's fortification, each new gate, peaceably in their stride. In the thirteenth century the system of walls had

Berlin Brandenburger Tor 1939

been expanded to incorporate the neighboring town of Cölln on the other bank of the Spree. By 1786 the map of Berlin listed some thirteen gates in all, named for Brandenburg, Oranienburg, Hamburg, Rosental, Schönhausen, Prenzlau, Bernau, Landsberg, Stralau, Silesia, Cottbus, Halle, and Potsdam. Soldiers with bayonets fixed to their rifles and their hair braided under three-cornered headgear, were standing guard everywhere.

The most famous of the gates, the one still standing, is Brandenburg Gate. It constituted the western opening in the city wall. Tiergarten, a royal hunting ground, stretched out *ante portas* toward Charlottenburg. The structure of the gate, as we know it today—the traces of the 1945 Battle of Berlin largely removed—was built between 1788 and 1791 by a famous Silesian architect, Carl Gotthard Langhans. He had been to England and had been very much impressed by the first mock-Doric temple erected near Birmingham. The Berlin gate was his answer to the neoclassical trend. The sculptor Johann Gottfried Schadow had been just as impressed by the high-bosomed wife of a Prussian officer, and with the permission of her husband she was allowed to sit half nude for the artist. Her likeness, restored in 1958, graces the Quadriga chariot above the gate in the image of the goddess of victory, laurel wreath in hand.

Ever since a Red Army soldier raised the red flag of victory over Hitler's forces above Brandenburg Gate, it has been the boundary line between East and West. The requirements of modern traffic with its street-cars and buses, felled the other historical gates, or what was left of them, one by one, their former existence only remembered in names of streets and squares. Berliners, every so often struck with the gentle bug of nostalgia, did not take too kindly to the destruction and lugged antique substitutes into their city, two museum attractions of the first order: the Ishtar Gate of Babylon and the market gate of Miletus in Asia Minor. The latter had collapsed in an earthquake around the year 1000, but luckily its ornate marble slabs had not altogether crumbled to pieces. In 1905 it was excavated and transported to Berlin. Once, traders from all over civilization had passed through the awesomely beautiful structure donated by a rich citizen of Miletus during the time of the Roman Emperor Hadrian. Much of its splendor was preserved and Berlin is still able to levy "toll" for it. A visit to the Pergamon Museum in East Berlin costs an entry fee, and even if Hadrian himself were to return to admire the treasures exhibited there, he too, would have to pay his dues at the museum's ticket office.

In Berlin, too, the distance from a gate to a representative and impressive portal was only a few steps up. The Ministerial Council of the GDR resides in the Old Town Hall of Berlin between Klosterstraße and Parochialstraße. The pompous columns, heritage of the year 1911, are a sight to behold. Here, as with many other places of similar authority, it is advisable to approach with slow dignity—the sheer number of steps to be climbed takes your breath away. It seems hardly surprising that most popular rebellions in Berlin ran out of steam before they reached the portals of the halls of power. One wonders whether architectural design took into account dissenters storming up the long flights of stairs, only to lose their momentum in the process. Government from above not only increases stature, it also preserves distance and adds to security.

It stands to reason that public gateways and high portals do not fail to inspire respect and a sense of smallness. The Egyptians first built them to symbolize the entrance into the realm of the dead. Today they more often than not adorn the access into the realm of bureaucracy. Fortress-like old schools with their imposing portals and flights of steps are just as awe-inspiring. Does the daily routine of being swallowed up by one of these monsters in the morning only to be spit out

Berlin Grunewaldturm   Jürgen Zettmeißdt

again in the early afternoon leave any traumatic effects? Or are perhaps those modern, more functional educational buildings to blame for the gradual disappearance of Prussian order and discipline? Who knows! The former head office of the publishing house of Ullstein in Tempelhof still presents itself, stern and sturdy, with a portal which resembles a raised eyebrow knowing about the joys and sorrows of bookmaking. The owl of wisdom hovering above the doorway may know the answer to why the building now houses a number of textile companies. The industrialist Borsig probably had a similarly powerful entrance gate for his locomotive plant in mind, but he contented himself with but one half of the effect, one Gothic tower next to the gate rather than two.

The entrance to the Kreuzkirche in Wilmersdorf (West) seems like an exotic nesting box or a stuck-on Far Eastern temple gate. The brick building itself, massive and towering much in the way of a medieval silo, looks all the more menacing for it. But then, did the architect allow himself an ironical statement here perhaps? Maybe his dainty entrance stands in juxtaposition to the imposing pompousness of portals and gates everywhere else in the city?

Grunewald for Happy Wanderers

In the Berliner's mind the mere mention of Grunewald con-
jures up countless memories of pleasurable outings. And
quite rightly so. The huge forest park of that name offers a
wealth of outdoor activities. There is a residential district
called Grunewald, too, an area of country-style houses and
homes for the wealthy, which upon first glance does not
reveal its potential for leisurely pursuits. The housekeeper of
a mansion embarked on an entertaining conversation with an
unexpected, nice-looking visitor in the kitchen and remained
oblivious to the fact that the walls of every other room in the
house were slowly being stripped bare of valuable paintings.
The owner, a film magnate, returned and stood thunderstruck in the face of the imperturbable naïvety of his employee. He was lucky. The police retrieved his pictures.
Thanks to ample reporting in the media about the theft, none
of them had found a customer or trader, and the gang had no
connections outside of the city. What for? Normally, most
everything can be turned into gold in West Berlin.

To participate in a tour of Grunewald park, a major annual
event since 1971 called the "People's Hike," you need not
necessarily enter a sports club or hiking association, but you
can. In that case you will don the same colored woolen socks
as your fellow members, an unmistakeable trademark that
distinguishes you from members of other groups or stubborn
individualists. There are no longer wild boars grunting in the
undergrowth, and no descendant of the infamous, royally
protected black ibex will poke a berry collector from behind.
Even the berries, abundant just a few years ago, have vanished. Shooting up like mushrooms instead are restaurants
and kiosks every few turns of the path. "Somewhere about
there," a young sportsman in the know told us, "over there
was the film star Hans Albers' house." Then he talked about
the trees dying, but not about Nazi Minister of Propaganda
Josef Goebbels, who also lived in the house. Goebbels killed
his family, and then himself, in Wilhelmstraße in 1945.
Grunewald may be a fair distance from the city center, but
particularly in Berlin associations travel speedily across time
and space linking the present and the past.

At different times different Prussian kings had timber cut
down in Grunewald to be used on construction sites in the
city, which was forever bursting at the seams. A Scotsman

took the matter into his hands properly between 1882 and 1889. He founded a Kurfürstendamm Society with the declared aim of bringing the Grunewald district closer to the metropolitan center of political and financial power by improved traffic and construction strategies. His personal bad luck was that he started his endeavors during a peak of financial crashes and, though his private fortune rose quickly, the development of the Grunewald area proceeded at a snail's pace. For a long while only bridle paths through Tiergarten and over Kurfürstendamm led into the green woods of Grunewald. But then, by the time construction of a railroad was finally planned on paper, lumberjacks were already at work in the forest and the building boom along its eastern border well under way. Bismarck, the Iron Chancellor, had favored and actively supported the opening up of Grunewald into a future residential and recreational area for Berliners until in 1889 he himself was axed by his emperor. The folksy ballad about the timber auction in Grunewald, starting as a protest song of the "green peace movement" of the day, has remained a hit with Berliners of all ages.

The old hunting retreat Jagdschloß Grunewald went through manifold modernizations over the centuries and welcomes music lovers every summer to its delightful courtyard concerts. Shudders of fear are evoked by the castle's dark side. Rumor has it that a "white woman" has been haunting the place around midnight for ages. The explanation handed from one generation to another is this: Joachim II, tired of his mistress, had her buried alive at one end of a spiral staircase. So stubborn was the legend that successive Prussian rulers were asked to investigate the spot in question, a request they all refused. Historians are still guessing while Berliners enjoy the ghoulish tale. Anyway, the area is ghoulish enough because it took 22 million cubic feet of wartime rubble to cover the remnants of the Third Reich's Department of Military Technology under what is now "Teufelsberg," or Devil's Mountain, close by. It is not known whether a brown ghost moves restlessly about at night, and if so, nobody would think of excavating that laboratory of war. Berliners have a tendency to leave well enough alone.

The Grunewald observation tower with 104 steps from bottom to top impressed us so much that we stayed down. Its Byzantine style is not reminiscent of the Kaiser-Wilhelm-Gedächtniskirche for nothing, as both were created by one and the same architect. With your back to the tower you will

Berlin
Jagdschloss Grunewald

be able to take in a wide panoramic view across the Havel River. At a bend of Königsallee in plush residential Grunewald three political fanatics held up and shot the industrialist, politician, and author Walther Rathenau in 1922. The assassins, convinced by the glorified delusions of German chauvinism, were precursors of the Hitlerites. Even earlier King Frederick William IV, the romantic on the throne, had erected a memorial in Grunewald for very nationalistic reasons. He had a stone placed in Schildhorn on the bank of the Havel to commemorate a "historical" event: Jaczo of Köpenick, in his final attempt at fighting off the Christian Germanic colonizers had been defeated by Albrecht the Bear in 1157. To escape death, so the story goes, Jaczo swam across the river on the back of his horse, vowing to convert to Christianity if he were saved. He landed on a peninsula, laid down his sword, hung his shield up on a tree (hence Schildhorn or Shield Horn), and became a loyal Christian. This "historical event" had been the brainchild of an elementary-school teacher and was first published in 1823. The king was so much taken in by the tale that he wanted it to be true: the memorial is a reproduction in stone of *the* tree, complete with shield, on a pedestal.

Such wishful thinking became the underlying principle of National Socialism. Murder and war followed. On the Wannsee side of Grunewald the most powerful Nazi officials gathered in 1942 for a conference, where the "final solution" was proclaimed for European Jewry. It is a genuine relief to know that no more than trees are endangered in Grunewald today.

H

Heat's On

On old yellowed photographs of Berlin women and children push carts with pine branches along sandy paths into town— a tough way of providing winter fuel. Today, where there is still no central heating by oil or gas or from a remote source available, the coal man arrives once a month carrying a supply of briquettes on his back. The size of the storage area, be it basement, balcony, or pantry corner, decides the quantity to order. The man simply empties his basket, and away he goes, leaving his customer to deal with this "black day" of the month as best he or she can.

Rent in Berlin is charged either "warm" or "cold." Most modern housing is "warm" by now, connected to a long-distance heating system. The only question remaining—in either part of town—is how to get hold of such luxury. In the back courts of the old tenement buildings, in contrast, bins for dust and ashes clutter the cramped space; mountains of coal lie regularly on the pavement in front and the janitor hurries to shovel it through the cellar window for storage. The amount of black gold 4 million Berliners burn in a year is worth a bundle. As early as 1933, so contemporary reports tell us, a fierce war raged between the wholesale coal merchants of Berlin for that bundle. "In and around Berlin unmitigated battles took place. Coal from the Ruhr Valley had to fight its way into the marketplace struggling for decades against the uncontested predominance of English and Silesian coal merchants who had been dividing the market exclusively among themselves. With the disappearance of English coal [this, again, was written in 1933, the first year of the Hitler regime] a situation came about in Berlin in which Ruhr and Silesian coal struck about a fifty-fifty balance."

On West Berlin waterways we saw Polish barges loaded with Silesian coal on their way to the big Western power-stations. The Reuter Plant on the bank of the Spree had been dismantled completely in 1945 only to be hurriedly rebuilt three years later. Its three chimneys, each 100 meters in height, stand against the Berlin sky as characteristic land-marks. In East Berlin along the Spree Klingenberg Power Station runs at full capacity: a memorial to the engineer Georg Klingenberg, the first to develop the burning of coal dust in Europe.

Most Berliners are expert judges of the quality of coal dust compressed into the familiar briquette shape. Dealers who advertise unusually cheap heating material must put up with customers carefully checking the products they offer. If two small dots appear under the trademark profile cf a briquette, it originated in the soft-coal mining area of Senftenberg in the GDR and is considered OK. The pressed coal from Leipzig, however, is less well regarded, as too much sulphur dioxide is released into the air in the combustion process.

Such finesse bothered Berliners little during the icy winter of 1946/7. Countless tons of coal were, in fact, stored in a coal yard in Lichterfelde, but under strictest security and off limits to the civilian population. However when U.S. army trucks left the enclosure rumbling across the cobblestone pavement, a few pieces of coal always fell to the ground. Children trailed the convoy in droves, collecting the precious chunks in buckets or sacks. Soon they had learned how to yell "thank you," and "thank you" again, when a smiling G.I. kicked a few more briquettes off his truck. "Just imagine," sighed a woman who had been one of the youngters some forty years ago.

Briquettes, like no other fuel, suit the famous brickwork stoves encased in Dutch tiles. Strangely enough, open fire-places never became fashionable in Berlin. But a number of tiled stoves, those marvelous heating machines radiating warmth and cozy comfort, are still around. Strategically placed in a corner, they could heat four rooms at the same time and were a beautiful sight to behold with their glazed, often elaborately ornamented and painted tiles. Rare examples even ended up as museum pieces. One particularly splendid specimen from the rococo period, with a ceramic peacock on top, was restored and relocated, enhancing the elegant Ermeler House on East Berlin's Märkisches Ufer. Not long ago the prudence of a construction engineer and the protest of a preservationist prevented the destruction not only of painted stucco ceilings and ceramic bathtubs found in a Pankow house but also of unusual tiled stoves there. Thus (rather than falling victim to radical modernization), the home of an entrepreneur who had died without heirs was retained as witness to the cultured life-style of a past age.

While new housing developments in East Berlin, much like those in metropolitan areas around the world, may not one day be honored with like respect and museum-style caring, most of them are at least linked to a remote heating system. Older fuel supply installations, such as the gasworks in Dimitroffstraße, are no longer viable after a century or more in operation. They have to go. Rummelsberg, in contrast, boasts the latest technological advances and much improved fuel economy. In East Berlin alone 1.2 million households rely on heating from a distant source. Once the pipes delivered by West German companies are finally underground and Soviet natural gas is pumped to both East and West Berlin, the acrid smell of coal smoke will become a thing of the past (we hope). At any rate , the cold winter in Berlin will continue to provide young lovers with a welcome excuse to cuddle up a little closer in wind-sheltered corners.

Historical Sites and Sights—Part One

Berlin, if you will, is like an oyster. The hinge, where the two half-shells are joined together, can be compared to Brandenburg Gate. Lift the upper shell, spread it to the west, and what you have is the western part of Berlin as it unfolded from about 1880 onward and which constitutes West Berlin today. The other shell holds the actual oyster—the old city center—which Berlin historians savor above all else. In fact, what from the Western perspective is called East Berlin, is, in reality, the nucleus with its eastern districts, i.e. central and east Berlin. Many historical treasures were razed to the ground in the last war, vanishing forever, but quite a few were able to be preserved or even reconstructed along the lines of the old models.

To the east of Brandenburg Gate, the avenue Unter den Linden, lined by historical palaces, churches, the University, and the Grand Opera, forms a longitudinal axis. The streets running parallel to or traversing it had their names changed, in some instances, after the foundation of the GDR. Still, they are of no less interest to the historically-minded. East Berlin's Institute for the Preservation of Public Monuments is making slow but steady progress. Is it by chance that the windows of the institute look out upon a plot where the Gallows House used to stand? The name originated about 1680. The owner of the estate had accused one of his housemaids of stealing a silver spoon. The young woman was tried and found guilty, and judicial authorities had the gallows erected on the grounds. To the horror of all the other servants, the girl, protesting her innocence to the end, was publicly hanged. The spoon was found in the garden not long afterwards. A "nosy" goat, having the free run of the garden, must have pulled the spoon off a windowsill and dropped it between the flowerbeds. Whoever murmured even then that capital punishment was outrageous and an injustice has passed on long ago too, however.

Opulent baroque style characterizes not only castles, cathedrals and noble residences (since converted for public use), the Armory, and the Royal Mews. A mansion of an upper-class family like the restored Nicolai House, now home of the Institute for the Preservation of Public Monuments, exhibits the architectural flourishes as well. Friedrich Nicolai deserves military honors but for non-military reasons. A bookdealer, philosopher and author of renown, he won his battles gloriously, without shedding blood. Friend of many of the most eminent scholars of the Age of Enlightenment, he was one of the greats himself. He lived in the house from 1787 onward, during the years of the French Revolution. True, not even the capital of the GDR is blessed with many such architectural attractions anymore, but there are still some in existence. Traces of historical jewels in West Berlin are widely scattered through the outlying districts, where royal summer palaces, village churches, hunting retreats, and decorous inns have survived. The remnants lucky enough to escape modernization or outright obliteration are now protected and maintained as cultural heritage.

Anyone who enjoys walking can discover the historical center of Berlin in a few days. A city map and a guidebook will greatly enhance the tour and complement the chronicle in stone. The river Spree and its canal must be crossed over and over again; one may not necessarily realize the degree to which these once major traffic arteries have lost their importance. It may also be difficult to imagine how the city must have looked in the days when the banks of the Spree had not been fortified and the river was still winding its way through swampy ground, a natural border between the small villages of Cölln and Berlin. And not even the closest study of engravings of old Berlin will be of assistance in places where buildings, once characteristic geographical landmarks, have been moved to another location.

We would not have recognized, without prior knowledge, that on the stretch of the river bank called Märkisches Ufer one in a row of period houses had only recently been inserted, rebuilt stone by stone in 1966. Before that it had stood on Breite Straße for over two hundred years. Its first owner, a leather merchant, had made his fortune as a supplier of leather goods to the Prussian military forces. Then came the time when much was going up in blue smoke, and tobacco was the business to be in. The tobacco dealer and cigar manufacturer Ermeler bought the luxurious mansion and embellished it further—one of the first signals to the court and the nobility that the bourgeois classes had arrived with a purse to match their self-esteem. The estate was taken over in 1914 by the municipality, served for a time as a museum, but was finally moved to make room for traffic. Yet another exquisite home of the same architectural period, Palais

Ephraim, owned by a banking family, was dismantled as early as 1935 on similar grounds. The individual building blocks were stacked and stored on what is now West Berlin territory. No wonder then that it took its time before East Berlin was presented with the raw material and could proceed with reconstruction. Today the Ermeler House offers gastronomic specialties and culinary delights in three restaurants. Visitors make their reservations early. Owing to their popularity, the eating places are forever overbooked.

Inevitably under crowded circumstances one gets into a friendly conversation with one's neighbor. The new acquaintance we made rambled on about his favorite subject, his Berlin, in the way Berliners do with enthusiasm and imagination to fill the gaps. "Saint Gertrud, the one who stands on Gertraudenbrücke, carries a lily for virginity and a distaff for her social work. There was a hospital for the poor on Spittelsmarkt, you know." Suddenly pondering, he drew a deep breath and continued: "Actually she was no virgin in the regular sense, because for the normal virgins there is the Jungfernbrücke next to it." (We suppressed a chuckle at the associative connection he drew between the two bridges, one named for St. Gertrud and the other dedicated to the young innocent maidens of Berlin.) "Saint Gertrud can be glad she is still standing there," he continued. "The Nazis had already taken her down for melting and she would have ended up as ammunition. But a few workers covered her up pretty well with rubble, and that kept her safe." And what about the goose and the bronze rats climbing around the pedestal, we ventured to ask. "That I cannot tell you exactly," the man confessed. "Anyway, she is just handing a jug to a thirsty journeyman and that is why she is our beer drinker memorial."

Historical Sites and Sights—Part Two

The annals of Berlin, seven heavy volumes of parchment dating back to the fourteenth century, are under lock and key in the municipal archives of East Berlin. Visitors may, at best, catch a glimpse from afar since the priceless documents of local history are too delicate to be handled. A few documents in their care are older still, but the town hall fire of 1380 did not leave much unscathed. The city annals were, in fact, started in the aftermath of the fire to fill in the historical gap, recording existing property titles and privileges reconstructed according to contemporary depositions. One of the seven volumes suddenly appeared on the free market in 1749—unthinkable today—and was acquired by a printer from Leipzig for two reichstalers (older cousins of the dollar). The book resurfaced in Bremen, and how it got into Czechoslovakia during World War II remains a mystery as well. After the war the volume was finally returned to its place of origin, the early history of which it records.

This historical source has had to be studied on different occasions for very practical reasons. During digging operations in front of the church steeple of Nicolai-Kirche, for instance, the construction engineer had noticed a thick layer of clay for which he could give no immediate logical explanation. Historians were called in to solve the riddle and they, in turn, consulted the annals. As it turned out, as early as the thirteenth century that clay had filled the space between two timber walls long since rotted away. The basement of the oldest residential building in Berlin discovered thus far had been laid bare. Scientists also supervised the excavations on the grounds of the former Klosterkirche, heart of the Franciscans' Grey Cloisters. Almost three and a half thousand roof tiles could be saved for future use, all of them of the special "cloisters format" we have been unable to duplicate nowadays, in spite of our technological advances. Every Saturday a walking tour is organized to the sites of historical interest in East Berlin guided by a knowledgeable expert. Point of departure is the T.V. tower pavilion on Alexanderplatz.

From time to time mummified bodies are brought to Berlin for closer scientific examination. It is at the medical center of Berlin's oldest hospital, the Charité, in the eastern part of town, that such autopsies are performed. Their investigators are the ones who decide, whether "Knight Christian Friedrich von Kahlbutz died of natural causes in 1702 or was expedited into another world by means of a vicious poison." As soon as historical detectives had ascertained dubious elements in the nobleman's background, the pathological checks became part of a belated forensic study. The young bride of a shepherd in the knight's service had refused to abide by the *jus primae noctis*, the overlord's right to her during her wedding night. Later the bridegroom was found murdered and his master was accused of the crime. When released for lack of evidence against him, the defendant publicly proclaimed: "If I am guilty, may my soul find no rest and my body never rot." In 1704 his corpse was found preserved in a coffin during remodeling work in a church in the Mark Brandenburg region. For a century and a half the reasons why the body had not decomposed remained a mystery. Now we know that conditions in the vault were such that the corpse had

[111]

Berlin um 1900 Kurfürstendamm

dried up, like an Egyptian mummy—a logical rather than a mythical end to the story.

In West Berlin such matters may first be referred to the criminal police whose officers probably welcome the change in their daily routine. At a building site on Kochstraße, a large number of skulls were unearthed. Workers had hit upon a burial ground in use at the time of the Crusades, during which Jerusalem Church in the vicinity was founded. Could it be that the ground had covered victims of oriental revenge, the disease then believed to be of Middle Eastern origin, the one we now know as syphilis?

Throughout its history Berlin has tolerated the oldest profession in the world, which operates rather openly in West and discreetly in East Berlin. The police department responsible for prostitution control east of the Brandenburg Gate therefore have much less on their hands than their overworked colleagues on the other side. The latter have to keep a close watch on the region around Nollendorfplatz, on Bülowstraße and Potsdamerstraße. The West Berlin avenue named after the 17th of June (recalling the date of an uprising in East Berlin in 1953) has long been established as a pick-up area frequented by motorized clientele. A native Berliner, a lady describing herself as of "historical" age, took her dog for a walk along a stretch of the Straße des 17. Juni one night. A resident of the upper-class Tiergarten district, she had walked her pets there when the long, wide avenue was still known as Siegesallee or Victory Boulevard. A motorist slowing down his car to invite her for a profitable ride completely unaware of the facts was gently fended off in unruffled Berlinese: "Well, young man, you had better repeat your offer after you've taken a good look under the next lamppost."

Horses in an Age of Horsepower

When Berliners talk about horses they do not necessarily have the racing results in mind. There are the wooden varieties too—rocking or hobby horses hunted by collectors, guaranteeing horrendous returns for antique dealers. And then there is the shop talk of hobbyists riding for the fun and the sport of it. Racing fever, though, spreads among fans in East and West alike—the same way it does among the susceptible all around the globe.

No matter what the weather may bring, the trotters run their course in West Berlin's Mariendorf. The old dilapidated stands had to be reinforced to accommodate the ever increasing number of spectators. Two and a half marks is the minimum you can lose, but the daily turnover in wagers varies between 0.5 and 1.5 million deutschmarks. East Berlin records a similar steady growth in enthusiasm. The tracks in Karlshorst or Hoppegarten not only attract the regulars, they have also become favorite places for family outings and workers' or staff parties, drawing in the crowds of people who follow events on the turf, take their chances at betting offices, or sip champagne served in the track restaurant—a welcome change from soccer or ice hockey. Optimists can even back a horse running in Longchamps near Paris by placing a bet in one of the eighteen state-owned bookmakers throughout East Berlin. Local favorites—all horses in fact—are property of the people's own riding stables. There is academic blessing for racing even, as one of the prizes bears the name of Humboldt University.

The Berliners' obsession with horses is not new. For over 200 years Berlin and Potsdam showed off their world-famous cavalry regiments of the guard, tournaments brought the best military riders together with the elite of private horsemen, horse breeding flourished, and Hoppegarten just outside East Berlin provided a training center for the whole of the German racing community. In 1872 Berlin's Society for the Protection of Animals called for a much-needed improvement in the road system. With horses sliding on bumpy pavements and falling, insurance companies were no longer willing to carry the loss. There were some 13,500 coach horses, over 500 saddle horses, and countless military mounts in Berlin. Forage for the latter had to be supplied by farmers in the vicinity at strictly regulated prices (though the official price lists were always being "delayed in the mail" or "misplaced" by village elders, and constant wrangling ensued). When in December of 1701 the court of Berlin moved to Königsberg to witness the elector's self-coronation as "King in Prussia," his subjects had the honor of providing no less than 10,000 horses for the procession—free of charge!

A former bridle path between Zehlendorf and Kohlhasenbrück, at one time a vital link between Berlin and Potsdam palaces, is still known as "Königsweg" or "Royal Route." Located about halfway between the two lies Düppel Manor. Counting on a long tradition, the old buildings were, appropriately enough, taken over by West Berlin's Institute of Veterinary Medicine, and the estate was turned into an equestrian sports center. Where there are horses and ranges, there is no lack of manure. Where that is in abundance, bureaucracy cannot be far away. Indeed, West Berlin authorities found it necessary to differentiate not only between saddle and farm horses but between their dung as well. Legally speaking, manure from riding horses may, under no circumstances, accumulate on terrain reserved for the droppings of "horses used for agricultural purposes." So what is a horse owner or a private riding club to do with all that manure? A troubled citizen complained in a letter to the editor of a West Berlin newspaper: "Manure on the paddock behind our house breeds millions of flies. We simply cannot open a window, and we spend a small fortune on insecticides every week. I counted 140 flies on my ceiling alone. It's the Senate's job to do something about it."

Calling for the authorities in connection with horses has got others in trouble before. The small hamlet of Lübars in the French sector of town, under national protection now, is a horseman's paradise with its stables, blacksmith, nicely decorated inns and surrounding fields and parks. Here a tradition is being carried on. The same tradition recalls the sad story of Michael Kohlhaas of Kohlhasenbrück at the other end of the city. An upright and honorable man, Kohlhaas was accused by a nobleman of stealing two horses, which were confiscated. When the defendant had finally been cleared of the charge, he refused to take the horses back, as they had been badly mistreated and worked to skeletons. Litigation continued and Kohlhaas lost his case. In revenge he formed a gang of highwaymen who haunted the area with Robin-Hood-style ambushes. He was hanged in the end, not for writing to the editor of a paper but for robbing a silver transport.

The above-mentioned letter of complaint from Lichtenrade did receive an official and straightforward answer: "We hereby refer you to the ordinance on fighting animal pests. Matters involving rats fall under the jurisdiction of the district council. Flies, even in great numbers, are the responsibility of the citizens themselves." A hundred and forty horseflies on one ceiling, counted one by one, seem to be keeping the spirit of Michael Kohlhaas alive to this day.

Housing—Battleground for Owners, Occupants, and Occupiers

The man at the center of Berlin's living comfort is without a doubt the janitor, called "Hausmeister" in German. Cleanliness of staircase, courtyard, and sidewalk—through summer and winter alike—are not the only duties in his masterly hands. He is in charge of repairs, tends to the heating system, functions as arbitrator and ultimate authority. Though Prussia customarily pressed anyone into a uniform who could make life miserable for someone, the "housemaster" had to do without one. (Even as late as the turn of the last century state wine-tasters had to employ tailors at their own expense to fit them with jacket and collar ornamented by vine leaves.) Berlin janitors had to forego such proud decorum. And, unlike their Parisian counterparts, the concierges, they had no business intercepting the mail to poke their noses into it. Their powers more resemble those of British caretakers, but, here as everywhere (especially when you need them), a note on their office door tells you to "check again, when I'm back."

Thanks to the professional pride of the janitor there are green areas, where, without loving care, nothing would grow for lack of direct sunlight—as, for example, inside those typically somber and dark courtyards of Berlin built during the boom of an early industrial age. According to imperial regulations they only needed to leave enough space for a fire-engine to maneuver in case of emergency, thus measuring no more than 2.5 meters from wall to wall. Of course you will not find those back courtyards in the wealthier residential areas of Dahlem and Grunewald. They were characteristic of the places where workers lived, in Wedding to the north, Prenzlau to the east, or in Kreuzberg. The social deprivation rampant in those monstrous tenement barracks was to become Berlin folklore. Heinrich Zille, who photographed the "milieu" and sketched it with his sharp pen and even sharper critical wit, highlights the misery: a young boy is looking up a barren brick wall, while his little consumptive sister hovers on a stool. "Mom," he shouts up to the kitchen window, "throw down the flower pots, Liese wants to sit in the garden."

East Berlin is taking the greatest of care in modernizing old tenement buildings. Entire streets such as Prenzlauer Allee are being remodeled, back-court buildings torn down to give light where there was none, lofts extended, and shops opened on the ground floor. The occupants of these buildings, who have to move out temporarily while work is in progress, are provided with accommodation nearby. They should not lose their neighborhood contacts. Large high-rise buildings have been shooting up in all areas of the city since 1976, a program designed by the GDR authorities within the framework of their master plan to tackle the housing shortages. Here the sense of neighborhood and community is lacking. A young East Berlin woman told us laconically: "There is a lot of switching of apartments going on. And when they carry out a whole lot of furniture downstairs, nobody bats an eyelid anymore. It just happened that a tenant came back to find the apartment empty—everything stolen."

In West Berlin even the staunchest advocates of huge apartment blocks have conceded that the blind craze of pressing so many people into anonymous giants of concrete is a mistake, and voices warning of unforeseeable social consequences have been right after all. The effects of human isolation, as the increasing crime rate in these housing developments shows, confront the city elders with ever intensifying problems. Walter Gropius, the famous architect (who died in 1969), still lived to see his idea of more humane, interconnected residential settlements perverted by megalomania. It took decades before the public as well as the West Berlin authorities were ready to consent to more carefully planned urban renewal than during the first twenty-five years after the war. As with all good intentions, realization may be far off. An employee in the Schöneberg district started on his own beautification scheme and bought himself a can of paint. His doctor had advised him against a trip to sunnier parts in southern Europe, so instead he created an Italian landscape, complete with cypresses and pines, on his terrace wall. Should he have wanted to add to the atmosphere and break out into an Italian aria, however, he had better beware. A sign in the hallway warns: "No singing in the courtyard!"

Half of all living quarters in Berlin were built before the First World War. Even excluding the damages caused by the second one, renovation would be in order everywhere. Those very real problems of housing shortage and dilapidation led to rioting, political agitation, street fights, and police raids in West Berlin. An anarchical program of self-help mushroomed into a full squatter movement spreading rapidly and violently into all run-down areas. Not only private homeowners—neither paid any rent nor given access to their barricaded property—were at a loss. The Senate, too, had its worries. Social plight led to crime, as many homeless people knew of no way out but to occupy houses standing empty. Breaking and entering and willful damaging of property posed as social plight. The police had a fight on their hands. As Berliners are no friends of compromise, the fronts polarized; only the media were able to capitalize on the heated battle.

The old spacious apartments on Kurfürstendamm with their ten and more rooms are beyond the means of private tenants today unless converted into boarding houses, small hotels, night clubs, art galleries, or brothels. In modern apartment blocks in East Berlin units of two rooms plus kitchen, bath and storage space (including perhaps a balcony), are the rule. Only one-third of all housing is of the three-rooms-plus variety. In cases where diplomats and other foreign representatives need a more comfortable and roomier abode, a solution is found which is out of the question for all but the luckiest citizens in East Berlin: by breaking through a wall two smaller apartments are joined together. The state as landlord cashes in at a rate of 20 marks per square meter rented. East Berliners only pay between 0.80 and 1.25 marks, depending on their income. Upkeep and urgent repairs, here as everywhere, remain a constant bone of contention.

I

Industry Between Boom and Bust

It had taken generations of the most wide-ranging and extraordinary talents to build up the industries of Berlin; until 1945, when everything in town had been destroyed as never before. By that time it did not matter anymore whether the founder of Schwartzkopff Torpedo Company had been appointed Privy Councillor by the emperor in 1884 or whether a Stralau palm-oil mill had mass produced the basic ingredient for that newly invented "workman's butter", margarine. Useless too was the idea which made a Berlin cook famous, who had pressed puréed peas into sausage skins and had sold his products, easily stored and long lasting, to the Prussian army. In 1945 Berliners rummaged through the storerooms of such enterprises for anything and everything usable, edible, saleable or otherwise marketable.

In spite of the fact that the major production plants of Berlin's heavy industry were moved into West Germany, the electrical industry, which ranked first long before Berlin's division, still leads any other branch of industry in either part of the city today. The plants of the General Electric Company (AEG for short in German), of Siemens and Borsig had always been spread around town, and their installations still survive, operating in the West under their original name, while in the East their new designations are prefixed mostly by VEB (short for "company owned by the people"). AEG in West Berlin, a public company listed on the stock exchange, was unable to withstand international economic pressures

[119]

and had to let a lot of their workers and employees go. They barely managed to avoid complete bankruptcy. In the course of developing "high-tech industries," the manufacturers of electrical equipment have increasingly shifted toward electronics in the hope of regaining a share of the international market. On both sides of the Wall attention focuses on the fabrication of robots for instance. Approximately 30 percent of the industrial output in Berlin (less 5 percent in the West and plus 5 percent in the East) is connected with electro-electronics.

There was a time, when the Prussian state communicated with its more distant realms via a clear and simple form of telegraphy. From village to village watchmen with signals (much like the ones used in the railway system) were positioned on top of church steeples. They waved their coded messages syllable by syllable in the direction of the recipient, weather and visibility permitting. Morse code, wireless, telephone, television transmission, and satellite communication perfected the basic idea of getting the message across. Research into the workings of the telephone was greatly accelerated by Werner Siemens, a lieutenant of the artillery, and his partner Johann Georg Halske, a mechanical engineer. They introduced the first telephone network in Berlin, which in the beginning connected three dozen skeptical customers. Ever since, Berliners have been known to call a simpleton a "weak-current engineer" or—with reference to the famous Berlin light-bulb company Osram—have been known to quip: "Send him to Osram, he needs a new bulb."

Berlin is involved in most every kind of industrial production. Behind the uncontested leadership of the electro-electronic industry the most important industries in East Berlin are machinery and vehicle production, production of foodstuffs, chemicals and fuel, and light industry. In the West foodstuffs take the lead followed by machinery, chemical products and fashions. When the Wall was built, 60,000 East Berliners were suddenly unable to commute to their working places across the border. Foreign labor, particularly from Turkey, was imported to take their place. East of the divide, in spite of labor shortages, understaffed or open positions, no significant number of "guest workers" from Eastern European countries has been introduced; nevertheless, East Berlin is the most economically viable capital within the Warsaw Pact. Problems of a geographical as well as political nature and unemployment in West Berlin have forced the Federal Republic to support the Senate and the economy; enormous subsidies are poured into the city to keep it economically and politically stable.

The working climate in East Berlin's ministerial offices, for instance, suffers from its very affability. A brief explanation to the doorman, and the afternoon is free for a visit to the dentist or hairdresser. Objections from above meet with passive resistance. In contrast, we heard an out-of-work welder in West Berlin cheerfully announce in a bar: "I'm doing fine; my wife Rosie has a job for life at Grieneisen's." (Grieneisen is West Berlin's largest funeral home.)

P.S. News just arrived that Rosie is out of a job too. Funeral business is not what it used to be either.

Italian Motifs

The young man selling Italian ice cream from a motorized cart in Tiergarten (West) couldn't care less about the ruins of the former Italian embassy behind the trees nearby. And yet the structure—built in 1940–1 and, due to wartime damages, only partly in use—recalls the days when a petty bourgeois like Adolf Hitler toyed with the idea of competing with the once glorious Roman emperors, regarding his Italian ally with less than high admiration. Germany and Italy had teamed up before, in 1882, when King Umberto I committed his country as a third partner to Chancellor Bismarck's brainchild, the Triple Alliance (which included the Austro-Hungarian and German empires), against France. The king graced Berlin with a state visit in 1899. Did he know that a Berlin artist and writer, August Kopisch, had been the one to rediscover the Blue Grotto of Capri, that romantic stage setting so beloved by Australians, Americans and Europeans alike?

Berliners have a close, long-standing connection with Italy. Even though they lack a Blue Grotto to attract hosts of tourists from all over the world, they can show off Capri's citadel ruins in replica, erected on an island in the Havel as a pleasure lodge. From GDR territory, the structure on Pfauen-insel is only visible through binoculars, but West Berliners can easily ferry accross on Sundays or during the week to admire the capricious building. Frederick William II had the mock castle built in 1794 for his mistress, Countess Lichtenau. Since marble was too dear, wood had to do, and a carpenter together with a few apprentices was able to finish the work to the satisfaction of king and courtesan alike. In recent years however restoration has utilized less stylish concrete.

Karl Friedrich Schinkel, one of Berlin's most famous architects contended in 1804 that nothing but scarcity of timber had forced the Romans and their descendants to chose slabs and blocks of marble, travertine and other hard rock for their main construction material. He traveled the length and breadth of the Italian peninsula, and his sketches of masterpieces and the panorama of Rome strongly influenced the architectural style of Berlin for generations to come. Sculptors like Begas (the creator of the Neptune Fountain near Marienkirche, now East Berlin) also refashioned their memories of Italy into monuments of stone or bronze, which stood out if not for their originality, at least for their longevity. Max Liebermann detested the epigonous copying of Italian scenes and motifs his painter colleagues from Berlin relished. Their pines, so he commented, reminded him of unopened umbrellas.

We shuttled to and from East Berlin in search of genuine Italian works of art. The engraving section of the Bode-Museum (East) contains sixty-one Boticelli illustrations to Dante's *Divine Comedy*, while the other twenty-seven silver-point engravings are kept in the Dahlem Museum (West). Italian masters in tableau size are relatively rare on either side nowadays. Whatever was counted among Berlin's greatest art treasures before the last World War had been stored in bomb shelters where, for unexplained reasons, they were destroyed in a raging fire after the end of the war. Other works of art came into the possession of the Allied victors; but the majority of those found their way back into that sector of Berlin controlled by the respective countries.

Hitler was fascinated by southern grandezza. Mussolini, his cohort, however, irritated him so much that only a square which Hitler regarded as utterly hideous was to be renamed after the Italian *duce*. The Führer had plans. Berlin was going to outshine Rome. Pompous edifices were drafted on paper, and prisoners from concentration camps were forced to work in special quarries to extract the building material. But the granite they were able to supply was of such inferior quality that it could only be processed into gravel or paving stones. Hitler's favorite sculptor, Arno Breker, received orders from Mussolini as well. Gigantic stone figures of his making still tower in Rome. But his sculptures disappeared from a building on Fehrbelliner Platz (West) just in time before they could become the subject of public ridicule after 1945.

The relationship between Rome and Berlin was off to a bad start when, in 1764, Giacomo Casanova seemed more impressed by his Berlin landlady than by His Royal Highness, King Frederick the Great. Frederick had offered Casanova the position of Director of the Royal School of Cadets. In the presence of the dignified Italian the sovereign read the riot act to one of the school governors in such abusive language (because of a cadet's unemptied chamber pot), that Casanova turned his nose and confessed in his diary: "And I should stay here? No thanks, I rather take the next coach to St. Petersburg." Off he went to more refined parts, much to the disappointment of the women of Berlin (not only the pretty ones) to this day.

J

Jewish Yortzeit

With 430 laws for the persecution and destruction of German
Jewry to back them up, Berlin disciples of the Third Reich
rushed forth to torment their 160,500 Jewish fellow citizens
shortly after the Nazis came to power. By 1939 only half their
number were still living in the city, in fear and mortal terror.
There had been Jewish communities in Berlin since the year
1671, and when Hitler took over some forty temples and
prayer halls were in existence. Today West Berlin counts five
Jewish synagogues for a community of 6,000. East Berlin has
less than 300 officially-registered members in its Jewish congregation, and its services are held in the Rykestraße Synagogue. The once beautiful temple on Oranienburger Straße
has so far been retained as a ruin, a memorial and haunting
symbol of warning. Now there are plans for its reconstruction.

Above a house on Große Hamburger Straße, a vocational
school at present, the inscription identifies it as the former
Boys' School of the Jewish Community. The Nazis had been
too busy to remove the letters on the wall, particularly from
1942 onward, when they herded Jewish Berliners together
next door in the now leveled home for the aged, prior to mass
transportation to the extermination camps.

Berlin, where some 5,000 of the persecuted survived under
most incredible circumstances, is generally considered one of
the centers of resistance against the Third Reich. Adolf Eich-
mann had 250 Jewish hostages shot and another 250 removed

to a camp when the Baum resistance group, in which a considerable number of Jews actively participated, fell into the hands of the Nazis. The twenty-seven group members were also executed. A memorial stone in the Jewish Cemetery of Weißensee bears their names, that of the traitor among them excluded. During a guided tour through this largest of Jewish graveyards, a Western journalist allegedly overheard someone call it "a burial ground for the Jewish plutocracy." Was there no mention made, for instance, of the numerous graves of Jewish First World War veterans? In the uniform of a country where the plutocracy has been abolished altogether, that is to say in Red Army uniform, many Russian Jews died in and around the capital during the Battle of Berlin. The tomb of one of them can be found close to the entrance of Weißensee Cemetery. The old family vaults gave some refugees shelter for weeks while the hunters were on their tracks. Only with these horrors in living memory are the intended innuendoes of the caustic remark of a Berlin taxi driver revealed: in the sixties he was driving a couple around town who had come from the United States on a visit. They casually mentioned that they did not recognize Berlin after an absence of thirty years. "Well," the driver commented, "you didn't miss much."

For many years now West Berlin has been inviting former

Jewish citizens for a visit to a city at once so familiar and so strange to them. An engineer needed a lot of persuasion to accompany his wife on the trip from the U.S. He vowed to stay as far away from conversations in his mother tongue as possible. Equipped with a hearing aid—the wire leading to his shirt pocket—but without a battery, he considered himself well-enough screened by deafness. After the first stopover—the plane had not yet left the state—he suddenly seemed to recognize a voice behind him. He turned around and looked straight into the eyes of a friend long presumed dead. The two men had been imprisoned in the same concentration camp. For the rest of the journey and throughout the stay in Berlin the hearing aid remained in the suitcase.

The former Fasanenstraße Synagogue has a permanent exhibition on display of artifacts from Jewish religious and secular life. On either side of the city divide government offices have been instructed to support the cultural activities of the Jewish communities, and here as much as there efforts have led to successes and failures. The temple on Fasanenstraße could have been saved, but the future of the Jewish community in Berlin was seen with such pessimism shortly after the end of the war that most of the damaged building was demolished. Only part of the portal arch was incorporated into the new structure of the Jewish Community Center on the same site, with a sculpture of a Torah scroll erected in the front. Visitors are welcome, but they have to open their bags under the sharp eyes of the guards at the door.

The "Mifgash," a restaurant in Wilmersdorf, was a favorite meeting place, mostly of young Berliners of Jewish descent, Israelis, and guests from many parts of the world. The kitchen was not kosher, but the menu abounded with Jewish specialties. In January of 1982 terrorists threw a bomb through the window. A thirteen-month-old baby girl was killed, her parents badly wounded. The unknown murderers escaped. After material damages had been removed the restaurant was reopened. Nobody was asked to show a passport upon entry. For it is written: In times of danger fear is the greatest one. The "Mifgash" has since been closed.

K

Kneipe—Home Away from Home

There are towns in Germany with four *Kneipen* or bars at every crossroads. If that's not enough for you, you'd better visit Berlin. Here you find at least five per intersection and various ones along the road. At one time these "haunts of the beer-drinking crowd" were pretty well of one style all over town. Late in the last century a chronicler reports: "Berlin with its one million inhabitants has some 800 clubs. They attest to the men's desire to be among themselves and drink together. And just like the frequent *Kneipen* socials they cut deeply into family life at home." Berlin was then a European testing ground for the design of industrial and tenement buildings. If a club was beyond your means, how much nicer to sit in a cozy *Kneipe* than in a dark, cluttered, and over-crowded apartment. A very practical and moral Berliner gave his bachelor friend some good advice: "Hey, Buddy, get married. It's time you know where you belong when you're plastered." *Kneipen* in Berlin, as a rule, are equipped with traditional furnishings: there is the bar with taps (at least for light and dark beer, if not more brands); the chromium top with drainage holes for overflowing foam and dripping beer; the refrigeration units below for bottled beer, sodas, wines and clear schnapps; and, last but not least, the sink or sinks with a brush handy for cleaning glasses. There would be an uproar if detergent were added to the dishwater. Germans detest flat beer; they like it with a crown. Behind the bar are the normal array of glasses, cognacs, brandies, liqueurs, and

[127]

bitters. There may be a few high tables for customers who prefer to stand up, standard ones are spread around the room; and the extra large one, usually round, called "Stammtisch" for the most regular of regulars, predominates.

The battles for bar licenses have led to ever more frequent takeovers of smaller concerns by big breweries so that nobody knows anymore who earns dividends from the sale of which brand of beer. According to special legal provisions *Kneipen* in Berlin are permitted to stay open twenty-four hours a day. Two and a half thousand pubs went on strike once to protest an attempt to enforce the more limited opening hours of the Federal Republic of Germany. A sense of sobriety prevailed. The Senate and the courts had no defense against the strikers' motto: "Don't turn Berlin into a sleepy town!" Even a pastor working with alcoholics joined the strike; his business, too, had been in danger of losing customers. So it's bottoms up!

If a well-reputed West Berlin businessman is seen taking the subway, he isn't close to bankruptcy by any means. He only lost his driver's license for a while for drunken driving. East Berlin knows no pardon for drivers whose blood test shows even the slightest trace of alcohol. The bars have to shut their doors on time; an eight-hour working day is a law broken by very few. Prices depend on the "class" of the establishment and on the level of luxury provided, which ranges from artificial flowers on tables to classy decor with a swing band for musical entertainment. Bars in East Berlin allow you to quench your thirst late into the night at the highest prices, and champagne flows in abundance. Motorists, however, stick to fruit juices. Supplies are delivered exclusively by the state-owned "beverage combines" at fixed prices.

Every stagehand of the Berliner Ensemble on Schiffbauerdamm can show you the favorite hangout of the theater's famous founder. The corner, where Bertolt Brecht and his wife relaxed on a sofa after performances, remains cordoned off, unless the guests can match the poet–playwright–director's fame. Similar couches of less renown but with equally worn-out springs are part of the *Kneipen* scene in West Berlin as well; though they are harder and harder to find, given the fast-changing fashions which do not fail to enter the Berliners' home away from home. Where too many slot machines beep or disco lights flash, the natives stay away, young ones not excluded. "That's for the gullible, not for us." Those who

[128]

agree, are quickly drawn into the family atmosphere.

Beer brewed from wheat, called "Weiße" for its light color, is served with or without a "Schuß," a shot of syrup. It is a favorite summer drink for tourists and locals alike. In years, when the rhubarb harvest is plentiful and the juicy stems can be boiled into an extract as sweet as vinegar, you may be lucky to get a taste of home-brewed "Faßbrause," straight from the vat. Normally the brew is mass-produced in factories and tastes a bit like watered-down root beer. But a "Molle" and "Korn," beer served alongside a clear schnapps, keeps even Grandma young. In all of Berlin those who imbibe can count on greater support and empathy than in any other German city. That's why their number keeps on climbing, and perhaps we'll be counting six instead of five *Kneipen* at every intersection soon.

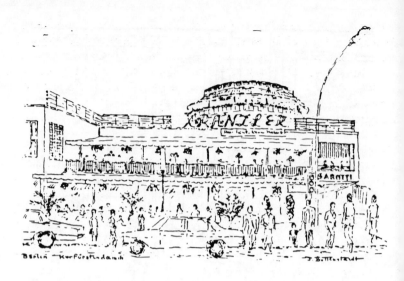

Kurfürstendamm on Parade

Whatever they may say about the Ku'damm, one thing—we checked it out ourselves—is true fact: the longest boulevard in West Berlin, three and a half kilometers from one end to the other, does not start with house No. 1. As early as 1925, when the Kurfürstendamm had reached the height of its fame, the eastern end was amputated and the addresses incorporated into Budapester Straße as Nos. 1 through 10. So exclusive was the area that no organ-grinder would have dared to disturb its noble atmosphere.

Nothing like Fifth Avenue, Regent Street or the Champs-Elysées, the Ku'damm, as it is affectionately called, has something of the Prussian line of the Hohenzollern about it. The ruling dynasty had always used the route to get to their hunting retreat in Grunewald. Chancellor Bismarck had seen to it that the old bridle path was widened, lengthened, fortified, and properly named—and set himself a lasting memorial in the process. Representative mansions with front gardens to line the avenue were planned but never materialized. For a long time horsemen and coach passengers would be grinding sand between their teeth as soon as they had left the paved section of the Damm. Today the whole length of it is paved, the center strip packed with parked cars. Wide sidewalks invite people strolling and window-shopping, who are forced to slalom around glass showcases every few meters or circumnavigate hotel and café verandas protruding into the walkway. The glitter of exclusive shops here, racks of mass-produced clothing there: the clash between elegance and tennis-shoe tourism is everywhere.

The postwar hit song "I'm so homesick for Kurfürsten-damm, I'm so homesick for my Berlin," brings tears to the eyes of some; others, who were not among the million or so people who left the city, are less impressed. In bitter honesty a Berlin writer observed that the flight from the city was not a forced evacuation. So why all that weeping, as if they were sitting by the rivers of Babylon, when they only "fled" to the full fleshpots of the Federal Republic?

It takes a close look at the façade of house No. 215 to discover the memorial plaque for the poet Max Herrmann-Neiße, whose mourning for Berlin, despair over the loss of his homeland and the separation from the living German language, was so much more stirring. The small man with his nickel glasses had sat among the greats and not so greats of literature, among actors and bohemians in the famous Roma-nische Café, until Hitler arrived. Exiled in London, a stranger in a strange culture, surrounded by a language not his own, he died of a broken heart in 1941. The pain had become too much, no poem could contain it any longer.

Artists can rarely be seen behind the panes of café verandas on Kurfürstendamm—prices take care of that. In bright sum-mer weather one can sit comfortably (but not much more cheaply) at tables outside in the open air. Passing by for the third time, you are considered an old acquaintance, a wel-come friend to be touched for a loan. To see and be seen is an integral part of life on Ku'damm. At the corner of Joachims-thaler Straße a Dr. Jovis banked on the proverbial curiosity of Berliners and visitors, and installed his wax museum up on the second floor of the building. The rooms at ground level had been rented out more profitably to shop owners and "serious" businesses. Dolls of flesh and blood appear on the Damm itself beginning at dusk. When a visitor from the "province," slightly taken aback, asked a Berlin taxi driver, whether there weren't any decent ladies around any more, the answer was: "Sure there are, only much more expen-sive!"

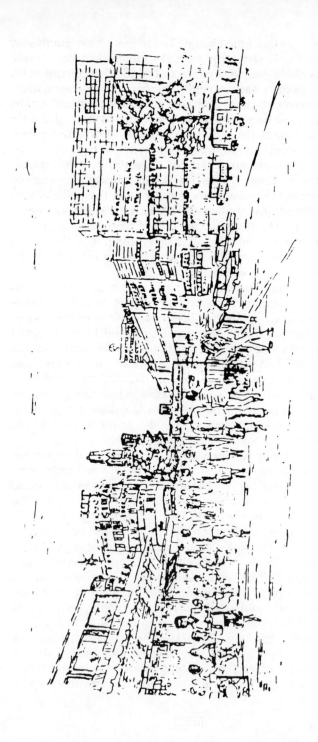

Galleries, furriers, jewelers and exquisite china shops are interspersed with movie theaters, sex shops, cheap boutiques and the like, all flashing their advertising at you. A dealer of very expensive cars threatened to move out and leave wide store windows empty. (Rent is astronomical on Kurfürstendamm.) He was persuaded to stay when offered subsidies by the Senate. Late at night traffic dies down, and fewer buses run. Suddenly blue lights flash, and sirens from police cars close in on a certain address. Two dozen uniformed policemen disappear through a door exquisitely fashioned with wrought-iron ornaments only to come back out laughing and joking. A lady had called the emergency number. She couldn't turn off the faucet in her bathroom.

L

Lighting Up

The darkness pervading Berlin during the early fifties can haunt the dreams of anyone who experienced it. On a wet night late in fall there was but one single light shining on Unter den Linden in the direction of Brandenburg Gate. It illuminated a guardhouse window in front of the Soviet Embassy, the only building which had been reconstructed at the time. Long power cuts in West Berlin evoked similar traumatic sensations of being lost and forsaken on the city streets. And yet, there was no fear of hold-ups or muggings then. How different is the realistic concern of senior citizens nowadays who avoid being out in the streets late at night. Times have changed. To what degree can best be exemplified by the words of warning against street lighting which appeared in the *Cöllnische Zeitung* in 1819. The paper rejected outright those newfangled ideas. Bright lights were having a bad influence on people's morality, undermining fear of the Lord and terror of the dark.

In the seventeenth century only every third homeowner was legally bound to hang up a petroleum lamp in front of his door during the "dark season" between fall and spring. In summer and when the moon shone bright fuel could be saved by leaving the lamps unlit. Later Berlin brightened up; gasworks began pumping coal gas through a regular network of pipes. Lamp lighting and lamp cleaning entered among the professional services. When electricity was introduced, there was an uproar. No matter that electric lights were much safer;

they were much more expensive, too. One cubic meter of gas cost only 16 pfennigs *vis-à-vis* 1 kilowatt of electricity at 40 pfennigs.

The noble Bauer Restaurant on Friedrichstraße was the first to glow under electric lights in 1880. Soon every business connected with lighting got off to a good start. Nothing better suited the self-confidence of Berliners than the assumed superiority of being the "light of the world." Thanks to the ingenuity of Berlin engineers and the willingness of banks to invest in the manufacture of cables, meters, dynamos and turbines, glasswares and suchlike, presumptive arrogance turned into pride. At any rate, the love of bright lights and beautiful street lamps have survived to this day in all of Berlin.

Whether out of local pride or a sense of tradition East Berlin takes great care in maintaining over 6,000 gas lamps still in use in four districts alone, while West Berlin claims 43,000 functioning ones, not all of which are turned on at night. Favorites by far are models designed by Schinkel, which are forever being copied. Along tree-lined pathways in Tiergarten, beautiful originals are exhibited as if it were an open-air museum of lampposts. And as if that were not enough West Berlin is involved in a worldwide trade with other cities—and the new acquisitions, faithfully labelled, are set up among its own. In recent times East Berlin has declared its traditional electrical streetlights, swaying for over a century on wires along and across its city roads, "historically valuable"—a welcome sign that the "peaceful" good old days are still with us. No matter that the lamps cast many a shadow and swing to and fro in wind and weather.

The former Schloßbrücke, Marx-Engels-Brücke today, had to do without its luster for some time. The beautifully worked railings and artful figurines had outlasted the war, but the candelabra, Schinkel originals, rested in a West Berlin storeroom, until they, too, were finally returned to their traditional location. They had illuminated the bridge before the war, and an underlying pride in *all* of Berlin, beyond any political division, made their return possible. Around the modern housing developments there is no longer any need for flashlights to prevent tripping in the dark. In Leipziger Straße (East) attractive streetlights have been installed.

An elderly Berliner called to our attention that Hitler must have detested any normal type of lighting, preferring substitutes instead: he entered Berlin in a torchlight procession through the Brandenburg Gate in 1933. Then flames rose from the piles of burning books that same year, when all of Germany's democratic literature went up in smoke. Two "hallowed flames" flickered on high pedestals in front of Hitler's New Chancellery to symbolize his "Empire of a Thousand Years" which lasted a dozen of incomprehensible terror. And, in the end, he took his own life during total blackout in the final days of the Battle of Berlin which closed the European theater of the Second World War.

Literature—Fiction and Fact

With few exceptions German writers of renown spent at least some time in the capital that was Berlin. They came from all corners of the country, a small number even grew up along the banks of the Spree. The public took notice of them, tolerated them all, but to this day still reserves the right to decide whose works find favor and whose do not.

After 1945, the majority of Berlin publishers moved their businesses into West Germany. In East Berlin the traditional names of progressive publishers were retained under new management and book production was soon budding again. There were authors who—driven into emigration by the Nazis—returned to live and work in what is East Berlin today. Johannes R. Becher who had spent his years of exile in the Soviet Union briefly went in the other direction settling in Charlottenburg (West) where he established the office of the League of Culture for a Democratic Renewal of Germany. When, in one of the first waves of anti-Communism, the League of Culture was forbidden in the West, the organization moved across the border. So did Johannes R. Becher. The literary scene began to split in two. In the West, the "Group 47" under the strategic command of Hans Werner Richter began to throw its weight around. Its star author, Günter Grass, became famous with his *The Tin Drum*. Erwin Piscator, back from exile in the U.S., fought, to the brink of despair, for recognition in West Berlin. His staging of Rolf Hochhuth's *The Deputy* (about the Pope's relationship with Nazis) stirred up a lot of controversy, but paved the way for a Jewish–Christian dialogue.

The art of giving oneself the air of a poet and attracting attention through appropriate bearing and attire (not new in itself), was tried and truly perfected in Berlin. At times the price of success was rather cheap, at times it was exorbitant. Heinrich von Kleist, born in 1777, shot himself with Henriette Vogel in 1811 near Wannsee; his fame came too late. The author Friedrich Spielhagen was luckier with his bestsellers, even though his characters seem more like two-dimensional mouthpieces for muddled agitation. Theatrical scandals and literary gossip usually hastened the rise, in rare cases the fall, of a writer and the popularity of a work.

The most "original" of Berlin authors often rested on their laurels, satisfied to portray local events and the idiosyncracies of the regional dialect, happy to be recognized by the indigenous population. On the other end of the scale, Arno Holz, who had set his hopes on a Nobel prize five times, died embittered in 1929.

The exception among the literary figures of Berlin is Theodor Fontane. His novels, poems, stories, and books of travel are almost exclusively dedicated to Berlin and his Prussian homeland, while his fame is international. And his memory lives on in East and West: no matter that the war destroyed his grave, and the memorial stone which replaced it could, for many years, only be approached by special permission of the East Berlin authorities; no matter that a parking lot occupies the space where he lived for years on Mehringdamm. The Fontane Archive in Potsdam protects his literary legacy and functions as a research center. A cultural and communications center in the modern Märkisches Viertel of Reinickendorf (West) carries his name; so does a valued literary prize in East and another in West Berlin. Peter Huchel, who left the GDR for West Germany, was recipient of both.

Writer-physician Alfred Döblin belonged to the acclaimed literary circles between the two World Wars. His portrait of Berlin, the novel *Berlin Alexanderplatz*, is set in the early decades of this century when, amidst the glitter of Berlin's "golden era," social problems among the underprivileged and disadvantaged increased sharply. Döblin fled to France in the thirties, but returned soon after 1945, living the final years of his life in southern Germany—there seemed to be no place for him in Berlin. Bertolt Brecht, the playwright and poet, was given his own theater company in East Berlin, the Berliner Ensemble, which still performs in the Brechtian tradition. His former living and working quarters on Chausseestraße 125, to which he returned from his Californian refuge, are open to the public for guided tours and for scholarly study.

East Berlin has remained the focal point of literary activities in the GDR, with its publishing houses, its literary magazines, and as the seat of the country's writers' association and PEN Club. In the West the "Group 47" has more or less fallen apart. The meetings held in Grunewald under Hans Werner Richter's leadership never could match those in publisher Samuel Fischer's private residence before the war. The literary elite around Fischer had been driven out of the country. Irretrievably lost were their stimulating intellectual and humanistic contributions, gone was the atmosphere of concerned liberalism which had carried them all. German history after 1933 proved a heavy burden on German postwar literature. Television, the new literary market, shifted the markings on the quality scales down even further. In an effort to turn the tide, each year West Berlin's senator for cultural affairs spends sizeable amounts on stipends and a wide range of programs for the promotion of literature.

The number of libraries in both parts of the divided city is considerable, their stock of books, both old and new, enormous. East Berlin's State Library can claim to be the oldest one with the greatest number of volumes. Berliners East and West still get a chance to see many writers in their midst. While East Berliners are known to be avid readers, there have been occasional reports about a writer encountering someone with a book under his arm in the Western part of town. The decision whether to pass this rare specimen of the reading public or enter into a literary conversation depended exclusively on the writer's personal courage. And it takes courage to face criticism from one of the most outspoken groups of metropolitans in the world. Berliners know it all—know it all much better.

M

Medicine, Magic, and Miracle

Berliners, especially in the West, are not allowed to forget their physical ailments: there are apothecaries at every street corner to remind them. The healthy ones couldn't care less about the flashy advertisements for this and that and the other thing. It's all for the birds, the ones that nest between the neon signs, chirping their disapproval, even dropping feathers, straw and other trash on the heads of those replenishing their supplies of pills and ointments.

The oldest pharmacy, preceded only by a pharmacological laboratory started in 1607 in the Grey Cloisters, operates at the junction of Schönhauser Straße and Rosenthaler Straße in East Berlin. It's a regular museum piece. Ernst Schering began as a druggist in the Wedding area (now West) in 1864; the firm he founded expanded into a giant, worldwide enterprise, while still maintaining its central offices and laboratories where it had all begun. Wedding, the "red" workers' district of the twenties, had long been considered the healthiest spot in and around Berlin, ever since a fountain of health, "Gesundbrunnen" in German, had been discovered here by Frederick I. The story goes that a miller's wife offered the king a drink from the spring, and by it he was cured of an unspecified illness. Perhaps he had been no more than thirsty. Whatever the truth of the matter, the spring was enclosed in 1701, and a court pharmacist later established a spa there that for a time was named after the Berliners' beloved Queen Luise, until in modern times it came to an abrupt end. Sewage from a tannery seeped into the waters and spoiled everything.

Medical progress, however, could not be held back that easily. Around 1900 Robert Koch founded a research lab for infectious diseases in Wedding, an institute which still continues its good work. Koch's mausoleum stands in the immediate vicinity. Also in this district and around the same time, the first hospital consisting of individual pavilions was built under the guidance of the eminent physician and municipal councillor Rudolf Virchow. Driven by a strong sense of social responsibility that seemed wanting in others, Virchow succeeded in realizing this ambitious project against all odds.

It was well-known that Virchow didn't mince his words. When the ladies of the bourgeoisie and the nobility of Berlin raved to him about the life of the divine soul, he was heard to utter that in all his countless operations he had never come across any such thing as a soul. Robert Koch's experiments he simply called "germ coloring." But the germ stainer Koch kept on going about his business, to be awarded the Nobel Prize for Medicine in 1905 for his successful battles against tuberculosis and cholera.

Long before a university was brought to academic life in Berlin, the Charité had gained European fame as an excellent teaching hospital. The former plague house inherited its French name from the Huguenots living in the area and kept it in spite of enlargements, modernizations, and the incorporation into the socialist health system. Like all Berlin clinics, the Charité was crowded toward the end of World War II with civilian casualties and wounded soldiers. A surgeon of the old school, Ferdinand Sauerbruch, labored with his staff in the operating theater under the illusion that he was contributing to a change of luck in favor of the National Socialists and their final victory. When the Soviet military authorities took over soon afterwards, it was with some regret that they saw him move to the western part of Berlin, for his reputation was that of a highly qualified professional. In his new surroundings, Sauerbruch failed to abdicate at the appropriate time, and among his colleagues mean jokes made the rounds such as "if the boss hadn't operated, the patient would be deader yet."

Many a modern doorway in Berlin is decorated on both sides with a mosaic of doctors' nameplates promising private or public medical care for any and every ailment possible. In East Berlin, where the health system is in the hands of the state and where patients are treated free of charge, there are nevertheless exceptions to the rule. In answer to a "Dear Doctor" letter asking "who pays for a cosmetic operation?" a local paper published the following expert opinion by a district supervisor: "If the reasons for such corrective surgery are purely personal, then such aesthetically motivated operations do not appear to be medically indicated. They can be performed, but as in the case of a face-lift to improve one's appearance, they are not performed free of charge. The legal consequences resulting from this principle of private remuneration . . ." and so on and so forth. Bureaucratese has always been unintelligible in Prussia, without exception.

"You're good in Latin, Doctor, aren't you?" a Berliner asked his amazed physician, who had just warned him that he was ruining his health by excessive drinking and eating and too many cigarettes. "When you have to repeat what you told me in the presence of my wife," the patient continued, "please do me a favor, Doctor, and tell her in Latin."

Monumentalistics

The most fascinating monuments in Berlin (and elsewhere) are usually those not only presenting to the sightseer their imposing exterior, but also allowing a close inspection of their inner life, a climb through their insides, and a crowning look from the top. The "Siegessäule" or Victory Column is a case in point. Strategically placed at the Great Star intersection in Tiergarten today, it is impossible to miss. The father and predecessor of the last German emperor had insisted that it be constructed of war booty, and his campaigns against Denmark (1864), Austria (1866), and France (1870–1) supplied the material. *Noblesse oblige.* By 1873 the column stood on Königsplatz with a tall gilded bronze angel of victory above, Victoria, the heaviest girl in town. In 1937 the whole construction was dismantled, only to be reerected in time for World War II in its present location, higher and more solidly based than before. Red Swedish granite encases the pedestal, sixteen columns hold up the ceiling of a circular walkway decorated with mosaic scenes of Prussian triumphs, and 300

Berlin Siegessäule

steps lead up to an observation platform at a height of 68 meters, opening up to a view over West Berlin and into the center of East Berlin. Here you almost forget the gilded gun barrels surrounding the structure and their origin.

It must have been more than irony of fate which in 1945 removed the four bronze reliefs around the base of the monument. They ended up war booty once again, this time in Copenhagen and Paris. Two years later, by order of the victorious Allied Forces, thirty-two tall statues lining Victory Boulevard, mutilated by artillery, disappeared. They were representations of "great" statesmen, soldiers, and citizens. Some were buried like corpses and dug up again thirty years later. Even in our enlightened era effigies apparently have not lost their magical powers. No one wants to believe that only the fuss made over them made them into the false gods, so much to be feared. Now they stand, for the time being, in solitary confinement in the courtyard of the pumping station on West Berlin's Landwehrkanal and in a storage space in East Berlin, wondering about the twists and turns of German history.

Close to the Victory Column, three of the "greats" under William I—his minister of war, his general field marshal and the Iron Chancellor himself—still enjoy the fresh Berlin air, none of them what they used to be. Roon was put on a higher and lighter base, Moltke has to make do without his coat of arms (and his motto: first weigh, then wager), and Bismarck's good name is missing a few letters. Bismarck once towered amidst allegorical figures in front of the old Reichstag, the ruined house of parliament behind which puzzling sculptures are now on view, products of an artistic competition of modern neolithics.

In East Berlin, members of a special unit of the people's army guard a memorial to which the public has access. An eternal flame inside the New Guard House or "Neue Wache" honors the victims of fascism and militarism. The memorial always was and remains a military monument through and through. It baffles the mind to see the changing of the guards in ceremonial Prussian style with goose-stepping soldiers in full gear and to listen to the drums and fifes that accompany the spectacle. The architect Schinkel must have been carried away already when he chose the style of an antique castrum for the building intended by Frederick William III to give his cannoniers a roof over their heads. In reality the New Guard House never served any other than a representative purpose, which goes to show that absurdities have the best prospect of prevailing. The new guards are housed in the old armory or "Zeughaus," which may or may not stand to reason. Much more reasonable is the existence of the victory memorial on West Berlin territory to the Red Army east of the Brandenburg Gate. Soviet soldiers are standing guard here in front of two tanks that rolled into Berlin in 1945. There is nothing absurd about that, but we noticed that nobody can even get close. Behind a barbed-wire barricade British military police watch over the safety of their colleagues from the USSR, since some maniac opened fire on them years ago. And that should not happen again.

A conical, sharply-pointed mock-Gothic contraption, the "National Monument" in Kreuzberg (West), rises 19 meters high—the most stately iron piece of art in Prussia when it was inaugurated in 1821. Its layout, too, both stately and metaphorically metallic, is in the shape of an iron cross, celebrating the "War of Liberation" against Napoleon, and in its wrought-iron construction the up-and-coming industrialization of Berlin as well. Incorporated are twelve statues of genii that closely resemble the military commanders of the 1813–15 campaign and some members of the royal family. When the trees in the vicinity began to tower over the monument, it was put on a high pedestal. An artificial waterfall rushes down from its base into Victoria Park with mock-alpine scenery to enhance the illusion of height, but with every step closer the impression dims.

The Senate of West Berlin faithfully and generously replaced every rusty part in the original style. But no pedestal of harmonious proportion could bring back the panoramic view over the city enjoyed from the top before high-rises and towering insurance buildings smothered the monument. The old order of things has been replaced by a new one. A better one?

Museums—Curiosities for the Curious

With fifty-three museums the two Berlins can well hold their own among the major cities of the world. The guide to New York lists only sixteen major ones, the largest public libraries included. Moscow, so the tourists are advised, maintains collections in thirty-two museums. But one museum is missing in Berlin, a collection of documents relating to the history of museums in town. Many a hair-raising fact would come to light. In hall No. 6 of the Märkisches Museum in East Berlin for instance "welcome cups" are invitingly displayed side by side with instruments of torture.

The National Gallery was the first to fall victim to Nazi art critics. Nowhere had German art of the nineteenth and twentieth centuries been so fully represented as in the Kronprinzenpalais (the Palace of the Crown Prince). The most important foreign artists of modern times were also exhibited here, until "degenerate" works of art were confiscated by the hundreds and whole sections closed in the end. Twenty years after the war, a Berlin film director showed us—in his private home—a considerable sampling of modern works of art—signed by the greatest of the greats. "I was in the German army," he casually disclosed. "A few crates with these pictures were sent to us in Italy, which we were to sell on the Italian market. I salvaged one of the crates by having it registered missing and sent it to my Berlin address instead."

In the light of such occurrences, who could be surprised about what happened to many prize possessions from Berlin

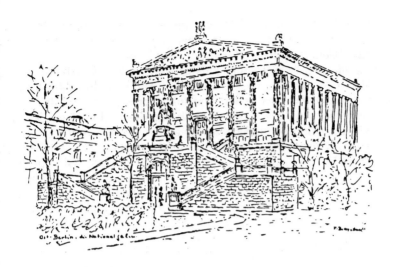

museums stored outside of the city for security reasons? Thuringia was liberated by the Americans, Berlin itself by the Soviets. The connoisseurs in uniform took their choice. Berliners had reason to be grateful for any item at all returned to their museums, where bombardments, artillery attacks, fire, and water caused more damage than the cruelest vandals could have done. Fire broke out in the bunkers of Friedrichshain after the battles had ended: its cause remains a mystery. Eyewitnesses still living keep their mouths shut. Gradually war booty found its way back to Berlin, from the Americans in Wiesbaden and the Russians in Moscow. Galleries and museums were repaired or rebuilt from the ground up. Exhibitions were held again, though none as wide-ranging and complete as before since the treasures were now split between East and West.

Since the number of collections had doubled and their individual values diminished by half, there are today two sets of museums specializing in Egyptian, Islamic, Byzantine and early art; there are twin arts and crafts museums, two collections of copper engravings, two ethnological museums, two National Galleries, and two Picture Galleries. No other city can offer that much in duplicate.

Traditionally the most famous of the exhibition palaces of Berlin have huddled close together on Museum Island, now in East Berlin, between two arms of the Spree. Each one of the buildings has its own historical reason for being. In 1815 the spoils of war taken from Napoleon were to be shown to

[145]

the public, so the Old Museum was founded. The New Museum followed not long afterwards. Space in the old one had been too meagerly apportioned. Berliners owe their Islamic Museum to the construction of a railroad line to Mecca. A castle in the desert stood in the way of a selected route and was torn down. The sultan presented the German emperor with a complete lavish façade of the place. The Islamic collection had been started. Postwar inventory revealed, however, that the beautiful carpets had vanished. The Great Elector had taken delight in collecting East Asian porcelain and art objects; they, too, disappeared—to the Soviet Union. Slowly both parts of Berlin have been able to replenish their halves of the various collections through donations and new acquisitions. Neoclassical interest in the cultures of the Nile delta—a trend inseparably linked to economic interests in the Suez Canal project—was at the root of the Egyptian Museum, whose large statues remained in East Berlin. The smaller, more easily transported works—the bust of Queen Nefertiti among them—are on exhibit in West Berlin.

New museums and collections in Berlin reveal a lot about the taste of the times. In a pavilion in Tiergarten objects were meticulously gathered which our grandparents would have ignored. "Street furniture" is the highbrow term used for these wrought-iron park benches, mailboxes, telephone-booths, and the like. East Berlin, which maintains the only hotel we know of exclusively catering to construction workers, preserves memorabilia relating to the history of reconstruction after 1945 in the "Traditionskabinett" of the regional building authorities. Photos, trade union membership cards, obligatory notebooks of workers with their foremen's remarks, documents of all sorts, even traditional construction tools keep a quickly forgotten social phenomenon alive.

A courageous pacifist had founded a Peace Museum near the Rotes Rathaus until the SA, Hitler's storm troopers or brownshirts, demolished it and closed it down. His grandson opened an "Anti-War Museum" in West Berlin in 1982 only to close it down again some time later. He and his club members could not come to an agreement about which kind of peace to show to school classes and other visitors—a remarkable testimony to the muddled thinking of today. One is reminded of the elderly Jewish gentleman in East Berlin who wanted to buy some tea and was asked whether he preferred the Russian or the Chinese variety. He sighed:

"Leave me alone with your politics and let me have half a pound of cocoa."

Music Sets the Tone

Only in a city as musical and music-loving as Berlin could three young enthusiasts from Neukölln get away with ordering just one glass of beer among them in a concert restaurant. To the skeptical waiter they explained that they wanted to be sure the music was to their liking before they ordered more. Closer to the truth was perhaps that their combined pocket money would buy them no more than one glass of beer, but the waiter gave them the benefit of the doubt. Times were hard before 1933—and they were going to become much harder still, as we know from history.

One of the most important contributions to the history of instrumental music originating in Berlin has been frequently overlooked: the invention of the bass tuba. Its significance, however, cannot escape those who, like us, spent some time in an apartment above a tuba player. His daily practicing convinced us of the power of his instrument as quickly as we began looking for another place to live. Thanks to the new invention, from 1835 onward Prussian military bands expanded their range and gained tremendously in volume and acclaim. Artillery, infantry, and cavalry became noted for their music more than their fighting capability. On the occasion of a visit from the Russian czar in 1883 the Prussian ruler held a mass concert which put to shame every musical event ever staged. One thousand wind instruments and 200 drums joined in thunderous harmony.

A few years later a cartoon appeared in one of the Paris papers depicting Richard Wagner next to a tuba mounted in cannon style firing a barrage of notes at the French capital. The tuba had conquered the stage against the strong resistance of French music critics. In Berlin, military concerts never failed to draw crowds around the bandstands of open-air cafés, beer gardens, and public parks.

Between 1741 and 1743 the architect Knobelsdorff built the German State Opera which, to the amazement of connoisseurs, has been reconstructed in its original style and location (Unter den Linden, East Berlin). Frederick II, expressing his love of music in his own way, showed little regard for German opera when he fell in love with a certain Barberina Campanini from Parma, star of the Berlin operatic stage. She was the talk of the town, less for her dancing than for her numerous affairs, so that the Prussian monarch was drawn into ever more complex diplomatic tangles. But eventually her looks and her charisma waned, at which point she retreated to a Silesian convent, where she died a respectable abbess.

When the first bourgeois vocal club, the so-called "Singakademie" was founded for the promotion of spiritual choral music, a center had finally been established for all those who detested endless military marches as much as they shunned the slippery road to fame in the musical world of courtly entertainment. The choral union flourished under the honorable and talented Carl Friedrich Zelter in Berlin, while all over the country patriotic glee clubs sprang up to exercise their newly discovered freedom of expression. Zelter could hardly have envisioned that the voices of patriotism he had set free would soon sing in support of a disastrously chauvinistic political development. Not far from his temple song, the university of East Berlin trains its musicologists today. The "Singakademie" itself was remodeled into a theater.

The functional structure of the German Opera, Berlin,

Deutsche Staatsoper Berlin

which was built in 1976 on Bismarckstraße (West)—site of the former City Opera—hardly resembles a temple of the muses. In 1924 a branch of the Knobelsdorff opera had been established here to serve the western part of town. Famous conductors once raised their batons here, in the State Opera on Unter den Linden, or in the Comic Opera on Behrenstraße. What has remained is the tradition of dressing up in festive attire for a performance of *The Barber of Seville* or *The Magic Flute*, or for one of the modern operas. A hard-working cleaning lady employed to keep front and backstage in top condition with broom and rag greeted us in the foyer with a proud and disarming: "I spend more time on stage than the whole ensemble put together."

Since Kurt Weill won world acclaim with his musical score for *The Threepenny Opera* which was first performed in Berlin, we searched for a memorial stone or plaque in his honor, but in vain. "For that you have to go to America," a Berliner enlightened us. A bust of Paul Lincke had just been moved from Paul-Lincke-Damm to Oranienstraße in Kreuzberg. The composer who celebrated the "Air of Berlin" and told that little glowworm to glow, no longer impresses young spray-can artists nursed on pop and rock, and his statue was invariably sprayed with all colors of the rainbow. Cleaning efforts resulted only in a new color scheme, much to the joy of the amateur artists and their followers. "Mack the Knife" or "Glowworm" meant nothing to them, were as ridiculous

[149]

as that "shashlik skewer"—a baffling metal sculpture in front of the box-like structure of the German Opera Berlin.

Asked about "Circus Karajani," even the youngest rascals knew and could give us directions. Herbert von Karajan enjoys the most amazing acclaim throughout the world, and of course in Berlin, too. So everyone knows "his circus," the home of the Berlin Philharmonic Orchestra, so christened in ironic reverence and loving mockery of the conductor's sensational art and artistic achievements. The story goes that he stepped out of the back door of the building, still in his tails, jumped into a taxi, shrugging off the driver's question "Whereto?" with an indignant and absent-minded: "Doesn't matter. I've got business everywhere!"

N

Naked Truths and Other Revelations

When the twenty-year-old daughter of a Swiss millionaire leaves West Berlin for a quick trip to the U.S. to have her picture taken "on a beach, dressed in nothing but a cowboy hat" the sensational press picks up the story, and nobody thinks anything of it. An elementary-school teacher, however, went into shock when his ten-year-old pupil, asked "What is the best thing in life?" replied, "to lie in bed with a naked woman!" The teacher demanded a conference with the boy's father the following afternoon, but the next morning the rascal brought the father's response: "Sir, my dad says hello, and he says I'm right. And if you don't think so, Dad told me to be on my guard."

The young ladies of Berlin were among the first to shed their corsets, once these had been declared unhealthy; since that time more and more restrictive clothing has been shed, occasion and weather conditions permitting. Heinrich Zille wrote of the sentiment in nudist colonies: "We walk around in the nude and think nothing of it." In this respect, at least, not much has changed in Berlin.

Berlin's bathing beaches usually have a stretch reserved for nudists nowadays, even though at the beginning of the century police could arrest "indecently" clad sun worshippers for failing to abide by the public code of conduct. It read: "Women are only allowed to bathe in public if they wear a swimsuit which covers chest and body in front completely, does not disclose anything below the shoulder blades in the

Berlin   Müggelturm

back, fits tightly under the arms, and is equipped with sewn-on legs and a gusset." This "gusset law" was, of course, ridiculed no end. Regulations notwithstanding, Berliners soon took to the bushes, undressed, hid their clothes under the sand and jumped into lakes and waterways in whichever state of undress they dared. Onlookers had to contend with a quick and sassy: "Don't stare or you'll go cross-eyed!"

Compared to the long winter months in Berlin, summer is always too short, so Berlin has obliged with heated swimming pools, where on fixed dates fans can bathe in the nude. In Lichterfelde (West) a large recreation complex with sauna, solarium, badminton, table tennis, volley and fistball facilities has been developed around a pool in a romantic South Sea island setting. The nudist club, registered as "Club for Body Culture," counts over 1,500 members, the largest in Berlin, and is filled to capacity. There are five smaller clubs in existence elsewhere in the city. East Berlin accommodates its enthusiasts in a slightly different way. The BBB, or Berlin Bathing Ball, held in the glass-encased pool hall of the Sports and Recreation Center is a sensational affair with a carnivalistic touch. Tables and chairs are set up in the water and most anything goes, except revealing your naked self. You can sit down, sip champagne, swim around, or dive under the water. Balloons rise to the ceiling, disco music blares, couples dance—it is a party the way Berliners like it. There have been no public announcements so far about the number of gentlemen in swim shorts and strawhats and ladies in Grandma's knee-length bathing suit who have become engaged after having first met at the ball.

While a summer vacation on the beaches of the Baltic Sea on GDR territory is in easier reach for East Berliners, Westerners too can book a holiday here through one of the East German travel agencies—for (hard) Western currency. "Beach baskets," those canopied double-seater wicker chairs lining the beaches, provide shade, protect from the wind, and allow you to change clothing in relative privacy. Streamers indicate spots where you can bathe in the nude. Those who prefer to enjoy their sunny days closer to home may console themselves. The beaches along the lake fronts and river banks of Berlin offer most anything the Baltic does, including beach baskets imported from those north-eastern shores. The first such chairs appeared along Berlin's "Copa Cabana" around 1930, the year of record attendance at this largest inland bathing beach in Europe: 1.5 million visitors. Though that number has never since been attained, the sandy areas along West Berlin's lakes and rivers are hopelessly overcrowded during the hot season, while sailboats and motor vessels race across the waters.

Whatever else West Berlin reveals as "naked truth" is not restricted to the late hours of the night. Papers and magazines leave little to the imagination. Former middle-class hotels have inadvertently become meeting places for prostitutes and easy pick-ups. Knowing full well that the natives like to frolic in the water and, hoping to attract the undivided attention of rich clientele, some West Berlin discotheques have built pools in the middle of their dance floors and filled them with girls in bikinis. And the naked facts have been met with financial return. But success can also be measured in different terms. In 1960, during the opening of an outdoor pool in Pankow, the lord mayor of East Berlin celebrated the event as the outcome of amiable cooperation among many volunteers, but admitted: "We built all this outside our regular budget. It would not have been possible without 200,000 hours of volunteer work. Now is the time for all those 'illegal'

[153]

workers to jump in with the best of conscience."

Solidarity is just as much in evidence on the beaches of West Berlin. In the nudist colony in Heiligensee the tent of a woman in her sixties went up in flames. Her gas stove had exploded. Even before the firemen arrived seventy bare-bottomed members of the club had brought the fire under control. Afterwards they passed a collection box around so successfully that the loss could be fully compensated. Said one of the participants to a newspaper reporter: "No, extravagant we are not. Just supportive among ourselves. Only the Internal Revenue has a hard time finding a pocket to pick on us."

Nazi Past and Aftermath

There is not one building or memorial inherited from the Berlin-based Nazi government which shows a touch of class or beauty. Office and administrative blocks still serve public purposes today, an external and by no means philosophical line of historical continuity. On Fehrbelliner Platz West Berlin's senator of the interior officiates in a massive edifice jokingly referred to as "civil servants' dormitory" by the sharp-tongued Berliners. East Berlin ministries, in turn, make use of some thousand office cubicles in the former Air Force Administration building—an utter monstrosity. The frosty air about these masses of ashlar and travertine blocks favored by Hitler is in no way mitigated by the icy silence of those asked about the origin of such edifices. The atmosphere is not much different around the Olympic Stadium and the exhibition halls near the West Berlin Radio Tower. It can also be sensed in Grünau (East Berlin) around the special facilities laid out for aquatic competitions of the 1936 Olympic Games. The monstrous structures can't be hidden. Their demolition and subsequent reconstruction out of the question for economic reasons, they remain warning symbols of German giganto-mania and political aberration to be borne with a sense of shame.

The young people of Berlin don't even notice; they grew up with them, and will probably grow old and die with them.

The city government of East Berlin had to be made aware that neither stone nor plaque honors the victims of Hitler's secret police, who here beaten and tortured in police headquarters on Alexanderplatz. The old building was torn down, but memories remain. By zealously renaming East Berlin streets and squares for prominent resistance fighters, the GDR authorities tried to erase as many remnants as possible of Germany's Nazi past. The historical lesson to be learned from it is taught in schools and publicized in every way. West Berlin has usually selected historical names for roads built in recent years.

The Wall now runs along the center of Prinz-Albrecht-Straße which became Niederkirchner Straße to recall a woman resistance fighter. On the Western side of the street the Prinz-Albrecht-Palais was demolished after the war. The palace had been the seat of the notorious Secret State Police. A memorial plaque points out this place of horror, where opponents of the Nazi regime were held and from where, after most gruesome torture, they were further expedited in stock cars to the concentration camps or called before the Volksgerichtshof. This court of Nazi "justice" on Kleiststraße housed the Allied Control Council from 1945 to 1948 and went on to serve as backdrop for important conferences on the future of Berlin.

In Tiergarten, Stauffenbergstraße 11–13, Hitler's Military High Command occupied the former "Bendler-Block." The courtyard was converted into a memorial place for those German officers who (on July 20,1944), had made an attempt on Hitler's life. The plot failed, and all those involved in the desperate plan to free Germany of its curse were executed. Count Stauffenberg had been the main defendant. Groups of school children are confronted here with the dark side of German history *and* learn about the resistance movement against the Third Reich (which is the topic of lectures inside the building). Another memorial can be seen in Plötzensee Prison, still a terrifying site even after the removal of the guillotine; however the gallows, where so many political prisoners were hanged, is still standing. In a newly erected Catholic church nearby memorial services are celebrated regularly for the 1,800 Plötzensee murder victims.

Haunting memories re-emerge for the older generation of Berliners wherever traces of the Second World War remain visible. There are still open spaces which have never been built over. Anhalter Bahnhof, formerly a main railroad station, stands in ruins; many a house wall still shows the damages inflicted by bombardments and mortar fire. No, the past is not dead. Youngsters react with unexpected aggression when faced with the results of recent German history. They, too, are affected by the aftermath, in spite of having been born a generation or more later. In the security of a private car an East Berliner pointed to a group of Soviet soldiers walking about town and hissed: "Those over there . . ." To him, "those over there" were responsible for all the miseries of the present. Young West Berliners throw plastic bags filled with paint at military vehicles belonging to the Western Allies. We heard policemen being referred to as "fascist fuzz." No, the past is not dead, neither is the glorification of violence at which the Nazis were masters. Unsuspecting, we stopped to look at an improvised altar in front of a house on Potsdamer Straße, West Berlin, adorned with red rags, slogans, tin cans and coke bottles sprouting with flowers. A child, probably twelve years of age, suddenly screamed at us hysterically: "Kneel down, kneel down, or I'll kill you." As we were told later, we had passed a modern "shrine," a memorial for a demonstrator recently shot by police. When we hurried off, nothing seemed to make sense. Something does now.

Understandable alarm spread among the population of West Berlin when, in two districts, ammunition and containers with poisonous gas were found in covered-up anti-tank ditches buried there by the Nazis. To facilitate the search for similar caches in the Spandau area, the Senate had to ask for aerial photographs to be sent from Great Britain. The Royal Air Force alone stores 10,000 such pictures in a university archive. They were taken between 1941 and 1945 during reconnaissance flights over the city.

"Why don't they grow mushrooms in them?" muttered an old Berliner showing us a newspaper article about twenty-six air-raid shelters West Berlin authorities just reequipped as "emergency storehouses" to add to 770 already in existence within the city limits. Of ninety-five above-ground bunkers built before 1945, seventy-eight are still considered "suitable for civil defense purposes." The Senate's budget will provide funds for the repair and restocking of further shelters, so says the report. It seemed to us a macabre phenomenon, like fingernails growing on the hands of a decomposing body.

O

Odd Jobs for Ordinary People

It would be hard to say just how many ordinary people perform most extraordinary jobs in the major cities of the world. Spanish matadors, Indian snake charmers and a host of other talents in law-abiding and not so law-abiding professions come to mind. Hard to say, too, what Berlin has to offer here. While limiting our report to what we personally observed and encountered, we must stress that in all cases the anomaly of the job was largely hidden by the normality and relative inconspicuousness of those performing it.

In a stroke of luck, a craft has survived in Berlin that has faded out most everywhere else. The craftsmen still employed in this traditional business are indeed fortunate. Lucky, too, the Berliners who meet one of these messengers of fortune. No other city in Germany, East or West, can claim as many coal-fired ovens for cooking and heating as the two halves of Berlin combined; chances here are considerably greater that you will catch sight of a figure all in black with a shiny top hat carrying a long-handled broom over his shoulder. The occupation of the chimney sweep is regulated in true Prussian style. The uniform is prescribed, and their vocational training from the first steps as apprentice, to journeyman, to the proud top of the ladder as master-sweep, is strictly organized. The customers, too, are subject to set rules, obliged as they are to employ the chimney sweep's services on a regular basis. Passing a member of the guild, better yet rubbing your left shoulder with him or her, will bring good luck. Equipped with rope, broom and weight and a small ladder to reach the tricky heights of chimneys across dangerous roof tops, the sweeps themselves need luck as well as skill in their precarious business. Maybe he has no business leaving his trademark, five black fingerprints, on the back of a housewife's blouse, but the skillful charmer who bragged about it was able to rely on his proverbial good fortune. The husband's return was delayed just long enough by the culprit's female apprentice who engaged him in a friendly chat.

Less endearing but mushrooming is the occupation of distributing mostly useless sheets of paper. Students hand out advertisements for companies and causes at every street corner. Civil servants are notorious for sticking a form under your nose at the reception desk of an office, institution, or organization. This circulation of waste paper can take on Berlin-like absurdity. At the office of the "Building Police"—such a department actually exists, no joke—we witnessed the following: an applicant carefully filled in name, address, date and place of birth, purpose of application, entitlement to apply, references etc. etc., on the appropriate form. Upon handing it back, he was provided with a second, identical questionnaire. He grumbled something about carbon paper and efficiency, and looked at the receptionist. "Right you are," the man behind the glass sighed. "You're not the first to come up with that idea. We used to have some carbon, but then it was gone and we didn't get any more. Doesn't matter. The forms are of little importance anyway. We only want to use them up."

A novelty in Berlin, capital of GDR, are the shadows of taxi drivers. Officially they do not exist at all, while the normal, licensed cabbies, who officially exists, are hard, if not impossible to find. Those drivers answering to the description of shadows have no business ferrying paying customers around, but they make it their business to do just that—in spite. They owe their unlicensed, unofficial, phantom existence to a scarcity of legal cabs, on the one hand, and to the near impossibility of getting a call through to the central taxi station on the other. Just imagine the scene. It is after dusk. A large sign hanging above assures you that you are at the taxi stand near the city railroad station of Lenin-Allee. The pavement is wet and shiny black, the street seems deserted. Suddenly, out of nowhere appears a private car, headlights dimmed, and a voice calls out: "Want a ride?" Naturally the young man driving counts on a generous tip on top of the low

[158]

Kleistermappe

normal fare so that he can afford the "new" secondhand car he wants so much and which is so very expensive to buy. "If the police stop us," the shadow instructs his customer, "my name is Paul, we are friends, and I am just giving you a ride."

Stop press: as of October 1, 1986 temporary taxi permits are issued to private motorists at hourly rates. The shadows can now step back into the light of legality.

"Pillar pasting" must be counted among the rare but not untypical means of making a living in Berlin. In 1855 a printer by the name of Ernst Litfaß acquired permission from the police to set up the first 100 samples of his new invention, the Litfaß pillar (sheet-iron cylinders for advertising), all over town. Today, "pillar pasters" stick so many posters, ads, theater and concert programs all around these contraptions that the coat of paper, when stripped off, may weigh over 200 kilograms. For more than 125 years now, troops of Berliners have been shouldering their ladders, picking up their paste buckets and brushes and tackling their jobs. Each services his

[159]

own, well-defined district. Together they adorn some 3,000 pillars with the flashiest placards and the latest in entertainment publicity. The Litfaß pillar stands sturdy and circular, so much so that one dark night a drunkard holding on to one wandered round and round, finally yelling: "Help! They've walled me in alive!"

Of Sand, Sewage, and Spooky Stories

Berlin is literally built on sand, but fortunately the metropolis is not in immediate danger of sinking. An extensive drainage system with ditches and canals was introduced early, and the ground has been reinforced. The Landwehrkanal and a number of other man-made waterways, since filled in, have not only carried vessels of all types to their landing places, they have also kept the ground water in check. Sand has earned the town frequent, although not always positive, literary mention. The French writer Stendhal summarized his impression in 1806 by asking: "How could anyone hit on the idea of founding a city in the middle of all that sand?" Seventy years later an author of less renown penned this rhyme:

A trip from Rixdorf to Berlin
Could mean a traveler's demise,
But if that sand didn't do him in,
He surely won Fortuna's prize.

Berlin sand grinds its way painfully into non-fictional areas as well—into shoes and socks, and between toes and teeth. In addition to these pleasures a pedestrian may enjoy in Berlin and in the surrounding countryside, a mixture of farmland scents—of sewage and gillyflower, as Theodor Fontane expressed it—may envelop him. The very consistency of the soil in fact provides the townspeople with a natural advantage in treatment of sewage (hence the smell): just over a hundred years ago sewage fields were established some distance away from the areas highly populated then. The latest in purifying waste at the time, these fields lie mostly within the terrain of the spreading cities of East and West Berlin today. A number in the outlying districts are still being used, so are some in East Berlin, while a single one remains in West Berlin in case of emergency, should one of the more modern sewage treatment plants be out of commission. These natural filters for liquid waste continue to produce organic fertilizer for garden centers and nurseries either side of the Wall.

Sandy, stony terrain lined with ancient riverbeds from the last Ice Age, dunes and beaches, rivers and fresh-water lakes, ponds and pools are characteristic of Berlin. Berliners take disadvantages in stride, making the best of advantages where they find them. In summer hardly a spot of open ground is visible for all the sunbathers. Swimmers splash about, boaters and water skiers are in their element, and even hobby fisher-men find the occasional lonely hideaway along the many waterways. In wintertime skaters race across the frozen ponds and puddles, like the ones in Schöneberg Volkspark. Houses alongside have to be evacuated when they begin to slide into the narrow depression formed during the glacial period long ago.

Since geological conditions change far less rapidly than political administrations, the scenery in East and West Berlin is of one design, at least where it remains intact for all the cityscape. In East Berlin, in Hohenschönhausen, hikers find recreation at a lake named after its putrid state—"Fauler See." Stems of toppled trees rot in murky waters among water lilies, reeds, and blooming irises to the accompaniment of all sorts of birds. Such lakes are endangered by a falling water table and pollution from chemical refuse. When the rain has washed in too many poisonous substances, the fish soon "swim" belly-up. The very same has happened with Lake Hubertus in West Berlin's Grunewald. The lake is now on a respirator, so to speak. A steady supply of oxygen is pumped through synthetic pipes into the water in the hope that the patient will soon be revived. Conservationists are keeping a watchful eye on the proceedings.

High moors, heaths, swamps, and dark pools have always attracted the likes of leprechauns and evil spirits. For centu-ries they are reported to have been lurking around Müggelsee (East Berlin), a lake deriving its name either from "muckle" for big or from "moegel" for the fog that hangs above it. Wanderers have lost their way around these parts, lured ever deeper onto the moors by "Will-o'-the wisp," and have vanished. People shudder at the mere mention of this land-scape of folklore terror. Even the scientific explanation for the eerie lights characteristic of the area has an air of the macabre. During the process of decay, particularly of cerebral and spinal matter, hydrogen phosphorus is released and self-ignites in damp air. Here, where the Spree River widens into Lake Müggel, sprites were at play in a fisherman's hut. Once the fishermen had dozed off, the little devils would come to pull the sleepers into a straight line atop, then afoot, atop again, and so forth until morning. They were sprites with a Prussian sense of order.

Originals, Types, and Other Eccentrics

Some proclaim Berlin devoid of genuine originals, the last of them having vanished even before the Second World War. We beg to differ, although we concede that in terms of quality and variety the city may not offer the same wealth it once boasted. Perhaps a further qualification is in order: eccen-tricity by profession should not be mistaken for the real thing; intentional originality as practiced by many an actor, artist, or writer simply to get attention, remains a mere publicity stunt. Neither does spirited nonsense qualify, which carries its own punishment: a super hangover the next morning.

But what about Rococo Pelle, a mouse-grey imp of a guy in his fifties we always happened to meet in pubs and never saw lifting a finger in honest work? Once he invited us into his lofty abode graced by a centerpiece the likes of which you may never see: a four-poster bed (rococo imitation), at best a theater prop acquired cheaply. It was his prize possession and sole breadwinner.

We overheard countless phone calls he made from bar telephones advertising the piece in colorful, ever changing terms, but with one constant refrain: "Circumstances force me to part with it at a give-away price." If he could be believed, everyone who was anyone in world history slept in his dream boat under the canopy. He himself crouched on the floor at night not to ruin his life's treasure. A lord mayor of Berlin even sent a valuer to Rococo Pelle to assess it.

Antique dealers, medical doctors with moonlighting money, lawyers hunting for a good bargain—whoever he could interest was first invited to a stylish restaurant for a "casual" meeting. The ice had hardly been broken, when the potential customer discovered himself suddenly helping Pelle out of a minor financial fix and footing the bill. By no means a blatant fraud, this original belonged in the category of plebeians with wit—Berlin wit that is. In the end he parted with his rococo bed no more than would a farmer with his only dairy cow.

According to reliable sources there existed in Pankow a certain Otto Witte whose death certificate of the year 1958 noted under profession: "Deposed King of Albania." After educational training of two years with foreseeable illiterate results, the young Witte worked temporarily as an animal tamer and later owned a boneyard. For five whole days in 1912 the people of Pankow fell for his act when he appeared with a tent of regal splendor, military escort, and harem in the phantasy uniform of a southern European monarch. He never revealed where he got hold of the costume, and even up to the end his papers identified him as the abdicated souvereign he most certainly was not.

In October of 1906 Berliners read the following report in the paper: "At 2.00 p.m. a company of twenty soldiers commanded by a captain arrived in Köpenick Station with the local train from Berlin, marched into the center of town and occupied Town Hall. The captain explained to the mayor that by order of His Imperial Highness, he was confiscating the town funds. He left the hall with 4,000 marks in gold." With this coup Wilhelm Voigt, a shoemaker by profession with a sizeable record of petty crime, had entered the list of Berlin originals as "The Captain of Köpenick." A dramatized version of his exploits became a notable German play by Carl Zuckmayer, and made film history as well. But it was the Berliners who most thoroughly enjoyed his prank. They laughed all the more, when it became known that the uniform—borrowed from a pawnbroker—showed major flaws and still had gained the bogus officer that typically submissive Prussian respect. Although he did land in prison once again, the emperor was enough amused to pardon him after two years. Not much later *Die Welt am Montag* published an interview with the shoemaker, now entertaining large audiences in an arcade on Unter den Linden. Here he also autographed and sold accounts of his story pressed onto those early sound disks. Only one such record survived, discovered by a collector and donated to the local museum of Köpenick in 1966.

Strawhat Emil, bicycle acrobat and comic, converted the streets of Berlin into his personal arena after he retired from the circus world. Whenever and wherever, the crowds loved him, as much for his unpredictable Berlin big mouth as for his bravado, his stunts, and his hat, the top of which would lift miraculously in acknowledgement of applause—and to the extra enjoyment of kids of all ages. In his declining years he enhanced his light summer attire by wearing cotton long johns, less for show effect than for a warmer bottom. Until his death some twenty years ago, he remained the East Berliners' favorite street character.

The proletarian areas of eastern Berlin have always been the nurturing ground for genuine Berlin dialect, wit, and personality. As he was able to procure, from rubber band to zipper, most everything unobtainable in East Berlin through regular channels, a mini-entrepreneur without business address or post office box was assured the greatest popularity among a wide clientele in those years of deprivation after 1945. He was a mere 130 centimeters in height, and always moved in the company of rather corpulent ladies with whom he ventured by train across the border to the black-market outlets on Potsdamer Platz, West Berlin. "When the customs officers check my identification and realize my name is "Riese" ("Giant"), they burst out laughing," he explained with an innocent face. "And when they have recuperated, my girlfriend with all that stuff in her bra or somewhere else has long since disappeared on the other train."

Anglers in West and East, along Landwehrkanal or Lake Müggel, must be among the most unappreciated of all Berlin characters. They seem to be as taciturn as they are patient. Wasting words on Berlin? What for?

We were reminded of the owner of a parrot who returned both bird and cage to the dealer after a year, furious: "The parrot hasn't uttered a single word the whole time. And you told me it was intelligent!" To which the shopkeeper replied: "What nonsense should it have blabbered at you? It is thinking, that's plenty."

P

Parades and Demonstrations—or Where are We Going Today?

Berliners resemble people everywhere: most of them prefer to be left alone, the others organize demonstrations. West Berlin is out front when it comes to demonstrating. The police register an average of 350 protest marches through their streets each year. East Berlin marches with considerably more pomp—at least on May 1st, Labor Day. The armed forces of the German Democratic Republic will put themselves on display on special occasions, too.

It is considered a great honor to be awarded a seat on the big stand allowing a close-up view of military units and workers' militia parading by. Tickets have been carefully distributed in advance, valid only in conjunction with other identification—as a government official, a member of any of the parties, diplomat, or member of a youth organization. These parades regularly stir up furor in the West unleashing a flood of protest by the three Western Allies. The status of the divided city, as laid down in the Four-Power Agreement, is at stake. Soldiers of the West German Bundeswehr are barred from entering West Berlin in uniform, let alone from parading through the city. But the bases of the United States, British and French armed forces organize their very own military shows every year. Shiny tanks, if not flown in on transport planes, arrive in long columns from West Germany for the occasion, driven through East German territory right past the watchful eyes of Soviet observers.

[165]

Under Prussian rule the streets of Berlin were even more conspicuously crowded by military formations marched to their drill grounds: to Pariser Platz perhaps, a rectangular one formerly called "Quarrée." Potsdamer Platz, another such destination, was a round square and lies deserted today. A third, of octagonal shape, known as Mehring-Platz in more recent times, bore the name of a small country inn in Belgium, Belle Alliance. General Blücher had taken up quarters in Belle Alliance Inn when the Battle of Waterloo was raging and Napoleon finally defeated. Prussian pride, rather than conceding victory at Waterloo, heaped the honor on a Belgian guesthouse. Waterloo? Never heard of it.

The patron of Mehring-Platz was a Social Democrat, and his party introduced Berlin to major demonstrations already in 1848. The March riots of that year cost 184 citizens their lives. The coffins were lined up on Gendarmenmarkt in somber accusation. The Prussian King who had ordered his troops to open fire made his appearance personally and bared his head in reverence. The masses of mourners were impressed. German republicans to this day remember the victims and place wreaths on their burial ground in Friedrichshain. Ever since those days in March of 1848 demonstrations in Berlin have either increased or decreased in popularity. There were almost commonplace after the First World War.

The Second World War made the impossible possible. Nazi legislation, which only knew enemies of the state or loyal Germans, wiped the streets of Berlin clean of protesters for a number of years. Once Hitler's legacy of rubble and debris had been cleared, the love of street assemblies, demonstrations, fiery speeches, and patient listening began to become popular again.

On June 17, 1953 East Berlin construction workers from the building sites on Stalin Allee, then prestige construction project number one, protested against unfair wages. Immediately supporters arrived *en masse* from West Berlin. The atmosphere was explosive, not least because of all the frustrations about the lost war that surfaced. Soviet tanks appeared on the scene, and the uprising was soon quelled. West Germany and West Berlin subsequently declared the 17th of June a national holiday, and West Berlin in particular is expected to commemorate it with public demonstrations. But slowly, over the years, the ranks of enthusiasts have thinned out, and the cold war has turned into cold peace.

The traditional imposing parades on May 1st, too, attract

fewer and fewer West Berliners. The police can handle them easily now, even directing them through side streets away from major routes, where traffic flows as usual.

In East Berlin, factory management takes care that participation in open-air assemblies and marches runs high. Party helpers appear at the doors of apartment blocks to impress on voters the need for a large turnout during this or that election. The reaction of a mother with screaming kids clinging to her apron was typical. "You've come for peace? Or what?" she asked the caller, barely opening the door. There is but one defense a Berliner puts up against the prosaic—attack in kind.

West Berlin authorities became less self-assured when, from 1968 onwards, students began to rebel—in the name of all mankind, if one accepted their slogans. The bourgeois order, maintained in part during the Hitler years too, was gagging them. They rehearsed the revolution and no longer gave way to the police. The older generation had not experienced such turmoil or had erased it from memory. Some conservatives actually believed that the ban on sword-fighting fraternities declared by the Allies for all of Berlin was responsible for this breakdown of discipline. Prominent personalities cheered the rebels on. The American Linus Pauling, twice recipient of the Nobel Prize, alluded to the example of similar movements overseas: "We in America know: Either we obey the police or we demonstrate; you can't do both at the same time." Noted a woman member of a T.V. camera team at the time: "Became witness to some sort of sadistic-masochistic orgy. Not only was it gruesome to observe the delight and energy that went into beating and kicking. Imagined that if police helmets were taken off the heads of one side and placed on those of the other, nothing much would change in the whole scene. Ecstasy on both sides."

When, in 1982, we were about to turn from a side street into Kurfürstendamm, a couple of policemen gestured us to wait for a while. The bicycle riders of Berlin were having their "demo." They came in a long, drawn-out procession on their colorfully decorated bikes, with children, cats, and dogs in baskets on their handlebars—bells ringing. They demanded improved bicycle lanes throughout the city. From Halensee they pedaled to Kaiser-Wilhelm-Gedächtniskirche, turned and rode back. No aggressive reaction anywhere—until a pedestrian appeared out of nowhere. The man began to hassle the policemen shouting: "Stop the bikers! Let me across! It's my right!" Congenially and calmly one of the officers turned to him, his hair greying under his cap. "If you want your teeth knocked out, go right ahead."

Post Me a Letter

The two postal administrations of Berlin hardly have any direct dealings with each other. Bilateral negotiations are conducted by the governments of the two German states—in Bonn and East Berlin. A few mail trucks and two postal trains carry out the exchange between Berlin and Berlin. Telephone connections from one part of town to the other were only re-established after the Four-Power Agreement of 1971. Cable lines can be counted without relying on an adding machine. Their sum is an uneven number: 471 lines run from west to east, eighty-four the other way round. A pitiful number for a major center of population whose inhabitants were described by Kurt Tucholsky as notorious callers: "The Berliner sits in a café, stares ahead, suddenly jumps up and shouts 'Where is the next public phone?' He finishes every phone conversation with 'I'll call you back'".

While telephone communication in Greater Berlin is not what it used to be, neither is the building at the corner of Leipzigerstraße and Mauerstraße (now East Berlin). Once the Imperial Post Museum, today it contains only a hint of its former collection and was badly damaged in World War II. From here Heinrich Stephan, son of a tailor, built up the postal system of Berlin. Here he is remembered, as he is in the Telegraph Museum, Urania House, Kleiststraße (West Berlin).

The district post office in Tucholsky-Straße stands in a traditional location as well. From 1713 onward postilions, the postal coachmen of old, lodged here above the stables for their horses and garages for their coaches. On a bas-relief in the inner courtyard Postmaster General von Stephan is peeping out of a coach drawn by four horses. The yard is not open to the public, and the relief is only visible through binoculars if the gates happen to be open. The scene von Stephan is looking down on seems relaxed (technological advances notwithstanding which promise us speedy service all over the world). A letter mailed within East Berlin can take six whole days from posting to delivery (which is still two days short of the record for a telegram within the city of Rome).

The postal services of Berlin keep their historical image well polished. Passing a post office on Goethestraße in Charlotten-burg (West), we witnessed the centenary celebration of the place. The street party included a postilion in traditional uniform blowing his horn over and over agan with gusto. The purchase of the building site had been effectively signed by the postmaster general himself as early as 1880, but it took him two more years to collect the funds necessary for con-struction. In the meantime he simply rented out the plot to a potato farmer for hard cash. Reason enough to have some fun one hundred years later and let the customers wait for a while.

During the Christmas season the sorting office at Nordbahn-hof (East) handles about a million items of mail daily. Who would have time to answer the bulk of letters addressed to Santa Claus with detailed lists of the youngsters' wishes? Something had to be done and was. A group of mothers volunteered to gather around a large table at the office and send each child a postcard in reply, however standardized it had to be: "If you've been good, Santa will try his best."

The Prussian mail services always saw to it that their customers remained good and law-abiding citizens. When it cost a mere 2 pfennigs to send a postcard, only the front could carry a message, whether it displayed a picture or not. And in 1879 the authorities ruled that a censor could open any letter suspected of containing socialist ideas. Today East Berlin officials are authorized under customs rules to check all postal matter passing through their hands for anti-socialist propaganda. Santa Claus is still watching, so be good for goodness sake!

Once again in 1948–9 a 2-pfennig stamp got stuck onto every letter and card sent from West Germany, a small additional fee to the regular postage. In this manner people contributed their share toward the cost of the Airlift by which the Allies kept West Berlin supplied with food and other essentials during the Soviet blockade. This little blue stamp is a much sought after collector's item now.

Emperor William I, in contrast, did not have to pay a single pfennig when, in 1882, he sent the following cable to U.S. President, Chester Arthur: "It gives me great pleasure to be

[169]

able to convey to you, Mr. President, by means of the first direct telegraph link just opened between Germany and America, my satisfaction with the completion of this project which will serve to further friendly relations between our two nations."

Cable links between West and East Berlin still exist, nineteen in all, and fully automated at that.

Potsdam—A Short-Distance Side Trip

When we left the New Palace of Potsdam, we had just been through a schizophrenic parting with our friends from East Berlin. Together we had enjoyed a beautiful concert in the exquisitely restored oval Court Theater, opened to the public in 1969 and noted for masterful performances, low prices, red velvet upholstery and gilded Prussian eagles. Now they were on their way back the long way driving a semi-circle well clear of the southern outskirts of town that form part of West Berlin territory, past Schönefeld Airport, and north-west again into the center of East Berlin to reach their apartment not far from the Wall. We, on the other hand, were heading toward a border crossing nearby and would be able to take the direct diagonal expressway through West Berlin to arrive at our destination not half a mile from their home, but on the other side of the divide—at least an hour earlier. Glienicke Bridge, once the closest connection between Potsdam and Berlin, was closed to us. Ironically called "Bridge of Unity," it may only be used by diplomats and people with special permits and, on occasion, by spies exchanged in a political deal between East and West.

Because of the division, Potsdam belongs to Berlin much less now than during the time when it served as residence to the Prussian court. The city palace of Potsdam had to be demolished; a tall Interhotel stands in its place. Potsdam itself remained a medium-sized but spacious urban settlement, in which Nikolai Kirche and the Dutch Quarters have survived from former days. Its claim to fame, however, are castles, pleasure palaces, and mansions.

Everyone in Germany knows the name "Sanssouci," the

palace "without cares," where Frederick the Great supposedly played the flute from dawn to dusk. Sanssouci as well as the surrounding gardens delight visitors from far and near no less than the New Palace, Charlottenhof Castle, the Orangery, Belvedere, the Roman Baths and others as well. Far Eastern scenes appear as the hiker approaches the Chinese Tea House richly decorated with gilded columns and groups of figurines. With elaborate surprises of this kind European monarchs tried to impress one another. Noble ladies invited to tea in the royal gardens (far be it from us to liken them to those gilded dragons of the Chinese variety) would surpass one another later in gossiping about the capriciousness of the court.

Potsdam's heritage was preserved thanks to Soviet Colonel J.F. Ludschuweit's foresight. When the town was conquered in 1945 he ensured that nothing was ransacked or stolen from the interior of the castles. A guided tour through these old treasures never passes without special mention of Colonel Ludschuweit. Not even the most conservative and chauvinistic Prussians can deny him his due for acting to save the art treasures (in marked contrast to commanders of Nazi troops in similar circumstances on Russian soil). He had been guided by respect for the artistic achievements of the defeated rather than by feelings of revenge.

The historical function of Potsdam has been enormous, as the example of a tower built near Glienicke Bridge may show. Behind its shutters patient observers engaged in political analyses which they based on the constant back and forth of coaches, horses, visitors, and couriers between Potsdam and Berlin. Every vehicle, each facial expression of a passenger was scrutinized. Interpretations and prophecies spread quickly (much like diplomatic horoscopes worked out by political astrologers).

In order that Generalissimus Josef Stalin be spared changing from his railroad carriage, tracks of the Russian width were laid as far as Potsdam in 1945. They are rusting in the grass now, unnoticed. The Conference at Potsdam, to which they brought the Soviet leader, became part of European history, not least of all for the impact it had on the development of the two German states and the two cities of Berlin. In Cecilienhof Castle in the northern part of Potsdam, a chip is missing from the wooden arm rest of a chair on which Stalin sat facing the heads of state of the other victorious Allies. An American souvenir hunter made off with it. John F. Kennedy

Berlin Potsdamer Platz
um 1930
J. Bittenstadt

was one of the accredited photographers at the conference. (No inference intended!)

Cecilienhof, an English country-style manor house, once held the distinction of having a room custom-designed for Emperor William II built in the shape of a ship's cabin and suspended on leather straps so that it could be swayed manually from the outside. The emperor loved to imagine himself ruler of the Seven Seas, but since reality spoiled his dream, he had to make do looking out on a calm garden lake from his rocking cabin.

Despite the abundance of water about town, physical hygiene remained low on the priority list of the early Prussians. Frederick I did put down in writing how often and exactly when his young son was to wash his hands (of course between other duties, all to be carried out according to a strict timetable), but baths and showers were not on anyone's agenda. Small wonder that large bowls with fragrant flowers and herbs were placed strategically all over the rooms, less for show than out of sheer necessity. The preference for orange trees, too, needs little further explanation—since the strong scent of their blossoms covered up what unhygienic conditions released. Neither does men's love for snuff. Frederick II owned a collection of 150 snuffboxes of which twenty-five are still around. Recently an antique dealer acquired one single box at a London auction for a mere 2 million deutschmarks.

Where there is plenty of water, someone will find a way of splashing it about—if only for visual effect. To feed the fountains of Sanssouci from the Havel River, a special pump was designed in 1840 with a two-cylinder engine from the workshop of the Borsig company. To this day the pumping station is discreetly hidden behind the walls of an imitation mosque, a minaret doubling as chimney. The people of Potsdam, a garrison town, hid their soldiers with similar discretion, though less stylishly. By law every household was forced to lodge military personnel in a room *with* a window. Clever and law-abiding citizens knew what to do. They housed their soldiers in basement quarters with a miniature opening just above street level allowing no more than a look at ladies' ankles or men's sturdy boots.

Up on Dünenberg, a hill in Potsdam Forest, rises a curiosity of the modern era, clearly visible when approaching town during wintertime, after the trees have shed their leaves. The Einstein Tower has been converted into a physics museum. It was designed by one of the many famous Berlin architects in avant-garde style as a research institute. Here Albert Einstein's relativity theories underwent experimental verification, at least for a brief period. The Nobel Prize-winning physicist had to flee Germany. His diaries reveal how much he cherished the memory of Lake Schwielow near Potsdam, the small town of Caputh, and the swans on the Havel.

Press and Publishing—Tomorrow's News Today

For publishers of newspapers and books the path of freedom of speech has always been bumpy, and not only in Berlin. It is paved by often contradictory manifestos issued by ruling dynasties and ministries. For the press of his time, the Prussian king called "Old Fritz" proclaimed the rather liberal motto, often quoted since: "Gazettes must not be incommoded!" By 1899, however, three Prussian ministers jointly signed a directive which proscribed: "Whosoever intends to sell printed matter in the course of an ambulatory trade is

[173]

required to present the local police authorities with a list, in duplicate, of all publications. To facilitate the investigation into whether these materials may or may not be offensive for moral or religious reasons, the applicant is asked to submit one sample of each of these publications . . . " et cetera.

Publishing in Berlin was not only a way to earn money, it also provided power over public opinion. As early as 1892 Theodor Fontane wrote in a letter: "Ninety-nine among a hundred people simply parrot what they read in the paper, nothing else."

Before Hitler came to power three companies had basically the entire press market divided among themselves. Mosse, Ullstein and Hugenberg published their widely-read papers in the capital until 1933 arrived and everything began to change. Germany's Propaganda Minister Josef Goebbels placed an order for rotary presses with extra-wide rollers to print the Nazi weekly *Das Reich*. Not only Hitler had to stretch his arms to handle the extra-large news sheets conceived as counterpart to the traditionally smaller "Berlin format" for working people in crowded subways, trains, or streetcars. The newspaper district in and around Kochstraße fell to ruin with much of the rest of Berlin just over a decade later. The Soviet military administration had the super-sized rotary presses dug out again to produce their journal *Tägliche Rundschau*. The Americans followed the Russian example with their *Neue Zeitung* in Munich, where Goebbels had formerly seen to the publication of a southern German edition of *Das Reich*.

Ten years after the end of the war, the journalist Erich Kuby pronounced his judgment on the Berlin press. In the Western part of town, so he maintained, mass appeal and profit were the exclusive guidelines, while in the East papers had become no more than official news bulletins. In all, they consistently kept their reporting at a level the provincial press of pre-Hitler days would have been ashamed of. In East Berlin the postal services are in charge of newspaper delivery, and they also maintain the newsstands on the city streets. In West Berlin publishers certainly can supply their customers by mail, but more often than not paper distribution is channeled through private intermediaries. We could not fail to notice that in West Berlin the popular *BZ* runs page after page of advertisements by male and female prostitutes, "escort services," and the like, while the classified section of the East Berlin paper of the same name attests to a flourishing trade in used cars.

[174]

Ullstein-Haus Kochstr. J. Bettenschildt

A catalogue of 1943 lists for Berlin about 250 publishing houses involved in the production of books ranging from factual to political topics, from the arts to pure sob stuff. "Racial hygiene" and other pseudo-scientific nonsense appears frequently in publishing programs, since everyone obviously strove, according to the trend of the times, to succeed by bowing to Nazi ideology. One company offered books on colonial territories and cacti, at a time when the loss of all colonies had become a prickly topic in Germany. Few of the publishers of that era operate in Berlin today. A judgment in itself. Some sixty firms, mostly small or even miniature enterprises, are holding out in West Berlin, as compared to around twenty-five sizeable publishers operating in the capital of the GDR. The latter began to publish again after 1945 under license by the Soviet authorities and under new, un-

[175]

tainted names. The situation in the Western sectors of the city was not much different, the Western Allies keeping a close watch on who was writing, translating and printing what, as well.

By now the free-market system allows anyone who dares to enter the business, and the market share of small publishers is rising slowly but steadily. But neither the mainstream nor the alternative makers of books can simply transport their products across the border into East Berlin to expand their sales territory, even though the reading public there might be very interested. Much more avid bookworms than their West Berlin brothers, the Easterners have to make do with the book production in their part of the world, and that can stand up to a comparison with any standard of quality.

The situation of a whole literature "brought into line" came about in Germany for the first time under the Nazis. In May of 1933 a Nazi journal reported that Hermann Göring had prohibited Ullstein Publishers from continuing a series of articles about his war experiences as flight lieutenant in World War I. "A Jewish junk publisher," so the paper read, "does not become a German National Socialist publishing house by quickly raising a swastika flag or adorning themselves with a personality decorated with the swastika." A slap in the faces of all those who tried to ingratiate themselves with the new rulers. It didn't work, and there was worse treatment in store for anyone declared an enemy of the state. Meanwhile the Freiheitsverlag or Freedom Publishers was at work in Moabit, churning out police literature.

Prussian Heritage in Gloom and Glory

Whenever the conversation turns to the reconstructed Schauspielhaus on Platz der Akademie (East), the natives show their true colors. For nothing is worth its salt to a Berliner if it doesn't top at least the rest of Europe, in height, depth, width, or quality. Even without the superlatives lavishly heaped upon the theater, it is truly grand. Berliners, however, need the whipped topping on the cake. The Armory is presented as "Europe's most beautiful baroque building." Unter den Linden is referred to as "via triumphalis," which

[176]

side-steps the admission that it is also a memorial to Prussian military style.

The Armory itself, accommodating the Museum of German History today, was begun in 1698 by the architect Andreas Schlüter and is beautiful enough, no matter that some of its inherent problems have contaminated more modern construction favorites as well. It is a brick building made of relatively bad material with stucco-covered walls. Only in spots, for accentuation, has natural stone been inserted, carved and polished. There was not enough money in the Prussian state purse for a more solid technical finish throughout—and herein lies the very reason for all those stucco façades recurring all over Berlin. When the building was modernized after 1949, the GDR authorities had to dig deeply into public funds, as the interior in particular had to be renovated and stabilized and the inherited problems eliminated.

Everything connected with the history of Prussia is superlatively inclined, an inclination which all too often ran into disaster. And then there are at least three distinctly different "Prussian Histories." There are the two sides of the coin, the Western and the Eastern pictures, each with its own interpretation of the forces that propel historical development, two perspectives of one and the same constantly moving object; then the third is the object itself, Prussian history as it truly unfolded. "And that's something nobody can improve, nobody can make worse, and nobody can make undone," a West Berliner with a clear view of things enlightened us—a window cleaner by profession.

On the occasion of the "Year of Prussia" in 1981, West Berlin filled its official calendar for three months with a barrage of retrospective exhibitions, shows, performances, learned and not so learned lectures, speeches, and pronouncements. What it all boiled down to was a mixture of facts and fiction, history and myth about the past. While the achievements of monarchy, empire and republic seemed to loom larger during these celebrations in West Berlin, East Berlin places greater emphasis on the popular resistance against autocratic rulers and militaristic traditions when presenting their interpretation of their very own Prussian heritage. In any case, the composite of these pictures drawn by the two heirs to Prussian fame probably comes closer to the truth than either alone.

The central power of the Prussian state, which later combined with that of the German nation, resided in castles and palaces as well as in the ministerial chambers in and around Wilhelmstraße, now in East Berlin. Though the royal and imperial era came to an end in 1918 with the abdication of the last German kaiser and king of Prussia, William II, Prussia remained a legal entity throughout the Weimar Republic and the Nazi period. Berlin, likewise, functioned as state and national capital until 1945. Again and again Prussian and later German soldiers answered the call to arms under the Prussian eagle, to be marched in all four directions. Victories brought spoils into the capital, defeats saw the spoils disappear again. The wars made some ever richer and the rest ever poorer.

The powers that took over in 1933 were sure to avail themselves of whatever Prussian tradition suitable to their purpose, most certainly of the military-style discipline and devout civil obedience ingrained in the people, as well as of the armed forces and the civil service machine to enforce these virtues.

In royal and imperial Prussia the supremacy of the military over the civilian population had been absolute. Uniforms of all types raised the self-esteem as much as the authority of the bearers while adding color to the life of Berlin. On the other hand, the traditional Prussian way of life proved a strong antidote against the virus of democracy and liberalism that swept Europe in the nineteenth century. The few liberal reforms that were accepted into the body of the law had powerful advocates from the upper echelon of society, such as Freiherr vom Stein et al.; demands for fundamental rights from the lower end of the social scale were silenced by force. Some democratic principles introduced by Napoleon during his occupation of Prussia had stuck, too, and could never be eliminated altogether.

Along with the speed of industrialization in Berlin near the end of the last century social problems rapidly multiplied. While the system showed little flexibility in answering the call for change, individual civil servants took it upon themselves to help. They administered the tiny welfare budgets as best they could, greatly assisted by private individuals with a heart for the needy and a sensitivity to social injustice. Berlin has always been famous for its excellent and committed social workers, for teachers who worked miracles in educating the underprivileged young and old. The stereotypes of the sternly disciplined Prussian soldier and the pedantic civil servant bowing to his superiors and exploiting his authority against those below him, though not devoid of realism, thus fall short of presenting the whole picture.

The Museum of German History in East Berlin has been in existence now for over two decades. West Berlin only recently decided to establish its counterpart near the Wall in a building named after the Bauhaus architect Gropius. In the Reichstag, too, aspects of the period around the turn of the century are on permanent display under the heading "Questions to German History." But the very mode of questioning is shifting continuously, the answers turning out ever more up-to-date.

The big "Prussia Exhibition" of 1981, advertised as an attempt at balancing the books, set out to present history in a new way for a change. But this view from the inside, according to a news report, unveiled its own complications: "The history of the Germans is not the history of the German Empire, the history of which is not identical with the history of Germany. The history of Germany differs from that of the two German states, and although Berlin represented 'The Empire' until 1945, it can only represent seventy years of Prussian Germany among the total of its imperial history." You figure it out! It's all a labyrinth, and not even thirty-two statues of Hohenzollern rulers with an additional sixty-four allegorical figures in stone can guide the way. These statues, erected under Emperor William II to clarify it all, once lined Siegesallee, the victory boulevard disrespectfully called "Puppet Avenue" by those who dared.

If you should attempt to study the city's chronicle of stone equipped with binoculars and an ample supply of literature, you are in for a few weeks of pure wonderment. The monument with a 14-meter bronze statue of Frederick the Great on horseback, at its base alone parades a whole cabinet of generals, who in turn are watched over by the cardinal virtues, one on every corner. Simultaneously on view are scenes depicting the birth of Frederick, Minerva handing him the sword, Frederick the protector of mercantilism, and the patron of the arts. The events seem to press upon each other in this escalation of graphic symbolism. On other memorials other generals again remind the viewer that they saw themselves as bigger than life and wanted to be regarded as such. Minerva appears frequently in this military accompaniment only steps away from East Berlin's Opera Café.

The wide-angle lens of dialectical perception apparently

[179]

doesn't take it all too seriously. The highest decoration for members of the National People's Army of the GDR is the Scharnhorst Order, so named for the chief of staff who: (a) was against the privileges of the nobility; (b) fought against Napoleon on the Russian side; and (c) introduced compulsory military service. GDR television dedicated a five-part series to him in 1981.

Louis Ferdinand, prince of Prussia, entered this world in Potsdam in the year 1907 and later worked as a mechanic at Ford in Detroit. In the U.S. he was also awarded his pilot's license. Two of his four sons lost their claim to the Prussian throne by marrying commoners; his third son died from wounds received during military exercises held by the Bundeswehr, the West German armed forces. Prussia never believed in a female line of succession, so the few royalists around have to set their hopes on Prince Louis Ferdinand's fourth son, Christian Sigismund. But while the song about wanting old Emperor William to return may occasionally ring out of a West Berlin pub in the wee hours of the morning, the chances remain pretty slim.

Public Places, Open Spaces

Berlin has long prided itself on its stately squares. Some grew out of old market places, others developed from military drill grounds, and a third type was custom-designed for effect— status symbols of a capital all. In more recent times additional open spaces have been left behind by war and subsequent demolition of adjacent houses. The largest and by far the most depressing is Askanischer Platz in West Berlin, a wasteland once occupied by buildings, shelters, and tracks of Anhalter Bahnhof. All but a relic of the station façade have disappeared. It evokes associations the designer of the station could not have dreamed of (even though secretly, in his spare time, he had been a writer and dreamer of sorts). The oval window in the front arch of the ruin resembles a monocle covering a cyclop's eye. The pigeons and the wind that pass through need no train schedule anyway. For the few tramps crouching on benches passing the bottle, time hurries no longer. They seem to have missed their last train to sobriety long ago.

In East Berlin many, but not all, squares are called by new names today, while Alexanderplatz, under its old one, has been completely refashioned. Here world standard has been attained with flair and spaciousness and the old livestock market converted into a remarkable city center above ground and below. One slip in the design or one convenience the architects failed to incorporate aggravates the Berliner's favorite (grouchy) state of mind. There are no ramps for children's strollers or wheelchairs alongside the maze of staircases that lead to and from subterranean walkways under the vast plaza. Should you offer to help a young mother carry her bulky vehicle, you might just hear a ruffled "Why? Do I look that old?"

Alexanderplatz served as a drill ground too. A figure in bronze, erect and imposing, stood here exposed enough to be seen and far enough out of the way for parading soldiers to run through their formations: Berolina, personification of Berlin. Her fate remains in the dark—she vanished without a trace. For a serialized television drama based on Alfred Döblin's novel *Berlin Alexanderplatz*, great care was taken to build an authentic-looking set. The set designers were lucky that, during the 1920s, the television tower, Europe's tallest structure, had not yet been built.

In West Berlin, around Nollendorfplatz for instance, little of traditional value has survived. The area has gone to pot. The newest fad: aggressive begging by young people with Red Indian hairstyle and punk costumes who step into the path of passers-by with menacing gestures. Teenage prostitutes by the dozen signal their intent and purpose. Firemen on occasion arrive in screeching trucks to pull a youngster from the booth of a public toilet—diagnosis: overdose. Only the blackened stone giants of the old Metropol Theater (long since converted into a disco) look down on "Nolle" in petrified equanimity. The rest of the surrounding architecture is of modern, stark bareness. The "House of Pop," as it is known today, saw revolutionary performances decades ago when one of the greats of the theater, Erwin Piscator, called the shots here from 1927 onward. Today concerts discharge teams of youngsters into a night sizzling with anarchical and destructive unrest. The prostitutes, as young as twelve, from Berlin or as far away as Korea, Vietnam, or West Germany, are out in force now. Their "friends" try the slot machines of cafés and bars while keeping an eye on what is going on outside. The takings better be right! A policeman, asked about the apparent complacency of the law, apathetically answered: "If we return them to their parents, they're back on the street tomorrow. We've tried."

Each one of the squares in Berlin is full of stories and historical anecdotes. Around Breitenbachplatz in Steglitz an artists' colony had established itself before the Second World War with studios for painters and sculptors and pads for writers and philosophers. A glance through the large windows of a café today proves that the tradition is alive, if more light-hearted, less argumentative, and more status quo than yesteryear. "Yesteryear" the secret police invaded the terrain to "move everything out," including anyone who opposed the Nazi state or called it into question by artistic means.

"For a day and a night with nothing on but shorts and a polo shirt I hid in the basement behind a mountain of coal until they found me." Such is the recollection of a painter who had come to Berlin from Poland to study. "The first one to greet me in SA uniform, grinning, I knew well. He had participated in studio parties as a declared Communist, had held provocative speeches, and had spied on us. I don't know, whether I have him to thank for the fact that I wasn't shot in the woodland near the border but shoved in the direction of Czechoslovakia with more than empty threats for guidance." This is what we were mulling over in our minds when we mingled among the young, well-dressed crowd of artists, would-be artists and their fans, and ordered two large ice creams with lots of whipped cream.

Q

Quenching a Superlative Thirst

Berliners spare no pains nor do they shun any distance to get to their beer. During the Thirty Years War already a shoemaker's apprentice proved the point. He came from Bernau, a town famous for the quality of its beer. The wife of his Berlin master told him to go and get a jug of Bernau Special, assuming the boy would hop over to the *ratskeller* nearby and be back soon. But he took her at her word and ran with his pitcher, ran back home to his mother's, never to be seen in Berlin again.

You can be sure that Berliners from the West on holiday in the Moselle valley, or from the East in one of the Hungarian wine regions, are the first to slide under the table. They gulp their wine like beer and only afterwards show surprise at the speedy effect of the unfamiliar beverage. The sweeter the wine, the closer it is to the Berliners' idea of refreshing lemonade. In centuries past there were vineyards along the slopes of the Havel River around Berlin, now recalled in names of streets and settlements.

Of course, given the prevailing climate, the final product in no way compares with Liebfraumilch or Hungarian Tokay. Berlin wines are "dry" to the point that they could well compete with the best of woodworm remedies.

In the Nursery on the Park in Kreuzberg, vines have been growing again since 1968. A two-hour harvest in 1986 yielded superior 341 kilograms of dark burgundy (and 502 kilograms of riesling). Both friends and foes of the Senate are gladly presented a bottle—friends to show their perseverance, foes to be shown their lack of stamina. The label not without reason identifies the red variety as "Kreuzberg Nero." The Nero of Kreuzberg, like his Roman namesake, sets aflame what hasn't yet crumbled to the ground.

By the fourteenth century the first beer kegs were rolling into Berlin from Bavaria and Frankonia. Brewers followed and soon local breweries sprang up. Not long afterwards, via Holland, Low German brewing recipes entered into competition with southern German ones. Today Berliners in East and West jump at the opportunity to celebrate the annual bock-beer tapping event. The peg is driven into the vat with a wooden hammer, and the first liter of beer spurts out in foamy whiteness until the tap is securely in place. Brass bands accompany the ceremony, "retiring" later to Resi's Ballroom or to the New World in the West, or to similar clubs and beer gardens in the East, for a night of fun, music, and drinking.

Once plenty of glasses, steins, and mugs have been emptied a strange urge comes over the ladies who suddenly find courage to climb up the steps to a grand slide and descend on their behinds. Squealing with delight they arrive at the lower end into the arms of their partners.

Berlin's favorite beverage has played not only a decisive role in social disturbances and brawls all over town, but has also been used as leverage. Beer drinkers once refused to partake of brands offered by breweries which failed to pay their workers a fair wage. It must have been the most successful strike action Berlin ever experienced.

A dissertation on "The Development of the Bottled Beer Business in Berlin" gained a German foreign minister of the Weimar years, Gustav Stresemann, his doctorate. He went on to receive the Nobel Peace Prize jointly with his French counterpart, Aristide Briand—both of them sons of innkeepers. When Stresemann died, an obituary announced: "None of the great statesmen of the nineteenth century, neither Pitt nor Talleyrand, Metternich nor Palmerston, Bismarck nor Gambetta, nor Disraeli, reached such world renown." He was sure, so the writer continued, that Stresemann would be the first true politician to enter Valhalla, Germanic heaven. Hurrah for beer, the lubricant of political progress! Economic progress in the beer business forced many a small brewer to sell out to the giants with a nationwide network of capital interests, and although the old names of Schultheiß and

Berliner Kindl are still in use, control of the companies lies in other hands. East Berlin breweries having to quench the thirst of equally dry throats are nationalized and centralized in a "beverage combine," producing a drinkable brew none the less. The traditional Berlin measure, a "Molle," or that summertime special "Weiße mit Schuß," are orders often heard. For kids large and small it is a "Faßbrause."

An East Berlin controller, off duty, accused a passenger of dodging the fare, assaulting him so violently that only a bystander with ju-jitsu expertise had the courage to haul her off to the transport police. The young woman, as it turned out, had managed to down twenty-four "Weiße" on a Sunday afternoon, the only excuse for her unusual behavior.

It remains questionable whether the collector of beer labels actually drank all 80,000 bottles of beer from which his prize possessions had been collected. The West Berlin winner of the "Golden Coaster" isn't telling. Serious heads of East Berlin families, in like manner, meet regularly at the "Beer Glass Exchange" to trade their treasures. The League of Culture supports this event which gives fans an opportunity to complete their collection or help someone else to do the same.

In Schöneberg (West), a construction worker found a bottle cemented into the wall of an old house. A note was attached: "Future finder, drink this in our memory. The plasterers of 1900." This is Berlin solidarity for you, sealed with a bottle. It contained schnapps.

R

Radio and TV—The Business of Floating on Air

Berlin can claim, among others, one first in the relatively short history of radio, even though it really is nothing to brag about: the introduction of a "listening post." A writer by the name of Arnolt Bronnen had been won over by the Nazis in 1933 to serve as informer from inside Berlin's station. Bronnen faithfully reported to the authorities when and by whom programs critical of the political rulers were smuggled into broadcasts. No other radio station had instituted such a "post" until that time.

Marconi's achievement of 1901, sending radio waves across the Atlantic to America by means of wireless transmission, captured the imagination of radio engineer Count Georg von Arco. By 1903 he had entered the Telefunken Company where he developed high frequency transmitters—just one of his many feats. Forty-nine Albrechtstraße, where the pacifist and non-member representative of the Independent Socialist Party to the Prussian trade ministry resided for over thirty years, carries a plaque reminding us of the historical reason why Berliners on both sides of the Wall are reasonably well-informed about one another.

In express recognition of an airwave plan agreed upon in Geneva, the GDR renounced the installation of jamming devices. At least half of the population of East Berlin listens to Western stations, believing most of what they hear. In sharp contrast, East Berlin's informational programs evoked pro-

found skepticism in the West until opportunities of visiting "over there" brought reality closer to home.

At the time of the 1947–8 blockade transistor radios were not widespread, and power cuts frequently interrupted reception in, as well as transmission from, the West. RIAS Berlin, short for Radio in the American Sector, remedied the situation by sending radio cars with loudspeakers through the streets, since the U.S. administration in particular was interested in keeping people informed about current events. That is something West Berliners have not forgotten.

RIAS had been founded as early as 1946. But the Soviets, according to the first-come-first-served principle, had retained radio installations in and around the "Funkturm" for their own purposes—even though they stood on territory occupied by the British forces. In 1957, finally, the SFB or Station Free Berlin was able to take them over and begin its work. Step by step East Berlin erected its own transmitters along the banks of the river Spree on Nalepastraße. But for a time after that expectations were confronted by harsh reality.

The buildings where engineers and production staff worked once belonged to a company manufacturing polished veneer for furniture. The language of radio, however, did not seem polished at all; the U.S.A. was indirectly responsible in a twofold way. Harsh barrages were fired back and forth between the U.S.-controlled station west of the border and its eastern counterpart directed by a man who had appeared before the Un-American Activities Committee in the States during his exile there. A refugee from Germany and a Communist, he had not wavered even when the committee condemned him to a fine as well as imprisonment. His flight

[187]

from New York harbor had all the makings of an adventure story, but there was nothing entertaining about his broadcasts.

Until the television tower on Alexanderplatz in the East topped everything, technically-inclined West Berliners looked at their "Funkturm" with gleaming pride. Still today an elevator lifts visitors 55 meters above ground to a restaurant with a superb view, or even higher to an observation platform with an even better one. To the tip of its antenna, the "Tall Fellow" or "Langer Lulatsch" measures 150 meters, while the "Tele Asparagus" of East Berlin rises to a height of 365 meters, thus surpassing the Eiffel Tower in Paris. If luck is with you, you may be able to book a table high up in the television tower and get a bird's-eye view of Berlin during its hour-long revolution. Over one million visitors enjoy the experience annually. "But not, when we are renovating," explains the manager. And how long does that take? "Well, if we get it all done, we hope eight weeks." We had discovered the highest basis in Berlin for the Marxist principle of hope.

Radio and television programs do not immediately reveal to the casual listener or viewer from which side they are being transmitted. Particularly in the field of entertainment both sides have apparently agreed to follow the path of mediocrity. Grumbling about and criticizing each other's output continues nevertheless.

The GDR television center is located in one compact area in Adlershof, while West Berlin maintains two sets of studios. The station linked to West Germany's "confederate" network servicing channels 1 and 3 occupies quarters in the vicinity of the Radio Tower, and the second German network maintains its Berlin branch at Tempelhof in the old UFA film studios. With cable and satellite T.V. in the offing, the only sane recourse may be to keep the set switched off.

Rails About Town

The beginning of the end for the horse-drawn coaches came in 1838 when the prince who was to become Frederick William IV inaugurated the first railroad line in Prussia between

Berlin and Potsdam. Smoky steam locomotives were soon pulling freight and passenger trains into the city's new stations from all directions. An immigrant work force for the budding industries was imported into the capital and required transportation to and from the factories, a service the long-distance lines were unable to provide. As early as 1882 Berlin boasted the first city railroad network on the European continent, called S-Bahn (short for "Stadtbahn"), and reported the proud number of 11 million passengers during this inaugural year alone, noise and air pollution notwithstanding.

A "scent of lacquer and the sparkle of shiny wooden benches and polished brass," so a contemporary writer observed, pervaded the new S-Bahn cars. They came in yellow for first- and in red for second-class travel. (For a long while they were "red" in more than one sense: under Allied regulations East Berlin operated the entire system, even where it served the Western part of the city. Recently parts of it were sold off to the West.) The speed of the S-Bahn inspired poets and storytellers. A trip on board the carriages gave the Berliner a rear view of his capital as the tracks, where above ground, led through densely populated quarters. Wherever obstacles appeared, the system went underground, even below the subway and the river Spree, or simply dug its way through tenement houses. The residents shook in their beds every time a train passed through. The efficiency of the S-Bahn as compared to the streetcar was obvious. It was able to go faster, in a straighter line and was interlinked with the bigger overland railroads.

From 1902 onward, thanks to advances in electrical engineering, competition for public favor came in the form of an ever-expanding subway network, which ironically goes above ground in spots. The ever-ready wit of the natives mastered the discomfort of overcrowded compartments with a typical: "Sorry Sir, the foot you are standing on happens to be mine!"

When the Berlin Wall was erected in 1961, West Berliners took revenge. They boycotted the S-Bahn system on the advice of the Western trade unions and former Berlin mayor Willy Brandt. What was intended as an act of protest proved a costly miscalculation for the city and its inhabitants. It backfired. A fleet of buses—polluting the city—had to take over where the city railroad had left off, public transport became increasingly expensive, (S-Bahn fares had been subsi-

Berlin Bahnhof Alexanderplatz
mit Fernsehturm.   F Bekostadt

dized by East Berlin), fuel costs rose, and the Bonn government had to step in with financial support. Meanwhile the
lines and stations on West Berlin terrain decayed, and East
Berlin received no revenue from the discontinued services
and hence could no longer afford their proper maintainance.
Further lines were cut in 1982 in spite of a much-publicized

strike. Only a skeleton service remains west of the border, while all along the eastern districts of the divided city have been well supplied with public transportation at minimal fares.

Now, after so many years, the Western authorities seem to have had a change of heart. They are willing to come to terms with the administration of the other side. An expensive (3 billion deutschmarks), long-term (thirty years) restoration program for the S-Bahn in West Berlin is in the offing. Useless to ponder: "If only we had . . . "

When the S-Bahn traveler today passes stations which are barricaded, walled-up or closed by iron gates while *en route* from one part of Berlin to the other, feelings of "gothic" terror may emerge with memories of 1944–5. By then war shortages had severely cut evening and night services. And when on April 16, 1945 the city was under direct attack, it took but ten days for the electricity supply to run out. People piled into the tunnels and bivouacked on the station platforms underground.

Hitler's storm troopers, in an attempt at preventing the Red Army from advancing, gave order to flood certain areas of the system. Many Berliners drowned. These haunting memories linger, as does the recollection that many Jewish citizens of Berlin committed suicide by throwing themselves under trains rather than be deported into one of the many concentration camps. A former superintendent, a woman in her seventies complained: "Hours went by before the bodies had been removed from under the trains. It was a really mean trick: under such circumstances how could you keep the trains running on time."

The city railroad and subway stations of Berlin are full of notices about what you may and may not do; regular customers and joy-riders; ticket machines and newsstands; even the occasional bench to rest your weary bones. On the platform of Friedrichstraße Station in East Berlin, open without border formalities to transit passengers from the West, there are a few stands selling articles and snacks, chocolates and alcohol, at lower than Western prices. A magnet for West Berlin tipplers.

One man of this type was asked by a nervous traveler, oblivious to the other's state of mind and body: "Excuse me please. When does the last train leave here?" To which the one so addressed replied pensively: "Young man, we are in Berlin. Last train? That neither you nor I will live to see."

[191]

Restaurants, Hotels, and the Hospitality Syndrome

A quick look at the menu cover and not only gourmets were delighted: the card itself was a *pièce de résistance*. Three naked graces leaned against a column adorned by laurel garlands reaching into a putto-inhabited sky. Two putti, one with a wine goblet, the other holding a harp, discreetly alluded to the excellent wine cellar and the musical entertainment by world-famous orchestras of the Adlon Hotel. Needless to say, that the Adlon fulfilled the promises so elegantly made, catering as it did to royalties crowned, uncrowned, deposed and yet to be. No glitter, only the very best upheld the standard, a maxim all but forgotten by too many West Berlin hotels today. In florid advertisements they promise to spoil the visitor where good service would suffice, and offer stylish decor where a bit less would have been a lot more. A nostalgic sigh in memory of the Adlon, long gone.

In 1907 Emperor William II stepped across the threshold as the first guest of the house where subsequently the most prominent visitors to Berlin resided, danced—and at times, broke or broken-hearted, hanged themselves. Had they done so in the Bristol, it would have been a fraction cheaper, but only a fraction. Young Berliners, asked today about the Adlon, shake their head. A few years after the end of World War II the only wing still standing was demolished, and the address Unter den Linden 1 incorporated into a new structure.

Of the old tradition of hotels in Berlin, only the waiter in tails remains in West as well as in East Berlin. In the latter particularly he keeps his customers in awe. Whether you are house guest or casual visitor, he will first motion you to wait at the door, no matter how empty the tables. This quickly settles the question about who is in command. If he is favorably inclined, the evening will be a memorable one; otherwise it will cost you peace of mind as well as money.

We shall refrain from mentioning the name of a large hotel on Kurfürstendamm where, instead of the order of fried eggs, a plate with cold scrambled eggs is shoved under the nose of the guest; where you have to ask for coffee no less than five times; and where the staff within hearing makes nasty remarks about other guests. We shall refrain from doing so because the letter of apology received from the hotel manager reveals the helplessness of management when the staff is asked to take care of busloads of people (paying concessional prices) in addition to individual guests (footing a much higher bill). The influence on behavior here as there reflects the situation. West Berlin hotels could not survive without group tourism, that's a fact. Before the Second World War, the writer Anton Kuh remarked that his debts accumulated in the bar of one of the grand hotels were so astronomical that he practically owned the whole house. Today, many a hotel owner will say the same about his bank.

The state-owned East Berlin hotel organization not only invented a system of hierarchically-arranged quality and price levels, but also the duty on the part of staff to refuse whatever tip is offered. The latter principle was soon forgotten. Groups of visitors from the Soviet republics, completely unaware of the tipping custom which invaded from the affluent West, have to expect the same cold-shoulder treatment here that tourist groups experience over there. These "delegations," as they are called, sit down at separate tables to a pre-ordered meal. This is as far west as any of the factory workers or farmhands from Uzbekistan or Novosibirsk will ever travel on their bonus trip of a lifetime; with an interpreter close at hand to guide them through big-city traffic and explain the sights and sounds so unfamiliar, so far away from home. The night watchman of the Berolina Hotel could write a novel which would paint a picture quite unlike the one presented in Vicky Baum's famous *Grand Hotel*. The tiny man seemed to grow as he confided: "Twenty-three years and not a day absent."

Niederschönhausen Castle (East), and Belvedere Castle (West), serve their respective governments as guest houses, in a style so similar that one is tempted to ask if there is a Wall at all. But everything in the line of marketable hospitality below this "top" class shows the divide between East and West.

Travelers in West Berlin, if they are lucky, can evade the rising costs of food and accommodation by putting the bill on their company expense account. In East Berlin the problems stem not from inflated prices, but from overcrowding. While in West Berlin it's easy enough to find a comfortable boardinghouse or a room with bed and breakfast, such private enterprises are rare across the border. Karl Marx declared private profiteering an obscenity. Accommodation problems of this kind he could not have envisioned. Would he have found them in order?

Russians—Distant Cousins of the Prussians

The Battle of Berlin not only cost the lives of many Germans; it also took a terrifying toll among Soviet soldiers who fought under Marshal Zhukov until the city surrendered. A wall of 560 meters was erected around the military cemetery of Schönholzer Heide (East), the last resting place of 13,200 men whose names are inscribed on the wall. In Treptow Park (East) another 5,000 Red Army soldiers were buried and a huge memorial built in their honor from the red marble blocks of Hitler's Chancellery. Visitors from all over the world, including from the two German states, leave the sites deeply disturbed.

Under the Four-Power Agreement Soviet military personnel has free access to West Berlin, and yet we never saw a member of the Red Army stroll along Kurfürstendamm or go on a shopping spree the way members of the other Allied forces do in Berlin East or West—due to lack of foreign currency. The Soviet Consulate for West Berlin is located in Dahlem. East of the border, Unter den Linden 55–65, stands the imposing Embassy of the USSR. Reconstructed between 1948 and 1953, the complex stands on the enlarged site of the former Imperial Russian Embassy and indirectly owes its location and size to a Prussian king. Nicholas I of Russia bought the plot cheaply from Frederick William III, his father-in-law. No wonder, then, that the king heaped laurels upon the czar, made him honorary citizen of Berlin, and presented him and the czarina with a Russian-style blockhouse named Nikolskoe (today a much loved destination for West Berliners on outings). Nicholas and Alexandra Feodorovna, former Princess Charlotte, should feel at home when on a visit in the Prussian capital.

The house was left in the care of a Russian coachman who soon began to serve food and drinks to members of the small Russian colony nearby. A Russian church dedicated to SS. Peter and Paul was built in the vicinity. A Lutheran pastor officiates here now, yet much of the atmosphere around has retained a flavor as Russian as during the days when settlers from St. Petersburg gathered for church services and vodka bashes.

Russian Orthodox services in Church Slavonic are still held

in the chapel of Konstantin and Helena in Tegel by a priest who was born and raised in Minsk. He was introduced to his West Berlin congregation by the Russian Orthodox archbishop for East and West Germany who resides in East Berlin. Thus it takes him no more than a short S-Bahn ride to set his foot on Russian soil. The little church without benches—the ritual prescribes that the congregation stands while singing and kneels while praying—was built on 4,000 tons of soil brought over from the homeland in 1893. Shortly before Hitler began his all-out invasion of the Soviet Union, in 1938, the Russian and Greek Orthodox congregation completed construction of its Ascension Church on Hohenzollerndamm (now West). Three onion-shaped domes stand out among the surrounding Central European architecture. The faithful assembled here throughout the war, many still in the hope that the revolution from which they had fled would pass.

In East Berlin, the Soviet Army settled in old Prussian and new republican socialist barracks in Karlshorst. Fences and guards near the turnstile keep civilians from attempts at fraternizing with the soldiers. The German–Soviet Friendship Society centered in the House of Soviet Science and Culture on Friedrichstraße on the other hand, invites and promotes what the military are forbidden to cultivate. The museum in Karlshorst, Fritz-Schmenkel-Straße, is the historic location where General Wilhelm Keitel unconditionally surrendered on May 8, 1945, conceding the fall of the Third Reich with his signature. One room shows the original map, on which Hitler marked, with red crosses, the way the war fronts were collapsing. On the Western side the museum is referred to as the former Armed Forces Engineering School, while on the Eastern side it is described as a former officers' mess hall.

No such question of historical interpretation confronts us in Tempelhof (West). House No. 2 on Schulenburgring had witnessed a similar ceremony of surrender a few days earlier. On May 2, 1945, Weidling, the general responsible for the defense of Berlin, met Soviet General Chuikov in a room on the second floor to confirm that the battle was over. Whoever continued to fight was doing so on his own account. Shooting ceased quickly. A table seating eighteen people must have been the decisive factor for the choice of this location. The table now stands in the local museum.

Only historians are aware that as early as the eighteenth century a Russian army was about to march into Berlin. But without fighting and shooting they retreated eastward again after a sizeable sum from the coffers of the magistrate had changed hands. Berliners of the older generation, however, might still recall the Russian restaurants of the Golden Twenties. Nobody was surprised to meet Russian generals and dukes there, not as guests, but in their new role as waiters. Russian specialties from caviar to bortsch were on the menu. Balalaika orchestras provided background music. Alcohol had to dull those awful attacks of homesickness.

During such festivities in the Tary Bary or in other bars frequented by Russian refugees, the owner was compensated in advance and the police asked to stay at the station. In the early hours of the morning, when the "exorcist" ritual came to a climax, every glass and piece of furniture was smashed to pieces. Then the party would stagger through the cool air of dawn to offer prayers at the church. Until the next such seizure the soul's equilibrium had been reestablished.

S

Science and Technology—Past Achievements, New Endeavors

Two Bavarians are sitting in a restaurant trying in vain to get salt out of the salt shaker. A Berliner can't help jumping in. Without a word he takes the shaker, opens the holes with a toothpick and pushes it back toward the two. Silence. Finally one Bavarian says to the other: "Darn those stupid Prussians—but technically they are one ahead of us."

The industrial wealth of Berlin can, in part, be traced back to the large number of "rational dreamers" who came up with innovative ideas and made them available to the city. Support for these ideas and acceptance of the inventions they produced depended largely on historical factors. Was the time ripe? Were the products needed? Who discovered the process for the production of Prussian blue, a dye traded worldwide? Johannes Kunckel, a seventeenth-century experimental chemist, considered "alchemist" in his own time, could he have been the early discoverer? He had a royal laboratory at his disposal on Pfauenwerder, the island called Pfaueninsel today. The monarch had set him up there to make gold. Kunckel dreamed of ruby glass, of Prussian blue. The export of the latter substance has in more recent days filled the purse of chemical concerns, including the VEB Kali-Chemie in East Berlin.

East and West Berlin are training their new generation of researchers—up and coming rational dreamers who have to come up with solutions for tomorrow's problems—in their universities, in scientific institutes, and technical colleges. An East Berlin natural scientist showed us a cartoon from the satirical journal *Eulenspiegel*, which he had pinned up on his wall for good reason. On it one of his colleagues is sighing: "10 percent of my time I can work on the solution of problems. The other 90 percent of my working day I have to spend convincing my superiors that they have to be solved." That sigh seems to be universal. Is that perhaps the reason why nobody has yet found a way to squeeze excess toothpaste back into the tube?

In 1747, with a Berlin invention of worldwide importance, tooth decay got a head start. The process of making sugar out of beets was developed. Large-scale production of the sweet crystals was realized forty years later under the influence of Franz Carl Achard, of Huguenot descent, who recognized and seized upon a propitious opportunity: Napoleon I had Europe under a blockade, which cut it off from cane sugar imports from the colonies. The answer was: substitute!

Relics from the history of beet sugar production are meticulously cared for in a museum in Wedding (West). The tower of the Sugar Museum is for once not fashioned in the likeness of a Prussian spiked helmet, but in the shape of a sugar beet. And that would stand to reason. Around the museum there is a whiff of malty molasses, for research continues in the scientific department of the museum.

Sugar sweetens your coffee, but how do you keep it hot? This problem was solved by a Berliner, too, by the glass blower Reinhold Burger (from Pankow), the inventor of the thermos bottle. And who actually invented the elevator? Not a Berliner! More than two thousand years ago Archimedes contemplated the principles underlying such a worthwhile apparatus, and by the middle of the nineteenth century the first steam-operated lift was installed in a New York department store. But it was Werner von Siemens who constructed the first elevator put in motion by an electrical motor, and that was in 1880 and in Berlin at that. From here on out it was upward all the way.

The Kaiser Wilhelm Institute of Physics followed just that trend. Albert Einstein worked here for nineteen years, as did Max Planck, Otto Hahn, and Lise Meitner, to name but a few of the greatest contributors. Under the auspices of this Berlin institute, universally important experiments, discoveries, inventions, and the development of the theories of relativity followed one another at incredible speed. In 1945 the Soviet

[198]

military administrator appointed Prof. Robert Havemann director of the umbrella organization, the Kaiser-Wilhelm-Gesellschaft. (Havemann died in East Berlin in 1980 while under house arrest.)

The Western Allies moved whatever they could from the research institutes out of Berlin to Göttingen, where the society reformed as the "Max-Planck-Gesellschaft." A house on East Berlin's Kupfergraben also carries the name of this eminent physicist. Here the Physics Society of the GDR safeguards the reference and professional library of Max Planck. With Berlin's scholarship and teaching thus divided, we are reminded that once before there was a division: into "Semitic" and "Aryan" science. Science by no means benefited from it.

NUTRIMENTUM SPIRITUS stood in large letters above the old Royal Library. It was called "Kommode" or "Chest of Drawers" for its shape, and stands reconstructed today on Bebelplatz, East Berlin. Those familiar with Latin will translate the motto into "Nourishment for the Intellect," but Berliners have no particular inclination for antique languages— the speed of the city doesn't make any allowance for it. Instead, they are more frequently original, no matter what the consequences. Above the Otto Weise grocery store on Prenzlauer Berg 9 the sign once read, on the left: "Potatoes— Herrings—Cucumbers;" and on the right: "Fruit—Vegetables— Oranges." Which goes to show that to a Berliner potatoes and cucumbers do not rate among the vegetables, and oranges do not belong in the category of fruit. The Latin inscription above the Royal Library was thus translated by the metropolitans with Berlin logic into: "Alcohol is a means of subsistence."

Social Problems, Special Problems

A West Berliner in his mid-forties, insurance agent turned drop-out, abbreviated his life story as follows: "When that thing happened with my wife, a colleague first put me up in his garage. Then I hung out around Savigny Platz, sharing everything with the others. When it got cold, I locked myself up at night in a public toilet and slept there. No tax collector can get hold of me. He wouldn't know where to send a letter." Then he offered us a drink from his bottle. We politely declined and he nodded: "You're right, this stuff is bad for you," at which he lifted the bottle and took a big gulp himself.

Social services in West Berlin are divided into a great number of independent agencies. At the turn of the twentieth century everything now provided by a state-supported network of public health care, welfare, and emergency centers was in the hands of charitable organizations for the poor. As in any large urban settlement problems are plentiful, and the number of people in need of assistance is enormous. Not infrequently problems are compounded by alcoholism and drug addiction. Each year the Senate spends over a billion deutschmarks on relief work. Some 150,000 citizens receive aid, either in the form of cash payments or in goods and services. The district offices employ teams of social workers and staff to scan through applications, give advice, send out checks, distribute winter coats and blankets, and see that children are cared for.

When youngsters run away from one part of the city to the other, the Senate office in charge of internal affairs has to contact the Interior Ministry in East Berlin to ask for assistance. On rare occasions when a child has crossed the border going in the opposite direction (border controls are so much tighter on the eastern side), it is the West Berlin Senator for Family, Youth and Sports who is responsible. In Königsheide (East), a home has been established for those juveniles whose parents deserted them rather than deprive themselves of a chance to flee to the "Golden" West.

In West Berlin the situation becomes problematic when, in times of high unemployment, the younger generation no longer accepts the rules of the social game. A group of punks had to be forcefully removed from a house they illegally occupied; but they couldn't be turned out into the street. A girls' dormitory in Reinickendorf had to be requisitioned to give them shelter. A more permanent solution was proposed to the tune of 800,000 deutschmarks annually, paid from the public purse. Modern services at modern prices.

In their resolve to find practical, long-term answers to dilemmas of such proportion, East and West Berlin are not much far apart. The city throughout its history has brought forth more pioneers in social work and more dedicated social workers than its condition would let you believe. Alice Bendix created the profession of kindergarten teacher. Deported to Auschwitz, she died in the gas-chamber. It was the example of women like her, their philosophy and devotion, that guided socio-pedagogical movements in the years after the Second World War. Rash experimentation and the sudden boom of *Kinderläden* claimed their ideals as well. It took a while until these self-help day-care centers modified their adamantly anti-authoritarian approach to pre-school education. Meanwhile a whole generation of young adults struggles with the after-effects of such libertinism.

In East Berlin the network of nurseries and day-care facilities is taken for granted. The emancipation of women as well as labor shortages account for most women of working age holding down a job or practicing a profession. The right to work is safeguarded: state-subsidized centers for pre-school children are therefore a necessity. The political organization of the Young Pioneers was instrumental in the construction of recreation camps for children, such as the one in Wuhlheide. Proceeds from a lottery provide many of the funds allowing West Berlin to send a great number of children on holiday in the Federal Republic. Socio-political programs cost money here as there, more than obligatory or private insurance contributions can support..The state must step in. Volunteers are needed in East and West.

There are alcohol-free social centers in West Berlin. Across the border drinkers are kept from too much beer and booze by colleagues at work, organized in closely-knit units large and small. Production plans must not turn into chaos.

As a rule a shop delegation is sent to visit a co-worker believed to be slipping. Greifswalder Straße, East Berlin: two visitors are on their way with a bunch of flowers to see a friend from the street-car depot. A neighbor fills them in. Yes, the man called in sick. But unfortunately just now he was out—around the corner in a *Kneipe*.

When the two comrades check there, he has disappeared again. First he needed a drink to find courage to commit himself voluntarily; now he's on his way to the hospital to "dry out." The waitress gets the flowers, the delegation of two parties till three in the afternoon and then returns to the depot.

The neighbor continues the story: "When I go down later for my evening paper, who is leaning against his apartment door trying to find the keyhole? Our friend. Wet as a washcloth. I stop to chat in front of the house for the better part of an hour, come back up the stairs, and who is still standing there trying to get in? I see nothing, say nothing, quietly pass him by. No use helping, his wife would be so jealous she'd have a fit."

The GDR spends 12 percent of its gross national product on social programming. In the Federal Republic and West Berlin the chunk is bigger still—18 percent, in fact. Add them up and see. Faced with a jealous Berlin wife watching over her alcoholic husband, powers far greater are forced to capitulate.

Spandau for Keeps

Spandau, so the natives tell visitors if given half a chance, has almost nothing to do with Berlin, even though this once independent town was incorporated into the city in 1920. Looking around one cannot escape the feeling of approaching the Tower of London with its keeps and fortifications, towers and turrets. The gruesome stories and historical atrocities connected with the Spandau fortress, penitentiary, workhouse, dungeons, the infamous arms industry and its arsenals—all these associations came rushing in upon us. The author Ludwig Turek was incarcerated here shortly before the last emperor abdicated. Women prisoners had to sew sandbags; the men had to paste paper bags together. Rations were just above subsistence level, to avoid starving the inmates to death. A notice warned: "Eating glue is strictly forbidden."

In the armament factories, too, life was not much better. The kaiser had recruited "hands" even among the women and girls of Spandau and Berlin nearby. Grenades had to be turned and sent to the men in the field. Wages were miserable. (There is a war going on, don't you know?) Working conditions were appalling. Then, in 1918, the war was lost. It couldn't get any worse—at least so they thought.

Under military guard in which the four victorious Allies share—taking turns—the last of the interned Nazi war criminals sentenced to life imprisonment enjoys the questionable fame as the most expensive detainee in the world. Rudolf Hess, kept in a Spandau prison under top security, not only causes horrendous costs to the taxpayer, but his notorious crimes have cost him dearly as well. Some advocate amnesty on humanitarian grounds—Hess is in his nineties—and call his detention a senseless act of revenge. Others, in contrast, base their opposing view on the fact that during the funeral of an NS air force general a West German air force detachment, unauthorized though it was, flew above the graveyard forming an Iron Cross as they dipped their wings. What could happen if Hitler's deputy were to be freed?

When we stood on the other side of the street to gaze at indifferent prison walls a cyclist stopped and, one foot on the pavement, muttered: "There is so much talk about Siberia. But here they have stuck someone in a hole, too. . . ." The allusion was more than carefully formulated, and, when we showed no sign of response, the man disappeared. British guards were just marching off—another Allied guard had taken over.

We couldn't tell whether the cyclist was from Spandau proper. The natives there don't like to be called the "Bavarians of Berlin," a hint at their historical age. Much like their alpine brothers, their roots go back to the early Stone Age some 60,000 years ago. Later discoveries attest to a cultural mixture of Slavonic and Germanic tribes who continued to build fortresses and castles here throughout their early development. The name Spandowe first appeared in a document dating back to 1197, and in 1982 the town was able to celebrate its 750th anniversary. So the borough is actually older than Berlin—and prettier too.

On the terrain of the fortified citadel remnants of no less than eight former fortresses, one above the other, have been found. It is strategically located on an island formed by two waterways at the confluence of Havel and Spree. Imperial Chancellor Bismarck used a strong tower to keep 1,200 chests of gold francs safe which were paid by France after the lost war of 1870–1 as reparations. The archaeological institute is in charge of unearthing new excavations. No gold francs were discovered but an array of magazines, casemates, and dungeons, and even an early Gothic-style toilet facility have been found. The main tower of the citadel is open to sightseers, and a historic restaurant in the castle vault serves hearty German cooking to those whose appetite has not been spoiled by the history which seems to come alive during guided tours around the premises. It was from here that Carl Schurz liberated Professor Gottfried Kinkel, advocate of the

Spandau : Zitadelle und Juliusturm — J. Bitterstadt

democratic revolution of 1848, in a courageous coup. Not many other famous inmates were lucky enough to escape in this manner.

There is not another Renaissance fortress so well preserved anywhere north of the Alps. An Italian building expert of the sixteenth century, a time of preoccupation with building bastions against possible invaders, had imported some 200 guest workers from his home country to see the project through. Their assimilation into the local community has long been forgotten. The integration of Turkish immigrants still goes on, grudgingly and haltingly.

In downtown Berlin, visible from Spandau at a distance, only names of streets and dams recall the much greener periphery. Here, in the borough, a self-declared French king, the watchmaker "Louis XVII" claimed his "birthright," if only locally. Spandau had always welcomed separatist tendencies, so he may have been clever in his choice of "exile." Carl Wilhelm Nauendorff maintained he was the son of Marie Antoinette and Louis XVI which would have made him heir to the thrones of France and Navarra, and Duke of Normandy, had anyone taken him seriously.

More believable, however, was the fact that his wife was a Spandau native. In addition to Rudolf Hess and Albert Speer, Hitler's architect who was released from prison, Spandau almost harbored another famous participant in Hitler's war,

[204]

rocket specialist Wernher von Braun. Much like Hess he had harbored plans—once the Third Reich was falling to pieces—of making off to Britain with valuable documents. He was lucky that the Nazi secret police arrested him—thus indirectly saving him from the Nuremberg International Military Tribunal since he could claim anti-fascist intentions. In 1945 he was taken prisoner by the U.S. army, but was soon released and sent to the U.S., where scientists of his caliber were more welcome than former Nazi politicians. So he died peacefully in 1972 as one of the vice presidents of the American arms manufacturer Fairchild.

The V1 and V2 or "revenge rockets" he developed had once helped destroy parts of London and Antwerp. His professional career was indeed explosive, beginning with rocket experimentation in 1930 on the outskirts of Spandau (without ending in a Spandau prison).

Sports—Round One

So where do you go sailing for Easter—Lake Tegel or Wannsee? From Friday until Sunday racers compete for prizes in all classes of boats. Sailing ranks high among the Berliners' favorite sports. In West Berlin the boss at work is even legally bound to award his employees time off if they enroll in a sailing course (an educational holiday). If it's not the waves that attract crowds to the lakes, it is the icy surface during winter. On Lake Müggel in East Berlin surfers glide across the ice at speeds up to 120 kilometers per hour—without a motor. A person has really "arrived' if he or she is the owner of a car, a bicycle, and a sailboat with a reserved space to moor it. The dockyard may involve no more than a stake and a chain with padlock or it can include a safe, weather-proof spot in a boathouse. In any case, the pier, boathouse and possibly even the restaurant connected with it belong to the sailing club. The situation in East and West differs hardly at all.

Soccer must be the uncontested favorite among players and spectators alike. After World War II it became necessary to reorganize the sports clubs. In 1950, from the jumble of local organizations the German Sports Federation was established, administering Eastern and Western clubs jointly. It lasted until 1957, keeping alive a spirit of community and fair play among East and West German sportsmen and sportswomen long after the nation had been divided. But the split inevitably came, and East Germany founded its own German Gymnastics and Sports Federation.

As is widely known, "König Fußball" (King Soccer) rules in either part of Germany. During any weekend of the regular season, West Berlin can easily offer a choice between fifty friendly meets or competitive games. If Hertha BSC in the West and Dynamo in the East fail to live up to the expectations of fans, there is mourning for a whole week—until the next weekend. East Berlin does not subdivide its athletes into clubs but into sports communities. Out of a total of 750, 180 are dedicated to soccer alone. In stadiums and indoor courts alike the ball is kicked as if it were public enemy number one.

There was a time when the Prussian government considered gymnastics public enemy number one. In Hasenheide the legendary father of gymnastics, Ludwig Jahn, with his full beard and attired in knee-length cotton pants, set up his new gym equipment—a vaulting horse. The apparatus was confiscated by the police—Jahn was thrown into prison on Hausvogteiplatz. This sport was considered dangerous by the ruling classes as it might make progressive forces too fit physically; Jahn was too much for democratic reforms anyway. However, his followers continued practicing and, as time went by, they became superpatriots—a welcome audience for the politicians' rhetoric.

In 1935 Adolf Hitler ordered the trees along Unter den Linden to be cut down so that the Olympic Committee— along with the regiment of the Berlin guards and an enthusiastic crowd—could one year later parade to the pleasure gardens of the royal castle to the accompaniment of marching bands. With a forest of swastika banners for support, Propaganda Minister Goebbels extended his speech until the Olympic flame arrived. A contemporary journalist reports from the scene: "In the Olympic Stadium fanfares break the silence. Adolf Hitler, Führer of the Reich, patron of the Games, proceeds up the stairs. Upon arrival at his place, he greets his people." Those not belonging to "his" people were quick to realize their place as outsiders. They stood in silence, when the national anthem of the Third Reich was sung. Then the Olympic bell rang and the Games were officially opened.

The next Olympiad, planned for Tokyo in 1940, became a

casualty of the war, in direct consequence of Nazi politics. The bell was discreetly buried. Today, for an entry fee, visitors to West Berlin can take a look at it: 14 tons of cast iron steel unearthed in 1956, crack and all.

The Olympic Stadium has since been reduced by 20,000 seats, but our noses still seemed to get a whiff of that smell of uniforms and leather so reminiscent of Nazism. This was the famous "Field of May" used for Nazi cult assemblies. The amphitheater and "Waldbühne," or stage in the woods, had served similar purposes too. Statues of heroic youths clutter the place—gigantic nudes, gilded eagles on stone pedestals. Some of them are located behind the fence guarding the British Headquarters established here in the former "House of German Sports." The British tend to preserve national monuments, the principle of which—in this particular case— is hard to explain.

East Berlin took a much more radical approach. They reconstructed a huge sports building in 1950 and named it for Werner Seelenbinder, an athlete murdered by the National Socialists. That did not require much explanation. Seelenbinder Hall stands on a plot where, in former times, no shouts or applause had filled the air, only the bleating and squeaking of animals. It had been the old stockyard of Berlin. In the beginning the ice rink for hockey players was kept at appropriately cold temperatures by refrigeration units which once had kept nonpolitical pork chops and beef tenderloin fresh.

Berlin Havel mit Grunewaldturm   J. Bittestadt 1916

Sports—Round Two

"Sabri Mahir, the terrific Turk is coming!" proclaimed bill-board announcements of Circus Busch when the company was still in existence before the Second World War. "He will step into the ring and fight four opponents." And so he did, one after the other, winning against all of them. During the heyday of boxing in Berlin Sabri Mahir was a sensation—and a commercial success. Somehow as proof of his being genuinely Turkish, he surrounded himself with a team of Muslim-costumed cohorts with whom he prayed to Allah for victory. The name on his birth certificate had been Sally Mayer, and he hailed from Cologne, a fact easily detectable from his Turkish accent.

Later he became a skillful trainer. Franz Diener's bar on West Berlin's Grolmannstraße may be considered his memorial. It once belonged to a student of the legendary Turk and has been frequented by actors after performances for decades now. Heavyweight champion Diener had made a name for himself throughout Germany as well. But the rumor that his mentor, Mahir, was Marlene Dietrich's private masseur must be wishful thinking on the part of his fans.

A similar psychological twist lies at the heart of our friend Armin's contention that Bülowplatz in Schöneberg does not commemorate the chancellor known by that name, but rather a sports journalist. Arthur Bülow, chief editor of *Der Boxsport*, worshipped world champion Max Schmeling and other greats who left their mark with their fists. Bertolt Brecht even wrote sports poems in his day, thus setting himself up as a model for West Berlin authors who, in 1982, recited similar lyricisms on Reichpietschufer while movies of the most famous championship fights of their grandfathers' generation were flicking across the big screen.

Those famous six-day racing events for cyclists, another hallmark in the life of the German capital of yesteryear, contributed in a special way to the musicality of Berliners. It all began in the Sports Palace on Postdamer Straße. Two rows of light bulbs illuminated each letter of the advertising slogans high up on the front of the building. The race was on; musicians began to play "Wiener Praterleben." Whether it was the excitement over the race or over the Prater life of Vienna nobody knows. A faithful follower of the six-day events got up from his seat and could not help whistling on his fingers at certain moments during the waltz. Soon everyone in the palace whistled along with gusto. From that time on "Krücke," as he was affectionately called for the crutch that he had, would hardly need the enticement of a glass of beer to position himself in front of the microphone and lead the whistling contest in the hall. The song became the "Sports Palace Waltz," and the original name slipped from memory. But just like many no less clever and hard-drinking pensioners, "Krücke" continued to whistle even when the palace had been turned into an arena for Nazi propaganda meetings. He didn't whistle against Hitler, but for him. Decades after the war the ruins of the Sports Palace, where Propaganda Minister Goebbels had demanded "all-out war," were demolished. The Deutschlandhalle has since welcomed crowds of West Berlin sports fans under its massive roof.

It is characteristic for Berlin that in East Berlin's Seelenbinder Halle the Prater composition is only known as "Sports Palace Waltz" too. Here as well, bicycle racers get crowds excited, and everyone whistles along. Once around the oval track, and the racers have pedaled a distance of 171 meters. Indoor meets of this sort were delighting Berliners as early as 1930. For a murderous six days the competition kept going, even if individual racers and spectators didn't. Nowadays the length of time has been reduced, but so have attendance figures.

The "Avus," Europe's once "fastest" racecourse was raced to fame by the likes of Rudolf Caracciola and Manfred von Brauchitsch. Visitors arriving from the Federal Republic via checkpoint Dreilinden will pass its empty stands on their way into the center of West Berlin. In 1968 the track was opened to normal traffic; fourteen years later the Automobile Club of West Berlin risked a Formula Two competition here once again. Fear of bankruptcy keeps higher hopes in check. The best sports press cannot rally 100,000 spectators together whose entrance fee would make a Formula One race possible. At the very beginning of the history of motor sports in Berlin, newspaper publisher Ullstein sent a car on a test drive to the Riviera. That was in 1906. The driver mailed his reports along the way, and his employer received them no more than one day later in Berlin. During his adventurous endurance trip to the south of France, the driver did, in fact, happen upon other motor vehicles—three in all!

The mass media of East Berlin take notice of the interest of

[209]

their racing enthusiasts with an air of academic *noblesse* maintaining a certain "theoretical" distance to the subject. Desire for a private car must not be encouraged as long as, for economical reasons, the industry cannot meet the demand. The situation will change eventually. East Berlin, so we heard, was only free from terrorists because they had to wait at least two years for their escape vehicle. A Society for Sports and Technology is in charge of motor sports. Its membership numbers over half a million. 165,000 East Berliners are training for a sports badge, and nine-pin bowling is as strong as ever. Children of all ages compete in what is called "District Spartakiade," named after the rebellious Roman slave Spartacus.

During temperatures of two degrees Celsius in wintertime, a dozen or so die-hards take to the water of an East Berlin outdoor pool, among them Grandma Dorle Appelt, who is approaching eighty. Each one swears by the healthiness of their icy undertaking. All of them are rather well-padded—the cold gets to the core of slimmer people so much quicker. In Grunewald, on the other hand, staunch West Berliners of all ages participate in the annual "People's Hike." When he was still federal president, Karl Carstens joined the walkers one year. Among the inconspicuous "guardian angels" accompanying him, one was overheard frequently asking his neighbor in a low voice: "Much farther yet?"

T

Theater and Theatrics

Among the various means of becoming the talk of the town for more than twenty-four hours are, besides a political career, the fail-safe professions of actor and director in the theater. A pretty face is not enough—some accomplishment has to go along with it.

Heinrich Heine already found it difficult to take Berlin's thespian world all too seriously. The papers of the time didn't waste a sentence on the fact that plays by such greats as Heinrich von Kleist and Franz Grillparzer had been rejected. Instead their columns gossiped about this actor, that soubrette, and those master playwrights long since forgotten who, according to Heine, were the authors of such works as *Staberle's Adventures* from the provincial perspective of the boondocks. Honest theater critics today do not have an easy task either. Too much applause for East Berlin stages would produce a backlash, as West Berlin does the best it can with far fewer subsidies. Differences in quality can, to a large degree, be traced back to the disparate ways in which East and West support their theaters and encourage their talents.

But neither can East Berlin get around those stage sets which are called "modern" because they fell victim to cuts in funding. The Metropol Theater may well have to make do with ropes across the stage instead of scenery when the Ministry of Finance tightens the purse strings of the Ministry of Culture because the money is needed elsewhere. The press raves about the advent of avant-garde show effects (with which West Berlin has long been covering up for insufficient public subsidies). Necessity has been turned into virtue, too. In both parts of the city a considerable number of studio stages and theater workshops are laboring away with a young crew that make the most of the chance. In the East that rising generation of actors and actresses remain on the payroll, in the West they draw unemployment benefit.

During the "golden years" of theater in Berlin, some fifty stages offered a daily fare of drama, comedy, opera, and operetta, and the choice between them was hard to make. A page of theater programs in the *Berliner Tageblatt* of 1926 can easily take your breath away, so numerous are the legendary names which left their marks in the chronicles of European and even world theatrical history. After the burning of the Reichstag in 1933, Kurt Tucholsky's prophetic forecast became reality: "Once the real talents are driven out, the whores from the province come creeping in from every corner and fill their places." This was the way in which the Reich's "Drama Director" came to power who, in 1934, prevented a performance of Schiller's *Don Carlos* on the grounds that "the still rather dubious Berlin audience" should not be given "cause for a liberalistic demonstration." How right he was! During a performance of that very drama in the Deutsches Theater Berlin in 1937 Schiller's words "Sire, give us freedom of thought," caused frenetic and prolonged applause. Gustaf Gründgens produced Schiller's *Robbers* in 1944 in the Staatliches Schauspielhaus on Gendarmenmarkt but agreed to simply delete the author's furor against tyrannical usurpation of power as well as his appeal for peace.

The Schauspielhaus has now been reconstructed in style, between the German and French cathedrals in East Berlin. There was not a theater in 1945 in Berlin where—in spite of war damages, icy dressing-rooms and unheated auditoriums—the curtain failed to rise. Here, those theater people driven out of the country by Hitler attempted to re-establish contact with a public, which had become "a bit alien," as Walter Felsenstein put it. He, a Viennese, took over the Comic Opera in Behrenstraße, once known as Metropol Theater, and put it back on the road to fame. Bertolt Brecht and Helene Weigel took great care in their Berliner Ensemble on Schiffbauerdamm that nobody they didn't like got in their way. Erwin Piscator, back from New York, saw himself confronted with lots of work and an equal amount of problems at West Berlin's Volksbühne, which in fact thanked him for his endeavors

[212]

MAXIM GORKI THEATER Berlin-Ost J. B. Heupfalt

Früher Singakademie

with a letter of dismissal shortly before his death. Boleslav Barlog, yet another name from the gallery of famous theater people, didn't meddle in anything and kept on directing at the Renaissance Theater.

In East Berlin two million theater tickets are sold per annum on average. This would mean that every citizen of the capital attends more than one nightly performance in every twelve months—if there were not those from out of town to compete for a seat in front of the stage. *Fiddler on the Roof* and Broadway hits like *Showboat* are presented by guest companies or house ensembles; on the whole, many a solid Western success is introduced to East Berlin audiences as well. Variety shows have been staged in Friedrichstadtpalast in a brand-new building since the old structure suffered damages due to the sinking of the water-table. The posts under its foundation had slowly begun to dry up and gave way.

A memorial to Max Reinhardt was placed in front of his Deutsches Theater, which like the Kammerspiele next door goes on with one performance after the other. The name of

Max Reinhardt's Kleines Theater was brought across the Wall to Steglitz, where on a mini-stage literary delicacies are presented in grand style. Boulevard comedies entertain along Kurfürstendamm. Once in a while someone from the West Berlin Senate pronounces his lack of amusement about a show or play on the program—Berlin is no richer in theater scandals for it. Such official protests leave the public cold. East Berlin sends its directors across the border with temporary visas, which seem to be something like stamps of quality, if the press is to be believed.

A connoisseur of the theatrical scene in Greater Berlin came up with the lucid comment: "It is divided." New in this pronouncement is the apparent fact that banalities are no longer allowed to pass but are loudly brought to public attention, even on stage. In order to outdo television, that perfidious competitor, an author on occasion comes across a splendid idea, and if he is a director, too, he can even put it into practice. He will, for instance, present three actresses under the limelight, who, symbolically of course, tear a man into pieces; and the few spectators in the house laugh with relief, as they themselves did not fall victim to this sort of cannibalism.

Serious drama survives—in spite of equally serious attempts to ruin it. Box-office takings and revenue from season tickets keep it going, if barely. Berlin theater is much like an old-fashioned egg-timer: it stands on its head whichever way you turn it around. Around the turn of the last century the emperor had the director (who was about to open with a long-forgotten play) know in no uncertain terms that either the play was canceled or he would never set foot into this theater again. Upon which the director advised his staff: "Reserved seats in the royal box may now be sold." Today, however, it's the audience that stays away frequently. The director then advises his staff to send the bill to the Senate, the next best addressee now that the emperors, the real ones, are out of fashion.

Town Halls—One in Schöneberg, One in Red

For once it was the building material and not politics—the red bricks and not a colorful euphemism—which gave the administrative seat of East Berlin its name, "The Red Town Hall." In chronological terms it is the fifth and was inaugurated in 1869 in much splendor. Until 1945 the magistrate of Berlin governed an undivided city from these premises.

The imposing structure was nearly in ruins when the war ended. Reconstruction took place from 1951 to 1956 and, while this landmark could be saved, the once densely populated surroundings could not. Green lawns stretch around it now—emphasizing its massiveness. At a height more suitable for giraffes than human observers, a frieze runs the length of its walls, a picture book of thirty-six reliefs depicting scenes from the lives of peasants, craftsmen, and burghers. Especially noteworthy is the representation of a fourteenth-century inn. Waiters serving their guests in the Red Ratskeller may well be glad they do not have to carry such huge beer steins and wine pitchers as their colleagues did centuries ago.

The interior of the building is a mixture of local brickwork and Italian decor. Classical statues in alcoves along the walkways have a local flair, being allegorical figures of the Havel and Spree rivers. A boatsman's young daughter leans against an anchor, as if there were no better place to rest. As attractive and seductive as she is, she should have been able to find a Berliner willing to give her a safe harbor. By the way, the mayor of East Berlin has a bedroom available for his use in the house.

Magistrates and city parliaments began to hold their meetings in the Red Town Hall again in 1955. In 1945 Eastern and Western political ideologies had clashed so violently that the administrative unity of Berlin broke apart. West Berlin formed its own Senate and elected its own lord mayor, a development Theodor Fontane must have envisioned already in 1892, when he wrote: "A lord mayor of Berlin is unthinkable who does not have progressive ideas and a fighting spirit of the most loyal kind of course." How could a single lord mayor have been loyal to both sides? By necessity Berlin needed two!

The Senate of West Berlin took up quarters in Schöneberg

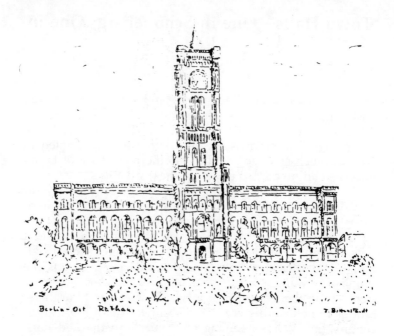

Berlin-Ost Rathaus,   T. Brinnelsdt.

Town Hall, and so did the House of Representatives, however provisionally at first. But the temporary arrangement
has lasted for over forty years now. If the tower of the Red
Town Hall rises to 77 meters above street level, with—at least
until the television tower rose higher—a red blinking light on
top of a mast to warn aircraft, the tower of Schöneberg Town
Hall measures only 7 meters less, while at its peak a similar
red lamp serves the same purpose. At least in this respect,
the same common sense prevails. If the political situation is
any clue the tower clocks of the two town halls should
actually be running in different directions.

The Town Hall of Schöneberg stands on the site of an old
water mill. There is no mill wheel turning anymore, but at the
stroke of twelve noon a special bell with a very special
inscription rings in the afternoon. "That this world under
God shall have a new birth of freedom!" This motto motivated 17 million Americans between 1949 and 1950 to donate
money for this "Liberty Bell." The Senate had to provide
another hefty sum in 1957 to safeguard 17 million American
signatures being stored in damp paper boxes. Thousands of
visitors climb the tower every year and many of them take a
good look at the balcony from where President Kennedy
spoke the famous words in 1963, often quoted: "Ich bin ein

Rathaus Schöneberg   J. Betterstadt

Berliner!" ("I am a Berliner!") Much less frequently does anyone care to have a look at the archives, also stored in Schöneberg, which contain many millions of entries—records of every soldier cared for in a German military hospital from the War of Liberation (against Napoleonic France) to the Second World War.

Such files say an awful lot about the style in which West and East Berlin like to practice administration in that they are orderly, meticulous, and complete. This led a nineteenth-century Prussian administrative official to inquire about the following—in a letter written to the minister of finance. Every basement and loft was full of files, there was no more space, and he did not know where to store more documents. He wanted to find out whether it was permissible to scrap tax returns of over fifty years ago. In a manner still practiced today, nothing at all happened for a good while. Then the written answer came: "Files may be scrapped after copies have been made in duplicate."

Turkish Delights?

There are some 170,000 (officially 120,000 Turkish) citizens living in West Berlin. Male adults arrived first, lured by advertising agencies, who promised them the Islamic version of paradise in diminuitive form. They entered the labor market when hands were short. A clean shirt, suit, and tie were prerequisite, as well as good teeth, if possible. The men later sent for their families.

This influx from the Middle East cannot be compared with other waves of immigration Berlin experienced throughout its history. Certainly not with the arrival of the Huguenots who, like the Prussians, were Protestant and who, because of their European background and their craftsmanship, could be easily assimilated culturally and linguistically. Islamic religion, dissimilarity of language and culture, and the lack of professional or working skills required in the industrialized West proved enormous barriers for the integration of first generation Turkish immigrants. The result: social discrimination, mutual distrust and misunderstanding, and—given the growing unemployment situation—an extra burden on the public budget. Not to speak of the flare-up of anti-foreign sentiments among Berliners.

Adventurous elements had swelled the steady stream, too, drawing others behind who wanted to forget Anatolia and adopt a Western lifestyle. Turkish Airlines maintains a regular route into East Berlin's Schönefeld Airport. Whoever travels there in transit to West Berlin and continues via bus to the border is not checked by East German customs. West Berlin customs officials and border police but rarely examine travelers arriving via East Berlin. Luggage brought in this way not always contains only what market stalls in Kreuzberg, the district nicknamed "Little Istanbul," display. Drugs find their way into West Berlin in this manner as well. And when, on top of it, brawls occur in or in front of bars, and knives are drawn—customs of fighting foreign to the former capital of Germany—then Berliners' nerves are strained. "Turks Out!" appears scribbled or painted on house fronts and walls. So far no outright pogrom has been incited, but at times all the signs point to a storm.

A horror for all Turkish families is the shelter in Kreuzberg, Legiendamm 30. They would rather accept any roof over their heads, no matter how grubby and dilapidated, to avoid that. The children attend German schools with special provisions made to serve their particular needs and overcome the language problem.

But problems enough remain: the political situation in their native country; the fear of expulsion; their conservative religious laws that are unfamiliar to Berliners. Twenty West Berlin schools accept Turkish children into about sixty classrooms. The boys adjust much more easily. Little girls with their traditional scarves around their heads shy away from their German classmates when they are called names. The meanest among them, "Kümmeltürke" or "Caraway Turk," is the most idiotic one used in a discriminatory way. Far from having anything to do with the immigrants from across the Bosporus, the term originated as a jocular way of getting back at the people from Halle, now in the GDR. The city colors, much like the flag of Turkey, show a crested moon. And since the housewives there seasoned their food with a lot of caraway seeds, student lingo of the nineteenth century coined the phrase.

There are many Berliners, predominantly young ones, who are trying to bridge the gap between the two cultures. A lot of effort and caring goes into their programs and endeavors. At times the well-meaning but not-quite-accurate argument is used that Turkey gave asylum to refugees from Hitler, so it is only fair and right that the favor be returned. There are much better reasons to treat people as people, without relying on a misconception. Turkey at the time accepted only refugees with a highly qualified profession that did not exist in Turkey itself. The former lord mayor of Berlin, Ernst Reuter, for instance, taught Urban Studies at the University of Ankara under the provision that he leave the country once enough students had mastered the subject. Often enough, residence permits were only extended after a present among friends, a good baksheesh, had changed hands. West Berliners who believe cultural integration can be advanced by concentrating on education for the minority may be flattering themselves.

Meanwhile political groups among the minority deride and denounce one another, and spy on each other in a language which did not become more European by the fact that the Latin alphabet was forced on it in the twenties by Kemal Ataturk and Western influences could take hold much easier in the country.

The radical right-wing faction of the "Grey Wolves" is

[219]

accused of terrorizing its own Turkish countrymen, even of murder. Historical precedents exist. In 1921 the former Grand Vizier Talat Pasha was assassinated in front of Hardenberg-straße 17, now West Berlin, by a 24-year-old student—an act of vendetta by Turkish Armenians.

In spite of serious labor shortages, East Berlin did not import foreign workers *en masse*, not even from the socialist countries, thus avoiding many of the problems experienced in West Berlin. When trouble arises with Turkish visitors from West Berlin, the People's Police acts with noted reserve, for a crisis could quickly reach the sphere of international diplomacy. Usually a low-key communiqué is issued, with an inaudible sigh of relief that the Wall prevents worse incidents.

U

Universities

Two West Berlin intellectuals enter a typical corner bar in the vicinity of Baumschulenweg, East Berlin, sit down at a table where four uniformed railroad workers are drinking their beer. Stared at in silence at first, they finally hear the judgment: "That one I don't believe a word from. The other is a student. He'd better watch his teeth." Neither of the newcomers had even uttered a word. This was an open invitation, though, to join in the conversation, provided they did not vent their high-flying political theories, the way young intellectuals do around the beer table. These seasoned workers had no use for that.

If universities are the nostrils through which a society can smell the scent of future developments, then the nose of Berlin, represented by Friedrich-Wilhelm Universität and the Technische Hochschule, was under violent bacterial attack throughout the Hitler years. Chauvinism distorted everything, egocentrism prevailed. Mankind became "Germankind." German physics, divorced from that evil "Jewish" physics, was the real thing. The humanities became inhuman, and the sciences in part pseudo-scientific. The end of delusion arrived only in 1945 with total destruction.

Academic institutions for theoretical studies were founded in Berlin relatively late compared to other European capitals and other German centers of learning. The Friedrich-Wilhelm Universität on the Unter den Linden originated in 1809. The Technical University in Charlottenburg, based on the Bauakademie (Construction Academy) of 1799 and the Gewerbe-akademie (Trades Academy) of 1821, came into being as late as 1879. Both had to be reconstructed externally and reformed internally after 1945. It was not as easy, however, as removing Hitler's portraits from the walls and hanging up pictures of the victorious leaders instead. Still, in 1946 the two centers of research and teaching reopened with one in the Eastern and one in the Western sector of town.

Only two years later, students and professors adverse to Marxist ideology left the university on Unter den Linden for West Berlin. The institution they left adopted the name Humboldt University tracing its roots back to Wilhelm von Humboldt, at whose instigation it had been founded in the first place. The new academic establishment they entered across the border in Dahlem owed its beginning mainly to U.S. patronage from the foundation which bears the name of an American car company.

"Veritas, Justitia, Libertas" became the motto of the Free University. Had the university considered adopting the name of Gottfried Wilhelm Leibniz, philosopher and founder of the first Prussian Academy of Science, a historical tradition could have been preserved. Given its current name, the term "free" has often been assumed to mean something like "free for all," particularly during the riotous late sixties.

In the beginning, classes started in large villas, requisitioned for the FU by US General Lucius D. Clay, commander in charge of the American sector. Under his successor, High Commissioner McCloy, professors and students were able to move into the new Henry Ford Building, while institutes and other facilities found their domiciles all over the district of Dahlem. Within the first fifteen years student enrolment tripled. Increasing almost at the same rate was a strong opposition within the academic community against U.S. policies. Aggressions were no longer released in the fencing rooms of sword-fighting fraternities: they exploded in violent form between students and police in the streets.

Since its inception, the university on Unter den Linden has been housed in a palace built between 1748 and 1766 for Prince Henry. Without a valid student or faculty identity card, nobody is allowed beyond the doorman's cubicle. By now even West Berlin scholars concede that, in spite of a heavy emphasis on ideology, research and learning in the GDR have advanced to a high level of competence, with special achievements being made in the fields of medicine,

Berlin Humboldt schloss

astronomy and space technology, optics, pedagogy, linguistics, and history.

Throughout the years twenty-seven Nobel Prize winners have taught at the oldest university in Berlin. The words of Karl Marx, that philosophers merely interpreted the world differently and it was time to change the world, greet students in the foyer of Humboldt University, through which Marx and Lenin entered the place in their times, the latter under a pseudonym to protect himself against the imperial Prussian and czarist Russian police.

In West Berlin, when students demonstrated protesting against a state visit by the shah of Iran to Bonn, and one of the protesters was shot and killed by police, 15,000 mourners attended the memorial service. Student politicians like Rudi Dutschke came to international fame in the chaos of riots, protest demonstrations, and arson attacks. There were times when more red flags were waved in West Berlin than on the other side. Then a whole generation of students discovered that their experiences with the police provided an unsatisfactory substitute for missed courses.

Already in the nineteenth century Heinrich Heine had observed that in Berlin, even more than science and philosophy, agitation and hate ruled the day. At that time students wore high hats à la Bolivar. Today the fad is Chilean ponchos, imported or imitated by clever tradesmen. Trendy fashions, like the wearing of bedouin scarves, signal solidarity with the Palestinians or, some say, veil latent racism with anti Zionism.

[223]

A bearded father from the 1968 student generation rode the subway with his little daughter on his lap. In a rather loud voice the little girl kept on asking questions for which there were no answers. The other passengers cracked a smile every time the child countered parental deficiency with a triumphant: "See, you don't know." To get himself out of the fix, the pestered father finally demanded: "Angie, hold your breath." Unperturbed the little one continued: "Then Angie will die. And what will Mommy say? See, you don't know."

Unter den Linden

From a road lined with lime trees in 1647 to a boulevard with four rows of linden trees with grand imposing buildings on both sides, Unter den Linden had by the turn of the century developed into *the* promenade of the capital that was Berlin.

Apart from tourists out for a stroll, most everyone else who frequents Unter den Linden today, is rushing about on official business, hurrying to or from the university or the library, or is perhaps busily watering flower arrangements and decorative greenery along the route. Doing just that is a gardener sitting in a small tank-like car who is watering the pansies to the point of drowning them. A good number of white chairs invite the weary sightseer to rest, but he or she is well advised to keep feet well back when the man with the motorized watering can is around.

Something which is unthinkable today happened in 1918 on this avenue not far from Brandenburg Gate, in the embassy building of the newly established Soviet republic. The German police, serving a German state which just months ago had become republican under a new social-democratic government, threw diplomats and staff out of the place. They returned only in 1922 and were welcomed by a powerful workers' demonstration.

This part of Unter den Linden, close to Brandenburg Gate shaded by big linden trees (the first postwar Soviet ambassador personally urged that they be planted), was once lined by big hotels and diplomatic residences. Today two ministry buildings, several embassies, and the central administration

[224]

nach altem Foto:

of the FDJ youth organization have taken up quarters here, along with a few exclusive shops. The window display of the Porzellanmanufaktur may seem somewhat strange at times, especially when signs in front of showpiece china read "not for export" or "not for sale." Bookshops, art galleries, and the cafés, however, do welcome their customers.

It sometimes takes more than good nature to call the often painful synthesis of old and new harmonious. Better not to look at it from that angle at all. Most students and office workers scurrying about don't either. So as not to stumble, they keep their eyes on the pavement.

It's only a few steps from boring apartment blocks, office buildings and unimaginative honeycomb-shaped windows to the baroque grandeur of historic edifices. Simply overlook those plastic umbrellas on the terrace of the Opera Café. The

Princesses Palais, in contrast, cuddles like a cat in lazy comfort nearby. Another reconstructed palace radiates no less warmth: the guest house of the city of East Berlin, formerly called Crown Prince Palais. State Library, University, Armory, and State Opera present themselves either distinguished or lavish according to their function. It is pleasant to take a breather behind the wrought-iron gate in the front garden of the State Library, even if the statue of a worker does not suit the aristocratic surroundings. Did it have to be set up here to please the artist? The brass fish, polished by millions of hands opening the library door, prefers to remain silent like the rest of its species.

Beautiful old architecture not only lines Linden Boulevard, but also stretches north and south. Intermittent gaps were left by the last war. "Berlin got its teeth knocked out," commented our friend Michel, "so that it could only repair its broken jaw by artificial dentures of concrete."

When looking at the Ministry of Foreign Affairs with its rigid ribbed structure one may well begin to wonder whether there was as little humor inside as outside. That would do injustice to the whole area where some of the greatest wits of German literary history have made their home. Wandering through side streets, one trips over memorabilia, mountains of rubble, and at least one policeman watching over them. He may not be fully aware of the historical importance of his beat, but he is ready to be engaged in a conversation—at least until one of his superiors appears. Then the topic quickly moves to more official chatter.

From Friedrichstraße Station in the direction of the Island of Museums, buildings still reveal the aftermath of 1945. Hopes for improvement run high since the first signs of reconstruction are evident. Dumbfounded, we stood in front of the house where the Swiss author Gottfried Keller had once lived. A tenant had simply bored holes into the front of the house to accommodate his idea of air-conditioning. A young woman visibly enraged, pointed to a door inside—solid carpenter's work—which was now painted bright lilac. Nearby the former residence of G.W.F. Hegel has been rebuilt. For a long time building activities proceeded at a snail's pace; recently they picked up incredible speed. And there have long been colors other than glaring lilac available for decoration. "Life is like a toothache!" philosophized our friend Michel once again. "When it's unbearable, it can only get better."

[226]

V

Vigil Over the Vast Vault of Heaven

If we are to believe the chroniclers, royal Prussians first observed the stars through tubular contraptions amidst horses' exhalations: the Old Observatory had been installed on the second floor of the royal stables. With due respect, however, it should be noted that the Academy of Arts as well as the Academy of Science occupied space within the huge building complex. That was around 1710.

Astronomy really got off the ground, though, only a century or more later, due to the influence of Alexander von Humboldt, a scientist and explorer known in South America as the second discoverer of the Americas. He was a strong advocate of bringing science to the people who were of course also attracted by the theatrical aspects of stargazing. Twice a month the Old Observatory (and later the new one) opened its doors for a small admission fee to the general public for a view of "moonscapes and celestial phenomena." When the sky remained overcast, the drama—much like the German revolution—took place in the darkened theater of theoreticians.

The story of the observatories of Berlin is one of intermittent wrangling caused by questions of finance. (What else is new?) The observatory of the Urania Society had been inaugurated in 1888. The astronomical instrumentarium exhibited during the 1896 World Fair of Trade and Crafts in Treptow Park first got a roof over its head in 1909. The funds for this new "People's Observatory" were collected from trade-union workers with the help of the astronomer Friedrich S. Archenhold. The observatory bears his name today, and his statue stands in front of the building alongside sculptures of the first man in space, Yuri Gagarin (USSR), and Siegfried Jähn (GDR), the first German astronaut. The observatory is known the world over for its refracting telescope, the longest of its kind at 21 meters. Zeiss installed a small planetarium in the close vicinity.

Wilhelm Foerster continued Humboldt's enlightened work. Until 1904 he served as director of the New Observatory. Erected in 1962, the new postwar substitute in the Western half of Berlin is named after him. It rises above the "Insulaner," an elevation of 75 meters in height-containing war rubble and debris.

The cosmic scientists of Berlin tended toward pacifism from the very beginning. The likes of Humboldt, Foerster and Archenhold had seen enough of the eruptions on the sun and the vast, overwhelming expanse of space to consider bellicosity and destruction on this small planet desirable. In 1915 another believer in peace, Albert Einstein, gave a talk on his theory of relativity to the Society of Friends of the Treptow Observatory. Another society promoting science and reason through public lectures and discussions was promptly banned in 1933: the Urania Society of 1888, of which Wilhelm Foerster had been a cofounder. The German Peace Society, since 1892 actively supported by Bertha von Suttner, Foerster, and other intellectual leaders of the time, met with the same fate. But from this nucleus has grown the peace movement in East and West Berlin today, a loose association of groups, committees, and individuals dedicated to the promotion of friendship among, instead of war between, peoples.

As with most everything in Berlin, the Urania has split apart. The West Berlin society by that name moved into a modern building on Kleiststraße (with a cafeteria open in the evening only; for lack of customers). It counts 8,000 members, holds lecture series, and is involved in the publication of works of popular science and related subjects. Its East Berlin counterpart spreads its activities far beyond the city limits and reports a total number of 60 million participants in their various programs for the 1981–5 period. Radio and television in East and West avail themselves regularly of Urania speakers for their educational and popular-science programming.

The study of astronomy can easily evoke melancholic reflections in Berliners. "Can you really imagine how unimportant we are?" we were asked by a young science fan and architecture student who had acquired his perspective during countless visits to the Archenhold Observatory. "If we reduce the Milky Way to the size of this room, our earth is less than a speck of dust, not even visible in a ray of sunlight. And now think of how many Milky Ways exist out there! You see that's why I'm so sure we'll not be able to cut that order of magnitude down to size—ever."

This brings an anecdote about Lise Meitner to mind, the physicist who had to leave her city and her country as Lise Sara Meitner, when every Jewish citizen of Germany was forced by law to identify herself or himself with the middle name of either Sara or Israel. Once during a lecture she mentioned some cosmic event estimated to occur in about 500 million years. "What did you say?" an excited voice from the audience interrupted. "In 500 million years," Lisa Meitner reiterated. A middle-aged lady sat down again with a sigh of relief. "That's OK. I thought you said 50 million."

(The) Wall in Passing Only

The construction of the Berlin Wall in 1961 was the result of East German deliberations at the highest level (as well as Soviet military decisions). Until that year, over two and a half million of 17 million GDR citizens had left their homeland declared to be within the Soviet sphere of influence by the Treaty of Potsdam of 1945. East Germany had tried in vain to stem the tide and avoid the economic catastrophe hanging over its head. For years Westerners, given the advantage of a favorable exchange rate, had been able to shop in East Berlin at bargain prices. The country was being drained of manpower and highly skilled professionals. With the Wall, the stream of refugees and basic goods and commodities rolling westward came to a sudden halt—and there was room to spare in Mariendorf Refugee Center. Today nobody can deny that much has changed for the better in East Berlin since 1961.

What began as a barbed-wire fence has in the meantime been reinforced and raised to a height of 4 meters. The material: concrete blocks topped with tubing that makes it hard to grip. A clearing of some 50 meters along the eastern side is further secured by watchtowers, floodlights, sensors, and dogs. Tenants living too close to the divide were evacuated. Windows were barricaded and houses torn down. Now at a total length of over 160 kilometers, the Wall cuts off West from East Berlin along a 50-kilometer stretch. "Without a doubt the ugliest structure in Berlin!" said a tourist guide. Well, thanks a lot. Should it be pretty to look at too?

Suffering and sensationalism were caused by it. Nearly fifty persons have been killed during attempted escapes. Withered wreaths and primitive crosses on the Western side recall their fate. East Berlin erected memorial stones for their border guards shot from across the West. The Western media gobbled up stories of daring escapes and foiled attempts, while those who have served as "flight helpers," collected information, and shot at the Eastern side remain nameless. The Wall Museum near Checkpoint Charlie in the West has two sides to it as well: it is a collection of documents about the Berlin tragedy *and* a thriving tourist attraction. So are observation platforms with a view across the Wall into the Eastern part of town.

Since nothing in Berlin is without precedent, neither is the Wall. Frederick William I, the Soldier King, declared an absolute ban on emigration in 1711, and in 1735 had a wall built—the third in Berlin's history. It served not to defend against outsiders, but to keep his soldiers from deserting and his craftsmen from emigrating. Deserters, if caught, were hanged. After a number of years, the king had to give in. First craftsmen were excused from active duty, then anyone living in the capital was declared free from military service.

Where there is a wall, there are passages to let people through after identification checks and passport and luggage controls, of course. That is not new either. A young man from Dessau got a taste of it in 1773 when he entered Berlin through the only gate among fourteen where Jews were allowed to pass. Many years later—Moses Mendelssohn had become a famous philosopher and, with his friend G.E. Lessing one of the outstanding personalities of the Enlightenment—he had to show his pass once again to Potsdam guards. He had taken the trip on royal order. Asked about the purpose of his visit, he allegedly replied: "I am to teach His Majesty a few magic tricks." No one caught the double meaning, but perhaps the most important magic trick he performed was that of human tolerance.

Apart from Checkpoint Charlie (reserved for foreigners, diplomats and Allied military personnel) there are nine other openings in the Wall. Some are for West Berliners, some for West German citizens—a few are for pedestrian traffic only and the rest are accessible by car. Since the thaw in the cold war—which to Berliners feels hotter or colder, depending on the way you look at it—West Berliners are again allowed to visit their relatives across the border. East Berliners can only

Berlin-West Check Point Charlie

travel in the other direction by special permission or once they reach retirement age. Day passes expire at 2:00 a.m. when a new shift of border guards takes over.

Every night there is a big hassle when drunken Westerners arrive at the barriers too late. Some Westerner might lift his hat to make identification with his passport photo easier and assert in jest: "Look, it *is me!*" The young lieutenant in charge might reply with a sharp: "In the last instance it is *I* who decides that!" Immediately the wind blowing feels a little icier. We prefer guards who do not hide the fact that they are human. One of them once commented with a twinkle in his eye: "If you looked in reality the way you look on that picture of yours, I'd feel sorry for your spouse." Relaxed laughter, and a friendly good-bye.

From the West you can get close enough to touch the Wall. It is full of graffiti, black on white, full color, in German, English, Turkish, or Arabic. Rarely reaching the mastery of their colleagues who decorated New York's subway, the local spray-gun artists do come close to the American sense of humor at times: "Rather red wine than a bullet in my spine" can be seen there, or the motto of a humanitarian optimist: "Mankind, I love you." An Indian guru fan and idealist successfully negotiated the Wall from West to East in 1984.

[232]

He crash-landed in his light plane, handed the East Berlin border police who picked him up a bouquet of flowers, and declared himself a missionary of peace. After some interrogation, he was led through a checkpoint back from where he came.

In the early days of the Prussian capital, shepherds grazing their flocks outside the city wall also had to put up with stringent controls both in the morning and at night when they returned home. Their sheep and rams had to hop, one by one, through a small opening to be counted, to ensure that none were lost or had been sold illegally. This procedure, called "Hammelsprung" in German, which means something like "Ram Hop," is still used in the Bundestag in Bonn for counting votes when important decisions have to be made.

Waterways—The Arteries of our Siamese Twins

In Berlin, if you follow the advice of a pop song which has you cross seven bridges, you won't get very far. Blame it on the songwriter— he's from Saxony. There are bridges everywhere, twice as many in Greater Berlin as in the city of Venice. Spree, Havel, and canals traverse East and West Berlin like arteries and, given the traffic requirements of a major population center, ever more crossings have had to be built.

There are curious structures among them. Old-fashioned and undamaged by war, the arches of Jungfernbrücke span Friedrichsgracht in East Berlin. The stone parts of the structure still show traces of original wooden padding. The movable gangplanks of the drawbridge are made of iron. Berliners of all ages love this little jewel. The Amstel and similar scenery in and around Amsterdam come to mind. Immigrants from the Netherlands built the canal, and the bridge has retained its shape since 1798.

Modern architects responsible for the construction of new, "aggressively" ugly apartment blocks were apparently not much impressed by the nostalgic surroundings. All they contributed to this corner, once famous for the picturesque

[233]

meadows along the banks of the canal, were empty ideas and miserable building material. Not even the security patrol, which regularly circles around the seat of the Central Committee of the Socialist Unity Party, can find pleasure in the sight. If only the maidens, the *Jungfern* of Berlin were still bleaching their washing down there!

Times have changed the scenery—and only in fairy tales do maidens retain their youth and innocence. It takes some poetic imagination to visualize—while leaning against the railing—apple barges which carried the fall harvest from Saxon and Bohemian gardens into Berlin selling their produce directly to customers on shore.

In Tempelhof (West), a million nuts—who has counted them?—were driven into the metal supports of a railroad bridge. It got the nickname "Millionaire Bridge." By the way, so did Swinemünde Bridge, a skeleton of steel. It earned its name because of the black-market trafficking between East and West that went on there after the war. Berliners may be sentimental when they so choose. But only then.

Schloßbrücke (now Marx-Engels-Brücke) was to be embellished in honor of the marriage of the crown prince to Princess Elizabeth of Bavaria, but work could not be finished on time. (Some things never change!) Quickly completed temporary railings could not withstand the onrushing crowds, and twenty-two well-wishers drowned in the Spree; others were saved. The princely wedding took place nevertheless, amidst the sound of wedding bells that, at least to some, were tolling for the dead.

Bridges in Berlin are never far from sluices, all of them under the jurisdiction of East Berlin port authorities. No difficulties arise from this state of affairs, and life on the waterways is surprisingly hectic. Industrial coal and freight from Hamburg, Rostock, and the Danube countries make their way on barges to the extensive port facilities in Berlin. Before the Second World War, Berlin was Europe's second largest inland port. With their warehouses, quays, and cranes, the Upper Spree area of East Berlin and the northern Tiergarten, Neukölln, and Spandau areas in the West, have that distinctive harbor atmosphere about them.

Onlookers watch the maneuvering of locks and hydraulic elevators with the same fascination as have their forefathers ever since 1650 when the first were built. The air seems to permeate bars in the vicinity as well. Sea gulls hover, diving skillfully for bread thrown by children and grown-ups alike.

Sahrower Kirche and Havel   J. Bettenstadt 1983

Berlin a mere half a century ago harbored a poet who used to disguise himself as a sailor: Joachim Ringelnatz, according to whom every gull looked as if its name was Emma.

Berlin's waters are just as much subject to border demarcation as the sandy soil. Luckily a *modus vivendi* has been found and, by mutual agreement, transport routes for cargo ships remain open—thorough inspection by customs and border police notwithstanding. Luckily too, an agreement has been reached that, in case of emergency, help can be counted on from either side or both. The American army maintains its only water patrol unit outside the U.S. here in Berlin. When their boats pass *Moby Dick* or any of the other sixty-nine vessels of West Berlin's pleasure fleet, there is a lot of waving back and forth. East Berlin's "White Fleet" sets out from Treptow during the sunny seasons. It is about half the size of the Western one. The names East Berlin chose for its boats attests to a love of literature underscored by the reading habits of their citizens generally. There is a *Bert Brecht* cruising the rivers and lakes, a *Heinrich Mann*, et cetera. Cruises of five to six hours, with or without a planned stopover are nothing unusual. There is water enough below and plenty of food, drink, and music on board.

Before the outbreak of the First World War the Spree Canal Steamship Society Stern owned a fleet of seventy ships transporting over 5 million passengers yearly. They went as far as Hamburg or Magdeburg, or merely to Potsdam. The pleasure

[235]

boats were actually developed out of paddle wheelers that had carried the mail for so long. The first steamer was launched in Spandau in 1816 when an Englishman was granted a Prussian patent to operate his service on the river. But the very first passenger boats in Berlin were constructed and operated by Dutch settlers as early as 1700. The voyage began near the center of town and ended in Charlottenburg.

Thanks to this type of service, Charlottenburg grew from a small hamlet into a burgeoning township, but was finally incorporated into Berlin proper. Two horses would draw the small boats on ropes, trudging alongside the Spree. The passengers sat beneath a canopy, the fare was no more than a few coins, and there was not an oil spill to be seen anywhere.

Berlin   Jungfernbrücke   J Bettenstaedt 1985

Wit and What Else Comes Out of that Famous Berlin Trap

Whenever Berliners invent jokes it is to tell them to their own kind—outsiders don't understand them anyway. Non-natives, should they dare to crack a few of their own about Berliners, only emphasize their ignorance about the city folk they are laughing at. It's just like the age-old Jewish question: does the Berlin species of humans live from inside out or outside in? And such a direct question can only be answered by an emphatic: "Yes!"

It's been said that a typical Berliner has little humor but one of the quickest wits around. Detached irony and knowing humor, understatement or resignation have long proved inadequate lines of defense for flexible, mobile, and adaptable metropolitans forever running up against Prussian drill and the hardships of city life. Only defiance, straightforward debunking, and disrespectful street sense could get them through. Humor is a gift—wit is tough work—and the natives with their one-upmanship, their big trap and unlimited range and variety of imagery prefer to use their head actively rather than put their trust in inner harmony. Even Berlin brats catch on early.

The stamina of teachers is regularly tested by school classes who celebrate a winning punch line for hours on end.

Religious Instruction: "Who was the mother of Moses?" "Pharaoh's daughter," shouts an eager student. "But she only *found* him," interjects the teacher. "That's what *she* said!" comes the irrefutable reply.

When an instructor lost his temper and told a pupil to run over to the drugstore and buy a dime's worth of brain, the object of his fury walked to the door, turned around and asked: "Should I tell them it's for you?"

Lessons in altruism usually fall short of the aspired result. A Protestant pastor in West Berlin recalled the following dialogue with a Sunday school participant: "If you have a big bag full of candy, what will you do with it?" "Eat it all." "Well, imagine you've eaten all but three, your tummy hurts and a poor boy is standing next to you, what will you do then?" "Don't worry, I'll force them down."

When a high official from Berlin was sent to Africa to teach postal workers "civilized" manners for their dealings with

[237]

the public, he was able to successfully accomplish his task. Upon arriving back home he encountered a customs officer who was so rude that he felt compelled to register a complaint with the local grievance committee. "Civil" is not an adjective frequently used to describe Berliners, and there are "ugly" Berliners, no doubt. But no mistake, these are not the wits of Berlin. True Berlin wit pervades everyday vocabulary; however caustic they may be, colorful comparisons and inventive nicknames temper the underlying aggressiveness and vulgarity. There are even funny aspects in insult and verbal abuse.

Berlin's artificial mountains under which wartime rubble and accumulated rubbish disappeared are "Hitler's Collected Works," the Opera House is "Sing Sing," the owner of a grocery store is referred to as "herring tamer."

Descriptive terms are always irreverent, so is "Halleluja Miss" for a female member of the Salvation Army, "pancake with legs" or "ironing board" for a skinny person—with the added explanation: nothing up front, and nothing in the rear. And there is no holding a Berliner back when he coaxes an opponent into or threatens him out of a fight: "One punch, and you can blow your nose at the back of your head!" Or: "I'll hit you in the head until your lice twitter." Or: "Man, I'll knock you out of your suit pound by pound." Then there are funnier versions of the same, such as: "I'll stab you with a frozen washcloth!" "Idiot, buy yourself a tail and go as a monkey!" Social satire postulates: "No one should go hungry without freezing too."

Unsolicited advice or comment is never suppressed either. A young passenger on a train had to endure: "Hey, you, if I were you I'd have my shirt collar tarred again. The white is showing!" A young woman, obviously in the family way, was at a loss for words when a casual passer-by approached her saying: "Well, Miss, already engaged, aren't you?"

Government and bureaucracy offer themselves as prime targets for aggressively political jokes. These are collected, told and retold, used, abused, worn out and then warmed up again. The best ones about the nuisance of the functionary system in the GDR, we were told, make the rounds among the functionaries themselves. It seems highly improbable, however, that this is the first sign of an impending counter-revolution.

One East German joke put us into an embarrassing situation. A museum guide judging us to be joke-trustworthy began to relate one about shoe supplies in Red China. A customer enters a shoe shop with only one pair on display and a huge picture of Mao on the wall. Underneath an arrow points into the next room. The customer follows the arrow and arrives in a second room, where the scenery is the same and the scene repeats itself. Suddenly the guide began to laugh and laugh . . . and left.

He was lucky, *he* knew the punch line. Our frustrating problem remains since we are unable to pass this obviously hilarious political joke on to you. We don't know how it ends. For that reason alone we continue our visits to the city in the hope that some day someone will let us in on the mystery.

X

Xmas Carols—New Year's Crackers

"What do swimming instructors do for a job when there is
snow on the ground?" a curious reader from Weißensee
inquired in the "Letterbox" column of an East Berlin daily.
"They play Santa!" came the to-the-point answer. Surprising
as it may sound, it is true and logical. In the "Polarium" of
East Berlin's sports and recreation center one such teacher
appears in Santa attire with skates under his feet. Gracefully
he glides over the ice alongside a professional "ice queen" in
miniskirt—over and over again to disco music. Children are
invited to join in the fun. Atheists in town console themselves with the fact that St. Nicholas of old now figures as
Father Frost of the Soviet tradition.

Christmas fairs in Berlin provide a fail-safe remedy for the
doldrums of long December nights. The ring of musical
clocks and the smell of roasted apples abound. In front of
Kaiser-Wilhelm-Gedächtniskirche (West) on brightly illuminated merry-go-rounds kids wrapped up in winter woolens,
their cheeks red and their eyes shining, scream with delight.

Sights and sounds differ little on Alexanderplatz (East).
Rows and rows of market stands hug a huge Christmas tree
aglow with lights. No heavy snowfall can spoil the excitement. On the contrary, it quickly transforms the whole scene
into a winter wonderland. One bazaar advertised as "the
largest Christmas market in the world" takes shelter under
the roof of an exhibition complex of 25,000 square meters near
Charlottenburg's radio tower. Three hundred booths and

stands are set up to sell treats and toys. Without fighting sleet and slush or hopping about on frozen feet, parents can stroll with their youngsters for hours in this commercial paradise. Crafts are beautifully displayed; Punch and Judy shows, movies and children's theater performances capture the attention. A corner has been equipped by some toy companies for kids to play and amuse themselves. A bakery has them try their hand at baking cookies. Tasting needs no practice.

Outside the halls a man paces back and forth, fir-tree-green in his face, chased out by the umpteenth repeat of "Silent night, holy night" over the loudspeakers.

During the last century, market policemen allotted each applicant precisely measured space for his or her Christmas stall. The city palace was still standing then overlooking the square. Vendors of glassware and cloth each had three meters of frontage while other merchants had 50 centimeters less. Crates and baskets had to be removed from under foot. No one was allowed to sleep here overnight. Alcoholic beverages were taboo. From nine in the morning until ten at night business was booming; on weekends, on New Year's Eve and New Year's Day trading continued until midnight. The public loved it, and the fair merchants held out to January 7th. And all that without a drop of booze?

Christian churches of Berlin celebrate the season festively. Nativity scenes are exhibited every year for which tickets cost 5 marks each. In East Berlin wax candles illuminate the Bethlehem manger. But the angels, in particular, posed a great ideological problem to the people there. What to call them was the problem. The solution, however, suggested itself. What had worked for many streets would work here as well. They were simple renamed "end-of-year figurines with wings." Honest. The laughter aroused by such linguistic creativity was, in spite of the holy season, indeed diabolical. Now angels are angels again—no two ways about it. And no two ways either about the old saying we found in a Christmas calendar: "Don't sit out on a winter day / too long without a coat, I pray."

Christmas plays seem to be among the most loved seasonal diversions of American military families. In city districts with old, for guests from overseas almost ancient churches, they rehearse over and over again alongside their German neighbors. At home such a romantic backdrop is only found in Disneyland. Christmas trees are everywhere, decorated and weighed down by electric candles, cut down in the Thuringian forests (in the GDR) which keep West Berlin in good supply; about 1 million spruce and pine trees arrive every year by truck or railroad prior to Advent. In bundles of 500 they reach the marketplaces. Once Christmas is over many of them end up on the sidewalk or in the courtyard after a not-so-elegant throw from the balcony.

By that time the New Year has arrived for which the famous chemist, Justus Liebig, a serious man through and through, invented the cracker. Few people remember that. If war were to break out, nobody would notice for all the firework explosions going on throughout New Year's Eve. East Berlin reports the sale of 2.5 million table fireworks, not to speak of rockets and howlers and more. Popping champagne corks sound like machine-gun fire. Pyrotechnicians have their work cut out for them to produce enough ammunition and make it safe enough as well.

Y

Youth—Is it Wasted on the Young?

Youngsters in Berlin, East and West, are faced with the eternal problem of contending with the older generation: parents, teachers, policemen, superiors. Since that generation—forty years after the end of World War II—has not been able to figure out a way to come to a political reunification of Germany, unsolved problems of world history also weigh heavily on the shoulders of Berlin's adolescents. It's a bit much when you're just sixteen years old.

Some react to the pressure by turning aggressive; others slide into anti-social behavior. Even the decision regarding what they want and how they'll get it depends on support from their elders who hold the purse strings: own concert halls, housing for communal living, youth centers—everything. Where money is involved, publicized or behind-the-scenes political decisions are not far off. Those who spend it reserve the right to spend it on what they think is best.

Young crowds all over the two Berlins care little about "who," and their unconcerned reasoning confronts the establishment on both sides of the border with ever new waves of questions, demands, and problems. In West Berlin they have turned the entertainment business political; and in East Berlin they have been forcing the business of politics to make room for their kind of entertainment. In either case the effect of *détente* is unorthodox.

In the Palace of the Republic under one roof with the GDR executive, the People's Chamber, mass concerts regularly attract crowds of youngsters. They are billed under the heading "Rock for Peace" or something similar, almost American-style. Tickets sell out in a hurry. Books, records, scarves, posters, and junk are on sale for the sake of peace. Missing from the scene are drugs—extremely hard to get here. In West Berlin smoking "peaceful" joints is widespread; in entertainment shows here the halls are filled with the sweet smell of incense.

"Peace" has just as much drawing power in West Berlin. Pop and rock concerts turn the open-air auditorium called "Waldbühne," with a seating capacity of 25,000 and located not far from the Olympic Stadium, into a veritable can of sardines for weekends on end. Once past the entrance with a high-priced ticket there is no escaping the vendors of sausages and soft drinks, posters and junk. You're caught for the day, since reentry is not permitted.

In East Berlin goods are delivered by state-owned stores which provide the sales staff as well. Across the border private vendors have to pay concessionary dues to the organizers. The young fans don't mind a bit, they don't even care.

A long, drawn-out tug-of-war went on between advocates and opponents in East Berlin before the first discos, fashioned after West Berlin models, were allowed to open their doors. Entertainment fashions, including psychedelic lights, disk jockeys, musical styles and types of dancing jump across the Wall like fleas. They also travel in the East–West direction and would do so increasingly, if there were active exchange programs between both parts of the city. "Deutsch Rock," an East Berlin invention, exchanged those meaningful American or English lyrics with equally meaningful German texts. For fifteen years now music lovers on both sides have remained ardent fans. Big bands and show orchestras from the Soviet Union, Czechoslovakia, Poland, or Hungary make their appearance on stages here and over there, all at a volume that drives the older generation into hasty retreat.

To be young in Berlin means to be exposed to two politico-economic systems at close range; a unique situation in Europe with which everyone has to come to terms. Whoever detests active participation, when around Pentecost GDR bigwigs are presented with teddy bears by youthful functionaries amidst festive excitement Berlin-style, withdraws to soothe a sense of melancholy by listening to one tape after the other. East Berlin produces 2.6 million tape cassettes per annum. That mixture of pessimism and rebellion takes youth as far out as punk masquerade, to the imitation of skinheads and new romantics. In Rummelsburg they meet in front of Erlöserkirche on motorbikes. The pastor of the church got the OK from the GDR state secretary for church affairs that he could let them play their music in the cemetery. At times the musicians are too drunk to accomplish setting up loudspeakers and amplifiers. Then it becomes a happening in which nothing happened—the pressure of emptiness. Once it's over they leave for home by the hundreds, some in cars on which they have painted the Mercedes star.

A bestseller, like the one based on taped interviews with an under-age prostitute recalling her adventures in Mercedes and other cars in the Western part of the city, would not be tolerated in the other half. Neither would the conditions described in the book. In East Berlin pupils, co-eds, and young female workers sit around the entrance halls of hotels frequented by international tourists and expect at least some romantic sweet-talk before they say yes. The young author of the book was interested in nothing but money. "If you don't like it, go across the border," is the stereotyped answer to criticism of West Berlin.

To be young in Berlin is only natural to those who are. And quite a few teenagers in West Berlin participate in a program organized by the Protestant Church. They pull weeds and plant flowers in Jewish cemeteries. Occasionally a group takes a trip to Poland not far away, to visit Auschwitz. And they return with an emotional burden that makes them noticeably more mature than their peers.

The village church in Tempelhof is associated with a crusading idea quite different from the one prevailing during the time it was founded by Jerusalem Templars. It is the only church in West Berlin where even the pastor arrives in jeans or leather outfit on an over-sized motorcycle. A convoy of male and female rockers follows him to the altar. Led directly from gas station to communion, they reverently take off their helmets when entering. Not much more is asked of them, though probably expected.

Z

Zoological Gardens (Almost an Epilogue)

The telephone rings in the office of West Berlin's Zoological Garden: "Are you missing a bumblebee?" Reply: "You better call the insane asylum. Or are you calling from there?" "Cut it out, I'm in my garden and was just bitten by that pest. It has a yellow number tag on its back."

The caller, by no means crazy, was a resident of Schöneberg, a lady in her sixties, victim of an enraged insect. Feeling misused by students of the Free University, violated by involuntary participation in a research project, the bumblebee had hit on the first human it encountered.

It might well be that, in a complex with several thousand animals, a bumblebee goes missing. There are no logical arguments against that assumption.

Founded in 1841 on a plot of land donated by the ruling monarch, the Zoo was once the object of financial speculations at the Berlin stock exchange. It was run as a public company.

About a hundred years after its inception it lay in shambles at the end of the war. Only ninety of the original 4,000 animals had survived. Yuri Waisz, Soviet cultural officer at the time, recalls that they were crying out from hunger. An emaciated German still in the uniform of the conquered Wehrmacht approached the Russian, who spoke fluent German, and begged: "Couldn't you do something for the animals?" The man apparently thought it quite in order that he himself was starving—a logical consequence of Hitler's war.

But his Berlin heart ached for the beasts in the Zoo; it hadn't been their fault, they had nothing to do with the fact that identity checks were just being run in Hitler's bunker in Wilhelmstraße, where the Führer had taken his own life and where his corpse had been charred beyond recognition.

During the harsh winter of 1947/8 in particular, Berliners developed a strong interest in all matters zoological. Their concern had little to do with scholarly pursuits or research into some exotic species. Their aims were more practical.

From the shaft of a lift in a badly damaged apartment block on Joachim-Friedrich-Straße came an odor hardly befitting the ambience. The porter was raising a piglet there. When the day arrived on which it was illegally (and secretly) slaughtered, he and his wife could not bear to eat one bite of it. They buried the carcass in Tiergarten in frost-hardened soil, and avoided leaving any traces for fear someone else might dig little Susi out from under again.

The Zoo and Aquarium on Budapester Straße, West Berlin, are as beautiful as in former days, richer in species without being poorer in attractions. We still saw that huge catfish found in the mud of a Havel tributary and moved from its hideout of a good 150 years into a rather small basin. Curled-up it pouted behind the glass partition, sporting a moustache any royal Prussian officer would have envied. Large wounds were clearly visible on its back. The construction workers from Berlin who had made the find during their draining of the tributary, had set their mind on getting the fish to the Zoo, while its resolve had been to the contrary.

The terrain of East Berlin's zoological garden was not the gift of a king, even though it had once been a royal hunting-ground. Tierpark Friedrichsfelde was opened in 1955 and during its first thirty years saw a proud 60 million visitors. When foot-and-mouth disease has broken out anywhere in the world everyone has to wipe their shoes on a disinfected floor mat; otherwise the Saxon director of the zoo acquires a bad case of contagious rabies.

The whole place is the result of countless hours worked by volunteers of all ages. Two stone lions moved here from the former palais of the Reichspräsident seem to be encouraging every animal family to procreate and keep the good spirit going. In peaceful competition with countries of the capitalist world, yet turning a cold shoulder to West Berlin, penguin eggs are hatched and baby hyenas fed with the bottle. West Berlin takes the easy way out: it has the animals given as presents, and publishes its thank-you notes in the papers.

The president of Indonesia sent a 3-meter cayman to West Berlin as a gift. Upon its arrival the already "naturalized" population of crocodiles and alligators got very excited. At night they surrounded the newcomer under the bamboo bridge in a moat with tropical water plants. "Go on, tell us about the world outside where there is no wall." No matter they are all tired in the morning. Not one of them has ever overslept feeding time. How could they in this city?

In the aquarium building we looked in amazement at an ingenious basin: an oval ring. There are fish of a strange kind swimming in circles, one behind the other, round and round. They must think that there is only one direction for them: forward into eternity. But when they open their mouth and are supposed to swallow what the one in front left behind, they must begin to wonder.

A city under seven flags—a city in two parts—produces many an indigestible chunk.

Two average chimpanzees are sitting in their enclosure staring down at the human beings in front of the cage. "Look," one of them says, "they descended from us. Didn't come to much! No higher aspirations—too lazy to climb."

Index

Achard, Franz Carl (1753–1821), chemist, 198

Adler, Leonhard, Berlin town councillor, 79

Ahmed Effendi, emissary of the Ottoman Empire, 86, 87

Albers, Hans (1891–1960), actor, 101

Albrecht the Bear (about 1100–70), margrave of Brandenburg, 103

Alexandra Feodorovna (Princess Charlotte), wife of Nicholas I of Russia, 194

Appelt, Dorle, octogenarian Berlin sportswoman, 210

Archenhold, Friedrich Simon (1861–1939) astronomer, 228

Archimedes (285–212 BC), Greek mathematician, 198

Arco, Georg von (1869–1940), radio engineer, 186

Arthur, Chester A. (1830–86), U.S. president, 169

Ataturk, Kemal (1880–1938), Turkish leader, 219

Augusta (1811–90), queen of Prussia, empress of Germany, 86

Baker, Josephine (1960–75), singer, dancer, 71

(La) Barberina (Barberina Campanini) (1721–99), dancer, 148

Barlog, Boleslav (b. 1906), theater director, 213

Baum, Herbert (1912–42), electrician, resistance fighter, 125

Baum, Vicky (1888–1960), novelist, 193

Becher, Johannes R. (1891–1958), writer, politician, 136

Beese-Boutard, Melli (Amelie) (1886–1925), aviatrix, 80

Begas, Reinhold (1831–1911), sculptor, 90, 122

Bendix, Alice (1895–1943), social worker, teacher, 201

Bethmann-Hollweg, Theobald von (1856–1921), imperial German chancellor, 37

Bismarck, Otto von (1815–98), imperial German chancellor, statesman, 7, 92, 99, 102, 121, 130, 143, 184, 203

Blücher, Gebhard Leberecht von (1742–1819), Prussian general field marshal, 92, 166

Bois, Curt (b. 1901), actor, singer, 35

Bolle, Karl (1832–1910), merchant, 69

Borsig, Johann Friedrich August (1804–54), engineer, entrepreneur, 100, 119

Botticelli, Sandro (1445–1510), painter, 122

Boucher, François (1703–70), painter, 92

Brandt, Willy (b. 1913), West German politician, former chancellor of the FRG, 189

Brauchitsch, Manfred von (b. 1905), race car driver, 209

Braun, Wernher von (1912–77), physicist, rocket specialist, 79, 205

Brecht, Bertolt (1898–1956), playwright, poet, 1, 2, 35, 44, 93, 128, 137, 208, 212

Breker, Arno (b. 1900), sculptor, 123

Briand, Aristide (1862–1932), French statesman, 184

Bronnen, Arnolt (1895–1959), writer, 186

Bülow, Arthur, sports reporter, editor, 208

Bülow, Bernhard von (1849–1929), Prussian statesman, 208

Burger, Reinhold, glass blower, inventor, 198

Busch, Paula (b. 1894), circus director, 54

Callas, Maria (1923–77), opera singer, 34

Calvin, John (1509–64), Protestant theologian, 49, 50

Caracciola, Rudolf (1901–59), race car driver, 209

Carstens, Karl (b. 1914), West German politician, former president of the FRG, 210

Caruso, Enrico (1873–1921), opera singer, 34

Casanova, Giacomo Girolamo (1725–98), writer, 123

Chamisso, Adalbert von (1781–38),

[249]

[253]